SCHOOL'S IN

AMERICAN GOVERNANCE AND PUBLIC POLICY SERIES
Series Editors: Gerald W. Boychuk, Karen Mossberger, and Mark C. Rom

SCHOOL'S IN

Federalism and the National Education Agenda

Paul Manna

GEORGETOWN UNIVERSITY PRESS
Washington, D.C.

As of January 1, 2007, 13-digit ISBN numbers will replace the current
10-digit system.

Paperback: 978-1-58901-090-1

Georgetown University Press, Washington, D.C.

Library of Congress Cataloging-in-Publication Data

Manna, Paul.
   Schools in : federalism and the national education agenda / Paul Manna.
     p. cm. — (American governance and public policy)
   Includes bibliographical references and index.
   ISBN-13: 978-1-58901-090-1 (pbk. : alk. paper)
   ISBN-10: 1-58901-090-6 (pbk. : alk. paper)
    1. Education and state—United States. 2. Education, Elementary—
United States. 3. Education, Secondary—United States. I. Title. II. Series.
  LC89.M223 2006
  379.73—dc22   2005027244

This book is printed on acid-free paper meeting the requirements of the
American National Standard for Permanence in Paper for Printed Library
Materials.

13 12 11 10 09 08 07 06   9 8 7 6 5 4 3 2
First printing

Printed in the United States of America

Table of Contents

v

List of Figures and Tables

ACKNOWLEDGMENTS

This book has benefited from the generosity and keen insights of several people who have offered their time, reactions, and encouragement. The full list would run several pages, so, unfortunately, I am not able to note all who contributed to the effort.

For financial support, I thank the Graduate School and the Graduate Student Council at the University of Wisconsin, the Dirksen Congressional Center, and the American Political Science Association. Teacher's College Press has also kindly allowed me to reprint portions of a chapter I had written on the No Child Left Behind Act; it previously appeared in *Political Education* by Christopher Cross.

The current project began as my Ph.D. dissertation at the University of Wisconsin. My primary faculty advising team of John Witte, John Coleman, and Don Kettl have been smart critics and supporters of the work ever since I floated ideas for the project several years ago. They continue to be fabulous colleagues and friends. Those three, in addition to Charles Franklin, Byron Shafer, and Julie Mead, as well as my other teachers at Wisconsin, provided me with great advice as I learned how to be a political scientist. Further, my student colleagues from Wisconsin—who are now faculty members scattered literally coast-to-coast—have been indispensable allies and sounding boards for my ideas. In particular, I wish to thank Patty Strach (my shadow advisor), Travis Ridout, Rudy Espino, Michael Franz, and other members of the Research Seminar on Voting and Politics.

Working on this book has helped me to realize that there are dozens of generous people in academia and the policy world. Their willingness to lend a hand, despite their own packed schedules, never ceased to amaze me. Bryan Jones and his team at the Policy Agendas Project and John Geer fielded several data questions that I tossed their way. Others in the political science community who read or commented on early drafts of chapters or offered support and advice include Jeffrey Henig, William Gormley, Paul Posner, Paul Quirk, Steven Schier, DeWayne Lucas, Lawrence Mead, Timothy Conlan, and Brady Baybeck. I also received great questions and comments on the work during visits to the College of William and Mary, Brown University, the University of Houston, and the University of Delaware. Two of my colleagues at William and Mary, Ron Rapoport and Chris Howard, provided sage advice that helped me to better understand the process of book publishing.

Beyond the walls of the academy, I am most indebted to my interview respondents, whom I list by name in the appendix. That knowledgeable group includes some of the smartest thinkers about education and policymaking, and I did my best to incorporate their wisdom into the pages that follow. Among the people I encountered who work every day in the policy trenches, Andrew Rotherham, Jack Jennings, Christopher Cross, and Ron Waterman deserve special thanks for reading and commenting on chapter drafts and for helping me to understand how American education policy actually works.

In the publishing world, I owe thanks and several drinks to Gail Grella, Mark Rom, the staff, and anonymous reviewers at Georgetown University Press. They have all had the patience of saints and have offered fantastic advice as the book has made its way through the publishing process. John Tryneski and anonymous reviewers from the University of Chicago Press also provided great feedback that helped to improve the work.

Finally, to Lisa, whom I did not even know when this project began: Thank you, my sweet, for making the completion of this book the second most exciting event of my year.

LIST OF ABBREVIATIONS

AASA	American Association of School Administrators
AFT	American Federation of Teachers
AYP	Adequate yearly progress
BCEE	Business Coalition for Excellence in Education
BRT	The Business Roundtable
CCSSO	Council of Chief State School Officers
ELC	Education Leaders Council
ESEA	Elementary and Secondary Education Act
GAO	General Accounting Office
IASA	Improving America's Schools Act (ESEA reauthorization of 1994)
IDEA	Individuals with Disabilities Education Act
NAB	National Alliance of Business
NAEP	National Assessment of Educational Progress
NASBE	National Association of State Boards of Education
NCEE	National Commission on Excellence in Education
NCLB	No Child Left Behind Act (ESEA reauthorization of 2001)
NCSL	National Conference of State Legislatures
NEA	National Education Association
NEGP	National Education Goals Panel
NGA	National Governors' Association
SEA	state education agency
SREB	Southern Regional Education Board

PART I

FOUNDATIONS

1

Introduction

AMERICANS GOVERN THEIR SCHOOLS WITH A SYSTEM AS COMPLICATED AS the country is vast. The nation's fifty states have created nearly 15,000 school districts to oversee roughly 90,000 public schools. For essentially the entire history of the United States, citizens and elected officials alike have considered the provision of elementary and secondary education to be the quintessential state and local function. With that fragmented system of governance—one strains to call it a system at all, actually—it is remarkable how much weight education policy presently carries in American national politics.

Events from 2001, for example, illustrate the growing role that K–12 education has come to play in the calculations of federal officials. During that year, President George W. Bush began his first term by noting that bipartisan education reform would be the cornerstone of his administration. Less than six months later, Senator James Jeffords of Vermont ended his life-long affiliation with the Republican Party in protest when the president and GOP members of Congress decided to use significant portions of the nation's budget surplus to cut taxes rather than increase special education funding. Jeffords's break with the party reverberated like a political earthquake and returned Senate Democrats to power for the first time since 1994. After the Senate reorganized, and Washington, DC, broke free from another humid August, the tragic events of September 11 riveted the country's attention on terrorism and national security. As they scrambled to respond to the devastation and shore up the nation's defenses, members of Congress still managed to pass with much celebration the No Child Left Behind Act (NCLB). NCLB extended the federal government's reach into the nation's public schools more deeply than ever before. Significantly, it was the only major piece of domestic legislation, other than laws to defend the homeland, to become law before the end of the year.

These three events from 2001—Bush's articulation of his administration's priorities, Senator Jeffords's declaration of independence to promote special education, and the passage of NCLB—illustrate how education policy has risen to the top of the nation's agenda like never before. Beyond the concerns of political elites, though, as figure 1.1 shows, Americans have increasingly identified educa-

3

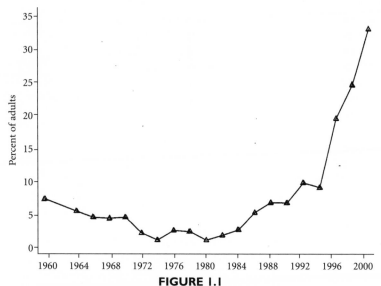

FIGURE 1.1
**Adults identifying education as one of the most important problems
in the United States, 1960–2000**
Source: Author's analysis of National Election Studies data. This question
was unavailable in the 1962 study.

tion as one of the most important problems facing the country. Even as terrorism and homeland security have risen to the top of the nation's agenda, public opinion polls continue to reveal that Americans remain concerned about education.[1]

My goal in this book is to describe and explain the increasing status of education on the nation's agenda and, in the process, to show how federalism influences agenda setting in the United States. Two questions motivate the overall study. First, if states and localities are the primary caretakers of K–12 education, how have federal policymakers so expanded their reach into the country's schools since 1965, the year the first Elementary and Secondary Education Act (ESEA) became law? Second, and more generally, how does the American federal system create opportunities for policymakers across the country to advance their agendas even in areas where they may struggle to wield influence?

These questions suggest several puzzles that I address in the chapters that follow. Consider, for example, the education policy initiatives of Presidents Lyndon Johnson and George W. Bush. Why was Johnson's administration, which in 1965 was backed by wide congressional majorities and committed to a liberal activist federal approach in education, unable with the first ESEA to affect much more than the educational periphery of the nation's schools? In contrast, how was it that almost a decade after the Republican revolution of the mid-1990s, a conservative president and a Republican House of Representatives would help enact NCLB in 2001 and extend the federal government's reach more deeply into American schoolrooms than Johnson and his allies ever could have contemplated?

As another example, it is curious to note that during the 1980s, state governors became increasingly enthusiastic about the federal government's presence in education and even called for more federal monitoring of state educational progress. These calls occurred at the same time that real federal expenditures on K–12 schooling were decreasing or remaining relatively stagnant. Typically, state leaders do not invite federal intervention on their policy turf unless federal dollars are also forthcoming. What were these state officials thinking?

Finally, looking more broadly at general changes in American federalism, it is useful to consider the insights of Baumgartner and Jones (1993), who have examined policy agendas across several decades since World War II. These authors note that the American federal system provides multiple connected venues for policy ideas and initiatives to emerge. The states and the federal government provide important arenas of action in this venue mix. One of the authors' claims is that the "flow of policies across jurisdictional boundaries is stronger in periods of nationalization and weaker in periods of decentralization" (Baumgartner and Jones 1993, 217). Education appears not to fit this pattern, though, given that federal interest and involvement in K–12 education expanded rapidly in the 1980s and 1990s, the two decades after the trend toward nationalization in the American federal system was supposedly slowing. That result seems to clash with Baumgartner and Jones's (1993) more general claim about what causes policies to flow across jurisdictions. What explains how the dynamics in education unfolded, then? And do those dynamics suggest larger lessons about how agendas take shape in the American federal system?

In addressing these puzzles and others, I argue that the evolving relationship between the federal government and the states has produced major changes in the American education agenda since the 1960s. In other words, education has not become more important simply because presidents have said more about it or because Congress has passed more education laws, though, certainly, those factors have helped. More important have been state actions that, when studied alongside the federal role, allow one to better describe and explain how education agendas have developed at both levels of government. Although Washington's influence over American schools has increased, it is wise not to overestimate the expansion of federal power nor to underestimate the resiliency and continuing influence of state education agendas in the United States. Recognizing a key process that characterizes federal-state interactions is critical for understanding how federal and state agendas have unfolded. That process, which I call "borrowing strength," occurs when policy entrepreneurs at one level of government attempt to push their agendas by leveraging the justifications and capabilities that other governments elsewhere in the federal system possess. Borrowing strength is the conceptual anchor that organizes my analysis and enables me to integrate previous scholarship on federalism and agenda setting. In the process, it provides insights about how education agendas in the United States have changed and will likely unfold in the future.

This opening chapter orients the book by doing three things. First, it briefly describes why a focus on federalism is crucial for understanding how the American education agenda has developed since the 1960s. Second, it provides a brief overview of major federal and state policy changes in education during this time. Finally, it previews the more general theoretical arguments that I use to explain changes in the nation's education agenda. I have two particular audiences in mind in this introduction and the chapters that follow: policymakers who are primarily interested in education and scholars or students of political science and public policy who are generally interested in the relationship between federalism and agenda setting.

EXPLAINING CHANGES IN THE AMERICAN
EDUCATION AGENDA

Several previous works have documented the development of federal and state education policy in the United States. Considering the ESEA in particular, which is also my primary focus in this book, an extensive historical and policy-oriented literature exists that has explored changes in federal education policy since the 1960s (Sundquist 1968; Finn 1977; Kaestle and Smith 1982; Graham 1984; Brademas 1987; Jennings 1995, 1998; McLaughlin and Rouse 2000; Borman, Stringfield, and Slavin 2001; Cross 2004; Peterson and West 2003). Similarly, researchers have documented the march of state education reforms, especially since the early 1980s (Doyle and Hartle 1985; Educational Testing Service Policy Information Center 1990; Bacharach 1990; Murphy 1990; Goertz 1996; Evans, Murray, and Schwab 1997). But other than the handful of scholars who have examined specific changes in federal policy in the context of the nation's intergovernmental system (Fuhrman, 1994; Elmore and Fuhrman 1990; Mintrom and Vergari 1997; Posner 1998, chapters 6, 7), no one has attempted to explain long-term developments in the nation's education agenda by focusing explicitly and in depth on the interrelationships between the federal government and the states.

Wirt and Kirst note a parallel shortcoming in their well-known work on the politics of American education. In highlighting areas for future research, they explain that "Political scientists have examined the path of policy from ideas embraced by a policy community to policy outcomes. But these analyses are partial and preliminary, and do not focus on education" (Wirt and Kirst 1997, 332). I would add that no major study of federalism and American education has reached beyond the policy specifics to offer more general theoretical insights about how American federalism and agenda setting processes work. My effort to link the federalism and agenda setting literatures begins to remedy this theoretical shortcoming. Further, by using the case of education to develop new theoretical insights about these two fields, I also address a further call from Wirt and Kirst (1997, 333) that "the concept of policy communities within education needs more definition and more research on their operation and impact."

A careful look over time reveals how developments in state and federal education agendas are related to broader changes in American federalism that have transpired during the last four decades. For example, since the 1960s, the nation's system of intergovernmental grants has mushroomed, and perhaps more important, but less appreciated, state governments have improved their policymaking capabilities. Shifts in federal and state education policy are related to these broader trends. Recognizing these dynamics in American federalism helps one to understand how and why the nation's education agenda has assumed its present form.

Scholars have sometimes used federal education efforts to make general theoretical claims about politics, including analyses of congressional behavior or government reorganization (Thomas 1975; Martin 1994; Radin and Hawley 1988). Researchers frequently describe intergovernmental relationships in education using top-down approaches that focus on how state agents respond to the preferences of their federal principals (Clark and Amiot 1981, 258; Guthrie 1983, 672–73; Chubb 1985b, 1985a; Hill 2000, 27; Volden, Cummins, and Woods 2000). This view tends to describe state behavior in reactive terms: the federal government shifts its policy priorities and the states respond in some way. Another perspective sees the federal government as relatively incapable of coming up with many good ideas on its own. Rather, Washington relies on states as laboratories of policy innovation, which in turn can provide fodder for federal law (Hedge 1998; Morehouse and Jewell 2004; Weissert 2000). This bottom-up perspective reverses the causal arrow and portrays the federal government as responsive to (but not necessarily controlled by) developments in the states. Members of Congress and presidents pick and choose from the range of policy initiatives available across the country, ensconcing some of them, in some form, into federal law.

In this book, I argue that one could characterize federal-state interactions in education as top-down and bottom-up, but neither of these approaches fully captures the complexity that has enabled the American federal system to influence education agendas in Washington and the states. Relationships between federal and state officials are much more pragmatic and fluid than either of these approaches, considered alone or together, would suggest. As Martha Derthick has argued, American federalism "is a highly protean form, subject to constant reinterpretation. It is long on change and confusion and very low on fixed, generally accepted principles" (Derthick 2001, 153). That constant reinterpretation means that perspectives on American federalism beginning with its dynamism as their organizing principle—rather than a one-way street approach looking down from the top or up from the bottom—will better explain both the central tendencies and variation in policy that federalism produces across time. Recognizing how federal policymakers and their counterparts in state governments influence each other's agendas not only produces better descriptions of how education policy has changed but it also explains more generally how leaders set agendas and make policy in what James Madison called America's "compound republic."

Madison used this term to describe the system the framers suggested for the nation's constitution. *Federalist No. 39* provides a concise description of the idea. In that article, Madison argued that the proposed document was "neither a national nor a federal Constitution, but a composition of both" (Rossiter 1961, 246). He extended this point in *Federalist No. 51* by noting how the government's arrangement would protect individual rights: "In the compound republic of America, the power surrendered by the people is first divided between two distinct governments [national and the states], and then the portion allotted to each subdivided among distinct and separate departments. Hence a double security arises to the rights of the people" (Rossiter 1961, 323). Madison emphasized that dividing power would frustrate leaders in any part of the compact who sought to control the nation. Interestingly, and most critical for my analysis in this book, that common view about federalism's roadblocks ignored the potential for leaders at one level of government to leverage officials in other levels to achieve their own political or policy objectives.

The compound republic does erect obstacles, as the authors of *The Federalist Papers* noted, but for creative policy entrepreneurs it also generates opportunities for them to build momentum for their ideas and to advance their agendas. Stated differently, at times the compound republic can stifle aspirations of federal or state policy entrepreneurs but at other times it can promote them. Despite the secular trend toward greater centralization that has characterized the American federal system since the New Deal, federal and state politicians have capitalized on opportunities that America's compound republic creates (Derthick 1987, 2001). The challenge of understanding changes in the nation's education agenda centers on explaining how officials across levels of government have leveraged those opportunities. For reasons I begin to describe in the next chapter, popular understandings of these federal-state interactions, which are frequently variants on the marble cake metaphor of cooperative federalism (Grodzins 1966), do not adequately meet this challenge.

DEVELOPMENTS IN AMERICAN EDUCATION POLICY

Later chapters will relate changes in federal and state education agendas since 1965 to the dynamic relationships in America's federal system. Before discussing those links explicitly, I first provide some context by briefly summarizing major federal and state education policies. This section will help to orient readers who are less familiar with the specific changes I will explain, but who are interested in the book's more general goal of providing insights about how American federalism influences agenda setting.

Federal Education Policy

Despite the federal government's limited role in education relative to the states, a complete accounting of federal involvement in K–12 education would easily run several volumes. I do not pretend to offer comprehensive coverage of that landscape in this book. Readers interested in important topics such as school desegregation and the federal courts or the expansion of federal laws that guarantee rights to disabled students should rely on other sources.[2] Some of those topics will briefly appear in subsequent pages, but generally they do not occupy a central place in my analysis.

In an effort to delimit the book and simultaneously explore major policy changes that can reveal novel insights about federalism's impact on agenda setting, I focus on the ESEA, the primary law that federal policymakers have developed to influence the nation's schools. Despite the importance of the other policy areas that I noted in the previous paragraph, the ESEA of 1965 does represent the beginning of a dramatically expanded federal role in K–12 education. It also provides a powerful tool that federal and state policymakers have used to expand their education agendas. Experts commonly consider the ESEA a "milestone in federal aid to education" (Hartle and Holland 1983, 418). In his study of policymaking in the Dwight Eisenhower, John F. Kennedy, and Johnson years, for example, Sundquist (1968, 216) noted that after the ESEA became law, "The question would be, henceforth, not *whether* the national government should give aid, but *how much* it should give, for what purposes—and with how much federal control." A focus on the ESEA, then, is substantively useful and provides opportunities for expanding what researchers presently know about the relationship between federalism and agenda setting. Chapter 4 describes the ESEA's development in some detail. For now, as a brief introduction, I consider the law's original features as it emerged from the legislative process in 1965.

Lyndon Johnson signed the first ESEA into law in Johnson City, Texas, on the site of the one-room schoolhouse he attended as a boy. On that day, he had at his side Miss Katie Deadrich, the teacher that LBJ said had taught him his earliest school lessons. After noting the wide majorities by which the House and Senate had passed the law (263 to 153 and 73 to 18, respectively), the president predicted "all of those of both parties of Congress who supported the enactment of this legislation will be remembered in history as men and women who began a new day of greatness in American society" (*Congressional Quarterly* 1966, 293). Two months later, at a Democratic dinner, Johnson said the ESEA would be "the most important measure that I shall ever sign" (*Congressional Quarterly* 1966, 276).

The original ESEA, known officially as Public Law 89-10, contained six titles. Title I provided help to educationally disadvantaged children by sending federal aid to local school districts with high concentrations of low-income students. It was, and still is, the centerpiece of the ESEA. For fiscal year 1966, for example, expenditures on Title I comprised 86 percent of the ESEA's total appropriations directed to the states. In fiscal year 2004, spending on Title I absorbed over 23 percent of the entire discretionary budget of the U.S. Department of Education.[3]

Title II was composed of grants for purchasing instructional materials. The focus of Title III was funding for a broad array of programs, generally called supplementary educational services. It was basically a catch-all and included things such as counseling for elementary and secondary (and even adult) students, remedial instruction, and specialized instruction for students taking advanced science or foreign language courses, among other programs. Title IV focused on educational research and training and allocated funds to universities and other groups to conduct and disseminate the results of this research. Title V was specifically designed to help states develop their educational infrastructure by providing grants to upgrade state education agencies.

The final component, Title VI, included general provisions and a statement illustrating that federal officials, despite their enthusiasm for the new law, recognized that the ESEA could provoke fears of a federal takeover of the nation's schools. Specifically, Title VI "stipulated that nothing in the Act should be construed to authorize any Government department, agency, officer, or employee to exercise any direction, supervision, or control over the curriculum, program of instruction, administration of personnel of any educational institution or school system, or over the selection of library resources, textbooks or other instructional materials by any educational institution or school system" (*Congressional Quarterly* 1966, 279). Politically, this clause was important given the Tenth Amendment to the U.S. Constitution, which leaves to the states any powers not assigned to the federal government. Because education does not appear in the U.S. Constitution but is a common topic in state constitutions, the ESEA's original authors included Title VI to recognize this division of labor even as they increased the federal role in the nation's schools.

The ESEA is the centerpiece of federal policy involvement in K–12 education, but as I alluded to earlier, it does not represent the whole of federal efforts in education.[4] Nor has the law remained static. Amendments to the ESEA have broadened its scope; most notably, these include important reforms in 1994 concerning educational standards, and changes in 2001 that introduced new accountability measures by requiring state testing in core subjects for students in grades three through eight. Subsequent chapters, especially chapters 4, 5, and 6, will describe and explain these changes in the ESEA in much detail.

State Education Policy

The development of comprehensive state education policy (not including laws mandating racial segregation in schools) really began to emerge in the 1970s. Before that decade, most state governments lacked effective analysts and full-time policymaking bodies that could innovate in a variety of substantive areas (Hedge 1998; Doyle and Hartle 1985). Education was no exception. Today, well-trained experts who are steeped in policymaking experience work in the states' legislatures, governors' offices, and agencies (Hedge 1998; Bowling and Wright 1998). These government employees also work in more mature bureaucratic systems and in state legislatures that tend to meet regularly throughout the year, rather than on part-time schedules. Without question, there is tremendous variation both across and within states in all these areas. Nevertheless, these advances in the nation's fifty states represent one of the major, yet often forgotten, developments in American politics since World War II.

Shifts in state education policy have occurred in what one might conveniently describe as three broad eras corresponding to the 1970s, 1980s, and 1990s. This brief introduction will follow that pattern for now, mainly to provide a concise overview of major changes. A word of caution is in order, though. Labeling these time periods as eras blurs the reality that the changes I describe have occurred in various forms across almost all years since the 1960s. While these eras may sometimes describe central tendencies of particular periods, they can blind observers to variation and interesting dynamics within those periods, as well. In later chapters, I will focus on this variation in more detail and eschew the eras approach.

State policy changes in the 1970s began with the rise of school finance litigation and the school finance equity movement. The U.S. Supreme Court's decision in *San Antonio School District v. Rodriguez* (1973) was an important factor in this development. The case arose when Texas students challenged their state's education finance system, which generated significant spending disparities across districts. In the San Antonio area, spending ranged from $356 to $594 per pupil depending on the district a student attended. In a 5 to 4 decision, the Court held that the Fourteenth Amendment's equal protection clause did not guarantee a right to equal educational resources. The majority emphasized that state courts should answer funding equity questions because many state constitutions explicitly address the provision of education (Fellman 1976).

Although disappointed with the outcome of *Rodriguez*, critics of state funding systems heeded the Court's advice and shifted their activities to state battlegrounds. Many state-level contests over funding equity ensued, and, in fact, efforts to equalize education spending across districts by breaking its strong connection to local property taxes continue to occur (Minorini and Sugarman 1999; Goodnough 2001). Since the early 1970s, plaintiffs in these cases have enjoyed varying levels of success and include nineteen who have won at the state supreme court level and twelve who have lost before their state's highest court (Minorini and Sugarman 1999, 41). While equity is by no means the rule across the nation's districts, figure 1.2, which illustrates the shift in relative sources of revenue for K–12 education across federal, state, and local levels of government, shows how a stronger state role in school finance has developed since the 1960s. Disparities still exist within states, to be sure, but in the aggregate, states have consistently outspent local governments since the mid-1990s.

In addition to school finance, support for minimum competency testing also emerged in the 1970s. Minimum competency tests established floors that define the lowest levels of student proficiency in various subject areas (Educational Testing Service Policy Information Center 1990). By the end of the decade, thirty-nine states had adopted this policy in some form. The degree to which these tests carried so-called high stakes, or significant consequences for students and schools, varied by state. For example, Alabama used its tests to make high school graduation decisions and Connecticut relied on them to guide counseling and follow-up teaching efforts while the state of Washington let local school districts and parents determine their use (Pipho 1978).

During the 1980s, a movement focusing on educational quality took the states by storm. The reforms during this period were extensive and included expanding

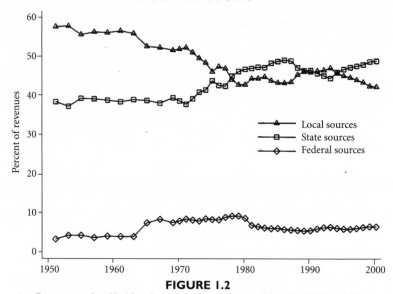

FIGURE 1.2
Revenues for K–12 education by source of funds, 1950–2000
Note: Years correspond to the beginning of a school term (i.e., 1950 = 1950–51 school term).
Data are not available for even-numbered years from 1950 to 1968.
Source: National Center for Education Statistics (2004, Table 156).

student testing, increasing high school graduation requirements, stiffening teacher certification requirements, and adopting measures to gauge school performance. Table 1.1 summarizes these changes. Many of the reforms resonated with recommendations in the National Commission on Excellence in Education's (NCEE) 1983 report, *A Nation at Risk.* In that publication, the Commission offered a startling and controversial assessment: judging by the success of American students relative to others around the world, the United States had essentially engaged in unilateral educational disarmament. Had another nation imposed the present system of American education on the country, the report argued, U.S. leaders might well have considered it an act of war (National Commission on Excellence in Education 1983). The blizzard of state reforms in the 1980s moved one review to call that period "the education reform decade" (Educational Testing Service Policy Information Center 1990).

During the 1990s, the standards movement became the primary engine driving educational reform in the United States (Ravitch 1995). During this time, states built on their work from the 1980s and extended efforts to write down explicitly what their students should know and be able to do. States linked those content standards to performance standards, which were designed to show how well students knew the material they were supposed to have learned. State assessments or exams were the tools that schools, districts, and state officials would use to measure student improvement.

TABLE I.I
Summary of major state policy changes in K–12 education during the 1980s

Reform Area	1980–89
High school graduation requirements	42 states raise standards
Student testing	47 statewide programs by 1990
Accountability	23 states go beyond test scores and use an integrated set of indicators
Teacher standards	39 states require passing a test to enter teacher education or begin teaching

Source: Educational Testing Service Policy Information Center (1990, 4).

By the end of the 1990s, the states' progress illustrated that moving to systems organized around standards and tests would not be easy. Just as President Bill Clinton's administration was leaving office in January 2001, the U.S. Department of Education reported on these efforts. As part of the 1994 reauthorization of the ESEA, called the Improving America's Schools Act (IASA), and another Clinton initiative known as Goals 2000, the department evaluated state progress. It found only eleven of the thirty-four states it reviewed had earned a mark of "full approval," indicating that these states had aligned their standards, curriculum, and assessments (Citizens' Commission on Civil Rights 2001, Figure 1). After conducting its own study, published later that same year, the American Federation of Teachers (AFT) concluded that twenty-nine states and the District of Columbia had made progress because they possessed clear and specific standards in core subject areas at the elementary, middle, and secondary school levels. Much work remained, however, to align state curriculum and tests with these standards (American Federation of Teachers 2001).

Not directly linked to standards but also growing in the 1990s was a movement for expanded school choice beyond the magnet school and within-district options that have existed for many years. During this decade, Wisconsin and Ohio began public voucher programs in Milwaukee and Cleveland. These programs channeled money directly to low-income parents to help them pay for education in private schools. Citizen entrepreneurs and charitable foundations also promoted this reform in other cities, creating privately funded endowments for this same purpose.

The Wisconsin and Ohio voucher laws have produced high-profile legal battles, but both have withstood court challenges. The Wisconsin Supreme Court upheld Milwaukee's program in *Jackson v. Benson* (1998), a decision that the U.S. Supreme Court did not review. In *Zelman v. Simmons-Harris* (2002), the U.S. Supreme Court turned back a challenge to a similar program in Cleveland. The law's opponents argued that the program was unconstitutional because parents could use their vouchers at religious schools. The Court disagreed in a contentious 5 to 4 decision.

Vouchers were not the only choice-based reform of the 1990s, though. Charter schools, which are public schools freed from many of the rules and regulations governing traditional public schools, have also expanded across the country. In fact, they are much more popular than voucher programs that involve private and public schools. By 2005, forty states and the District of Columbia had adopted charter school laws. According to the Center for Education Reform (2005), during the 2004–05 school year, there were roughly 3,000 charter schools serving nearly one million students in the United States.

KEY CONCEPTS AND THE THEORETICAL ARGUMENT IN BRIEF

This book develops a general theory of federalism and agenda setting to explain developments in the American education agenda. The overall theoretical argument is as follows: The level of interest and involvement that a government demonstrates in a particular policy area depends on the advocacy of policy entrepreneurs who mobilize the government's license and capacity to act. Lacking license or capacity at their level of government, entrepreneurs can acquire these ingredients by borrowing strength from other governments in the American federal system. This argument implies that federalism creates potential agenda setting opportunities for individuals who carefully size up their own weaknesses and then make up for them by leveraging the arguments or capabilities that exist elsewhere in the system. Borrowing strength thus enables policy entrepreneurs to advance their priorities, even in areas where, at first glance, they may struggle to wield influence.

I have crafted my borrowing strength theory of agenda setting in general terms. Thus, by government I mean national, state, or local governments. Interest and involvement, which I characterize as the two main components of a government's agenda, are straightforward concepts. Interest refers to the rhetorical commitment government officials demonstrate in a policy area. The number of legislative hearings devoted to a policy and the presence of the policy in major speeches, party platforms, or political campaigns all capture different aspects of this idea. Involvement refers to policy production. A government is involved in a policy area if it makes laws, issues regulations, constructs bureaucracies, and appropriates funds to address the area in some way. Unlike simply highlighting a problem through speeches or campaign ads, for example, involvement demonstrates that a government has committed itself to doing something about the problem.

License is the first key factor that influences government interest and involvement. It refers to the strength of the arguments available to justify government action. Clearly, some arguments are more persuasive than others, which means selecting compelling rationales for action is central to building an agenda. But if license justifies action, it by no means guarantees that policymakers will be able to act and to act effectively. That is why capacity, the second key factor, is critically important. Capacity refers to the ability to act once policymakers have decided they want to act. Capacity exists in the form of financial resources, the coherence and presence of bureaucratic structures such as regulatory agencies of government, and the knowledge, experience, and expertise of government personnel.

Policy entrepreneurs are the individuals who mobilize license and capacity to foster government interest and involvement in particular policy areas. Previous scholarship has described these entrepreneurs in many ways, sometimes focusing on their work within specific government institutions, such as Congress, while at other times discussing policy entrepreneurship more generally (Walker 1977; Arnold 1990; Baumgartner and Jones 1993; Schiller 1995; Schneider, Teske, and Mintrom 1995; Kingdon 1995; Wawro 2000; Sheingate 2003; Mintrom 2000). I tend toward the broader conceptualization and define policy entrepreneurs as individuals inside or outside government who champion particular ideas and attempt to increase the agenda-status of policy areas they care about most.

Overall, I argue that policy entrepreneurs are most likely to promote a government's interest and involvement in an area when the government possesses high license and high capacity to act. Conversely, where both license and capacity are weak, it is extremely difficult for an entrepreneur to promote government interest and involvement in the favored area. More interesting combinations occur when the government lacks either license or capacity but not both. For example, if policy entrepreneurs in Congress possess license to act but the federal government lacks capacity to alleviate some social ill, how likely is it that government officials will demonstrate interest in the issue and then get involved? Must these entrepreneurs give up making a strong push for their position and simply stand by and test their ideas behind the scenes by "softening up" (Kingdon 1995) potential supporters? If both license and capacity are required to foster interest and involvement, then one might conclude that the issue will not rise very high on the federal agenda. But this need not be the case.

When these congressional entrepreneurs and their staffers survey their options in the nation's compound republic, they find that limited federal capacity need not stifle their ambitions. In a federal system, creative policymakers can borrow capacity from other levels of government to help achieve their objectives. Lacking the capacity to reform the nation's schools on their own, members of Congress may pass laws building on state efforts. In the process, they rely on, or borrow, state capacity to make these initiatives work and to push their own agenda priorities. The result is that state capacity can enable policy entrepreneurs in Congress to build agendas in federal venues, something they could not have done by relying on federal capacity alone.

The process of borrowing strength described in the previous paragraph can also apply to state officials. For example, a governor may find herself possessing only weak arguments (low license) to justify a particular reform agenda. That may prevent the governor from persuading her constituents and other state officials to endorse her idea. However, the governor's task becomes less onerous if federal officials, in particular the president and his advisers using the bully pulpit, have charted a similar course for the whole nation. The president's own investment of

political capital can become a valuable resource for a governor attempting to develop license to expand her own agenda in her state.

Over time, the process of borrowing strength can influence levels of interest
and involvement that state and federal officials demonstrate in a policy area. The
process also reveals how the American federal system can be a source of positive
feedback that creates momentum and expands government agendas. This is unlike a view that sees federalism as replete with roadblocks that primarily foster
negative feedbacks and allow the national government and the states to mutually
check one another's ambitions.

Determining how to borrow strength is something members of Congress and
other federal officials must ponder as they attempt to assert their influence. In
other words, there is a fine line between borrowing capacity that effectively leverages state capabilities and imposing unfunded mandates that place unrealistic fiscal and programmatic expectations on state governments. Similarly, arguments
that can justify action at one level of the nation's federal system may be less persuasive in another. In short, borrowing strength may sound easy in theory, but in
practice it is not. Subsequent chapters will explain the source of these difficulties
and how federal and state policy entrepreneurs have responded to them.

OVERVIEW OF THE BOOK

This chapter has provided a broad overview of the arguments to come. Chapter 2
completes part I of the book by describing in more detail the theoretical model
that guides the study. The four chapters in part II are the empirical heart of the
work. Collectively, they examine how the American education agenda has unfolded since the mid-1960s. Chapters 3 and 4 focus on the federal government.
They include data from numerous sources that map out variation in federal interest and involvement in education during roughly the last half of the twentieth century. Chapter 5 analyzes that variation by using the theoretical model from
chapter 2 to explain how federal and state attempts to borrow strength from one
another have produced changes in federal and state agendas. I continue my analysis of change in chapter 6, which is an in-depth look at NCLB. In that chapter, I
show how the borrowing strength model of agenda setting can explain policy development and implementation of that reauthorization of the ESEA.

Part III examines several overall implications about education, federalism, and
agenda setting. Chapter 7 shows how developments in federal and state education
agendas have affected politics in the American states and inside the Washington
Beltway. Chapter 8 concludes by considering some general implications about education agendas in the United States since the 1960s. It also discusses some of the
broader theoretical implications that my study suggests for scholars interested in
the relationship between federalism and agenda setting.

I have written this book with two specific audiences in mind. For policy practi-
tioners and other observers of American elementary and secondary education, the

insights I provide will help reveal how the nation's education agenda has taken shape and what it might look like in the future. Similarly, political scientists who care about how the nation's compound republic shapes government agendas will find this analysis helpful and see potential applications of its theoretical ideas in other policy areas. To serve that latter audience, in particular, the next chapter reviews relevant literature on federalism and agenda setting before developing my theoretical perspective in greater detail.

NOTES

1. For example, a *Washington Post–ABC News* poll from September 2002 reported that 74 percent of adults said the issue of education would be "very important" in deciding their vote for the U.S. House. That number equaled or exceeded the number responding "very important" on the following other issues: war on terrorism (74 percent), the economy and jobs (74 percent), the situation in Iraq with Saddam Hussein (71 percent), health care (70 percent), prescription drug benefits for the elderly (63 percent), and Social Security (60 percent). With the deepening American commitment in Iraq, concerns over education abated somewhat during the 2004 election season. However, that did not necessarily suggest lackluster interest (*Washington Post* and ABC News 2002). In January 2005, a poll from the Pew Research Center for the People and the Press found that 70 percent of adults believed "improving the educational system" should be a "top priority" for President Bush and Congress in 2005. That was slightly lower than, but close to, the same number of respondents who said "defending the country from future terrorist attacks" (75 percent) and "strengthening the nation's economy" (75 percent) should also be top priorities. It was equal to or higher than concern over reforming Social Security (70 percent saying it is a top priority) and Medicare (67 percent) and much higher than other issues such as protecting the environment (49 percent) and lowering taxes for the middle class (48 percent) (Pew Research Center for the People and the Press 2005).
2. There are dozens of books and shorter studies in both areas. On the history of federal policy in busing and school desegregation, examples include Bell (1980), Wilkerson (1979), and Orfield (1978; 1999). Many titles also appear in a collection of articles from political scientists that commemorated the fortieth anniversary of the Little Rock drama of 1957 (Struggling toward Opportunity: 40 Years Since Little Rock 1997). For useful work on special education, see Hehir and Latus (1992), Hehir and Gamm (1999), McLaughlin and Rouse (2000), and Finn, Rotherham, and Hokanson (2001).
3. For data on the original ESEA, see the *Congressional Quarterly* (1966, 292). Current figures are available from the U.S. Department of Education at http://www.ed.gov/about/overview/budget/history/index.html (accessed on June 13, 2005).
4. A federal role did exist prior to 1965, even though it was quite scattered. Some of the more well-known efforts affecting K–12 education before that year include the Northwest Ordinance of 1787, which provided land grants to support educational institutions in the new nation; the Smith-Hughes Act of 1917, which initiated specific federal support for vocational education; Impact Aid, which was designed to assist school districts in communities significantly burdened by the presence of federal facilities or lands [Impact Aid became law in 1941, and essentially amounts to revenue sharing for

local districts; it is still one of the most popular federal programs, primarily because its eligibility criteria guarantee funds to school districts in more than 250 of the nation's congressional districts each year (Wear 2003)]; and finally, the National Defense Education Act of 1958, which became law after the Soviet Union's Sputnik launch [NDEA was designed to increase the nation's stock of scientists, engineers, and foreign language speakers; among other things, it funded everything from the development of elementary and secondary science programs to fellowships for graduate study (Dow 1991)]. While some of the specific elements of these programs no longer exist, like many federal education programs, they have continued in other forms. Beyond the ESEA, perhaps the most significant federal education law affecting K–12 schooling is the Individuals with Disabilities Education Act, or IDEA (originally passed in 1975 as the Education for All Handicapped Children Act). This act helped to reverse the nation's long history of excluding students with special needs from educational opportunities that nearly all citizens take for granted.

2

Borrowing Strength, Federalism, and Agenda Setting

IN THIS CHAPTER, I DEVELOP A THEORY TO DESCRIBE AND EXPLAIN HOW THE institution of federalism affects the process of agenda setting. My thesis is that a government's agenda, as measured by its level of interest and involvement in a policy area, depends on the efforts of policy entrepreneurs who mobilize the government's license and capacity to act. A lack of license or capacity need not limit a government's agenda, though, as long as entrepreneurs can make up for these deficits by borrowing strength from another level of government. This conceptualization proves quite useful in explaining how the nation's education agenda has unfolded since the 1960s. More broadly, it provides a generic tool for analyzing agenda development vertically across levels of the American federal system and horizontally into other policy areas.

The chapter proceeds in five sections. The first defines two key terms: agendas and federalism. The second describes some of the conceptual limits of previous research on federalism and agenda setting that prevent either field from shedding much light on the other. The third section examines three key concepts that are building blocks for my theory: policy entrepreneurs, license, and capacity. The fourth section develops a theoretical model that relates these concepts and the mechanism of borrowing strength to show how federalism influences agenda setting. The fifth section uses the theoretical model to derive predictions about how agenda dynamics are likely to unfold in a federal system. That final section also briefly describes the methods and diverse sources of evidence that appear in subsequent chapters.

DEFINING AGENDA SETTING AND FEDERALISM

For decades, political scientists have considered how policymakers, organized interest groups, and citizens determine the scope of government agendas (Dahl 1956, 1961; Schattschneider 1960; Bachrach and Baratz 1962; Olson 1965; Lowi 1967; Downs 1972; Cobb and Elder 1983; Riker 1993; Baumgartner and Jones 1993, 2006b; Kingdon 1995). In these studies, scholars have provided many answers to the questions "What is agenda setting?" and "What is the agenda?" For example, Riker (1993, 1) introduces his edited volume by describing in broad terms "the agenda function of setting alternatives and priorities." Studying that process includes three general activities, he argues: considering where issues come from in the first place; examining what makes some issues political and thus fair game for policy debate; and analyzing the strategies that advocates use to manipulate agenda setting processes, what Riker calls "heresthetics" (Riker 1986), to increase the likelihood that their favored alternatives will win.

Cobb and Elder (1983, 14, 85–86) take a similarly expansive approach and define the agenda as "a general set of political controversies that will be viewed at any point in time as falling within the range of legitimate concerns meriting the attention of the polity." Under this definition, they see two separate but related agendas. The systemic agenda "consists of all issues that are commonly perceived by members of the political community as meriting public attention and as involving matters within the legitimate jurisdiction of existing governmental authority," while the institutional, governmental, or formal (all synonyms) agenda "may be defined as that set of items explicitly up for the active and serious consideration of authoritative decision-makers."[1]

In his book on the president's domestic policy agenda, Light (1999, 2–4) characterizes the president's agenda as a "signal" that "indicates what the President believes to be the most important issues facing his administration. It identifies what the President finds to be the most appropriate alternatives for solving the problems. It identifies what the President deems to be the highest priorities." In short, in forming an agenda, presidents specify issues, alternatives, and relative priorities.

In Kingdon's (1995, 3–4) classic work, originally published in 1984 and mostly unchanged in its new edition, the agenda is "the list of subjects or problems to which governmental officials, and people outside of government closely associated with those officials, are paying some serious attention at any given time." Like others, Kingdon recognizes the existence of more particular agendas including the specialized ones present in government agencies; the general governmental agenda, comprised of subjects getting some measure of attention from public officials; and the decision agenda, which is a subset of the governmental agenda that includes specific topics that public officials act upon such as a House floor vote, an executive order, or a regulation.

It is interesting that in perhaps the most comprehensive work on agenda setting, Baumgartner and Jones offer no pithy definition of the agenda. Rather, the authors argue that "The agenda-setting process is much more complicated than the comparison of issues that are 'on' or 'off' the public agenda would imply" (Baumgartner and Jones 1993, 36). That moves them away from the level of detail present in the Kingdon (1995) or Light (1999) books and toward a focus "on the long-term trends in interest and discussion for much larger policy questions" (Baumgartner and Jones 1993, 49). Baumgartner and Jones conceptualize a number of different agendas. Media coverage reveals the public agenda, and the number of congressional hearings and public laws map out the governmental agenda.

They use these indicators to "trace an issue as it moves from one venue to another (if it does) and track how public or elite understandings of the issue change (if they do)" (Baumgartner and Jones 1993, 50).

Even though these definitions vary, all agree on one basic idea: a topic is on the government's agenda if public officials give it some attention, and possibly act upon it. My analysis begins from that basic starting point and in subsequent pages refers to three different but related agendas, which I define as follows. The public agenda contains items that are salient in the mass public, the media, and popular culture. Using this definition, for example, one could consider education on the public agenda if many people identified it as an important problem facing the nation. Because this project focuses primarily on the attitudes and actions of policy entrepreneurs, not the general public, the public agenda will play a supporting rather than a leading role in my discussion.

The political agenda measures how frequently and specifically government officials—such as legislators, chief executives, and their staff members—talk about particular topics. The political agenda captures the level of government interest in a policy area, one of my key dependent variables. I consider press releases from elected officials, campaign advertisements and issue briefs, proceedings such as government hearings, and presidential speeches all indicators of the content of the political agenda. Chapter 3 makes these ideas concrete by describing how federal interest in education has varied during the latter half of the twentieth century.

Finally, an item is on the policy agenda if it is reflected in laws, budget appropriations, government bureaucracies, or regulations. The policy agenda is sometimes the next stop after public officials have demonstrated interest in an issue. After discussing the topic in hearings or during campaigns, they sometimes pass laws or spend money to address it. The policy agenda corresponds to this study's other key dependent variable, involvement. Chapter 4 describes variation in federal involvement in education since the first ESEA became law.

"Federalism" is the other key term that requires clarification. In its common usage, the word "federal" has many connotations. For students and scholars of American politics, federalism typically refers to America's divided system of government, which contains a national government based in Washington, DC, and fifty state governments (Grodzins 1966; Elazar 1984). Because local governments are technically creatures of the states, researchers often talk about the nation's "intergovernmental system" when they want to explicitly include local governments, along with the national government and the states, in their analyses (Walker 1995, 22; O'Toole 2000a).

Lay people, news reporters, and scholars often use the term "federal government" to mean only the national government based in Washington, DC, and its associated courtrooms or departments scattered about the nation. When people complain about their federal taxes, for example, they do not mean all the money they owe to the U.S. Internal Revenue Service and their state departments of revenue. Rather, they are speaking of the portion of their earnings they pay to Uncle Sam.

This book will follow a couple of simple conventions to distinguish between different meanings of the word federalism. Phrases like "federal system" or "federalism" will refer collectively to the governments in Washington, DC, *and* the states. Statements about the "federal government" or the "national government" will refer to the government comprised of the U.S. Congress, the presidency and executive departments, and the courts. Following these general rules will be tricky at times. For example, politicians sometimes distinguish between education as being in the "national interest," meaning all citizens and governments (federal, state, and local) should care about it, versus the degree to which it should be a federal responsibility for the government in Washington, DC. Context should clarify the intended meaning where this potential ambiguity arises.

These definitions of the agenda and federalism can also work together to describe the agendas of different governments. Most broadly, general references to the "government's agenda" or the "governmental agenda" will refer to the political and policy agendas of a particular level of government, be it the states or the federal government. Further, when I use phrases such as the "American education agenda" or the "national education agenda," as this book's subtitle suggests, I will be referring collectively to the education agendas of the states and the federal government. An item is on the "federal agenda" or the "federal government's agenda" if members of Congress or the president, for example, demonstrate some level of interest and involvement in it. I will use "federal interest" to refer to those items on the federal political agenda, while "federal involvement" will refer to the federal government's policy agenda. Similarly, "state interest" will capture the political agenda in the nation's fifty states, while "state involvement" will gauge the states' policy agenda.

DISCONNECTS BETWEEN THEORIES OF FEDERALISM AND AGENDA SETTING

Federalism researchers and those who study agenda setting have made important contributions to what we know about the American political system. Their advances have often proceeded in relative isolation from one another even though casual observation would suggest that the structure of federalism in the United States can influence which policy issues become ripe for discussion and potential action. With the literatures on federalism and agenda setting relatively far apart, then, the result is that political scientists lack a tight set of rich concepts that can unite these two lines of inquiry. The disconnect stems from issues in both areas, which I consider to be a collective missed opportunity rather than a specific failing of any particular group of scholars.

Three main issues prevent the American federalism literature from promoting sharp theoretical insights about how agenda setting processes work in the United States. First, the metaphors that scholars have used to analyze federalism can make it difficult to link this work with other fields. Federalism scholarship has become somewhat overrun by labels and metaphors that describe the system's nuances. Walker's (1995) partial list of federalisms included more than twenty different variants; another study, which Anton (1989, 3) cites, identified 267. Walker (1995, 22–23) noted that these conceptions have been "diverse, discordant, and numerous" and have moved some researchers to "question their usefulness." While diverse perspectives can be good, this conceptual hubbub also can make it difficult at times for knowledge to accumulate in a theoretically elegant way. Anton (1989) has noted the field's general weakness at mobilizing powerful analytic concepts, in particular those that explore general mechanisms to explain change. The result, he argues, is that federalism studies have often been "empirically strong but theoretically weak" (Anton 1989, 2).

Even though scholars have identified many types of federalisms, any survey of American government texts would suggest that conceptualizations based on cooperation among governments enjoy much support. Ever since Grodzins (1966) coined the "marble cake" metaphor to extend the "layer cake" imagery of dual federalism, scholars have generally recognized that most policy areas in the United States involve actors from national and state (and increasingly local) governments (Elazar 1984; Zimmerman 1992; Peterson 1995; Conlan 1998; Derthick 2001; Agranoff and McGuire 2001; Gormley 2001). That swirl of activity, much like a marble cake, makes it hard to distinguish where one layer of government activity or authority ends and where another might begin. Without this perspective on federalism, Grodzins (1966, 8) argues, one "misses the most important fact of all: the system is, in effect, one government serving a common people for a common end."

If a cooperative take on federalism helps to simplify the conceptual landscape, it still leaves many theoretical avenues for others to explore. Arguably, the idea of cooperative federalism, and in particular its marble cake imagery, is more a metaphor than a model.[2] By that, I mean it provides a heuristic that can loosely characterize the system's broad features, but it does not necessarily specify the mechanisms that might enhance or retard cooperation. Because cooperation is often cast in very broad terms, the metaphor does not easily generate specific predictions that are amenable to empirical tests. For example, when Grodzins (1966, 11–12) describes various dimensions of federal-state "sharing," he notes that his claims are not "easy to test against actual events," which produces "difficulties of analysis that cannot be completely solved." Similarly, Elazar's (1984, 1991) elaboration of cooperative federalism as a matrix containing multiple centers of power may have enabled him to represent the system more precisely than previous authors. However, in contrast to his work on state political culture, which generates clearer predictions about the content of state policy, Elazar's explicit treatment of cooperation remains primarily descriptive.

Further, work on cooperative federalism tends to focus primarily on policy implementation and, in particular, implementation of federal policy rather than where policy ideas originate. That begs the question of why and how certain policy domains become ripe for cooperation and why others do not. Put another way, just because "governments constantly intrude into one another's policy space" (Anton 1989, 231) does not mean that intrusions or cooperation are equally likely in all areas. And surely, constitutional issues aside, given the nation's ambivalence about empowering the national government (Derthick 2001; Ellis 2000), federal officials often face major challenges when they consider embarking on cooperative ventures. So, even if one believed that ideas simply bubble up to Washington from the laboratories of innovation known as the American states, that still leaves unanswered how the bubbling up occurs and how the cooperation it might produce eventually takes shape.

To their credit, Grodzins and Elazar recognize how their work on cooperative federalism leaves much room for future theoretical development. The former reminded readers that the marble cake would not be the final word on American federalism: "The task of describing and analyzing the chaotic American government has been done many times by many hands in many ways for many purposes," Grodzins argued. "Yet it is a job that must always be done again. Circumstances are ever changing. New methods of observation supply new data. And most of all, the phenomena themselves are complex and baffling" (Grodzins 1966, 12–13). Elazar (1991, 69) made a parallel point twenty-five years later in responding to what he saw as pervasive simplistic assumptions about cooperative federalism; he noted that "the sum and substance of federal theory is not embodied in either dual or cooperative federalism, or in any of the other current slogans." More recently still, Zimmerman (2001) stressed a need for better theorizing that could account for the presence of dual, cooperative, and even coercive federalisms in the American system. Thus, forty years after Grodzins's (1966) work appeared, the labels and metaphors continue to proliferate, which certainly has provided more ways to describe the system's particular features. This crowded conceptrual landscape has made it difficult, though, to build bridges across areas of study. Thus, opportunities for conceptual breakthroughs that can elegantly link the institution of American federalism and the process of agenda setting still remain.

A second aspect of federalism research that makes it difficult to integrate this work with agenda setting scholarship is more easily described but no less important. It stems from the understandable desire of scholars who aim to explain federal-state interaction in theoretically precise terms that reach beyond the descriptive or even normative metaphors of federalism that sometimes crowd the literature.[3] Seeking more conceptually tight theories and explanations, several researchers have studied federalism by grounding their work in principal-agent models of federal-state interaction (Chubb 1985b; Hedge, Scicchitano, and Metz 1991; Hedge and Scicchitano 1994; Hill and Weissert 1995; Wood 1992, 1991; Nicholson-Crotty 2004). Generically speaking, these models attempt to analyze the strategic relationship between a principal, sometimes called the boss, and an agent, who is often portrayed as the principal's subordinate. In straightforward terms, principals hire agents to act on their behalf. Agents enjoy varying degrees of discretion as they work, and both principals and agents often possess dissimilar information and divergent goals that can complicate the relationship. In the context of federal grants, for example, scholars frequently draw upon principal-agent models to examine the strategic interactions between policymakers in Washington, DC, (principals) who distribute funds to state actors (agents) who spend these dollars.

One can reasonably praise federalism research in the principal-agent tradition for its conceptual precision and ability to generate hypotheses that invite empirical tests. As a building block for bridging the theoretical gap between federalism and agenda setting, however, the principal-agent approach is limited. Like work on cooperative federalism, these analyses typically focus on policy implementation by addressing questions such as: Do states strategically alter policies that Washington has directed them to implement? Do states respond to federal oversight activity when they issue regulations? Do states divert funds from federal grants to support their own policy priorities? By focusing on how governments carry out policy, the quintessential issue for agenda setting scholars of how policies emerge receives little or usually no attention. Despite the formal principal-agent relationship that appears to exist with federal programs, it is debatable whether states would necessarily consider themselves agents of Washington in policy areas in which federal dollars are quite sparse and for various reasons overall federal responsibility remains relatively low.

A third point worth noting is that much federalism research proceeds from a top-down perspective that suggests changes in the system emerge as the priorities of national leaders change. A popular narrative trajectory of federalism's development frequently begins with the cooperative and creative federalism of LBJ. It then moves to the New Federalism of Richard Nixon, which, according to these accounts, Ronald Reagan extended and stamped with his own mark. These descriptions, then, conclude with the devolution phenomenon of the 1990s that turned power back to the states (Nathan 1990; Conlan 1998; Donahue 1997). The principal-agent approaches to federalism also typically work from top-down perspectives, as the questions in the previous paragraph suggest. Even work on cooperative federalism, which stresses the overlapping responsibilities for state and federal governments, usually explores those overlaps in the context of federal programs. The unstated assumption is that cooperative federalism emerges when leaders inside the Washington Beltway decide that cooperation would be a good idea. States themselves appear as reactive or at best as supporters of ideas or philosophies that presidents and national leaders articulate. That understanding of federalism provides an important perspective but it understates the importance of states' own priorities and how they affect federal agendas.

The top-down bias sometimes also suggests a zero-sum perspective on power in the American federal system. If the national government grows stronger, as during LBJ's era, the states appear weaker. Fast forward to the devolution period in the 1990s and the story is reversed. Some approaches often portray federalism's dynamics as a competition between levels of government or as a clock-like machine with cyclical rhythm where ascendance at one level signals decline in another (Chubb 1985a; Nathan 1990; Walker 1995, chapter 11). These perspectives miss the ways federalism can enable actors at all levels of government simultaneously. Many authors have recognized the need to get past the zero-sum approaches (Grodzins 1966; Beer 1978; Elmore and McLaughlin 1983; Elazar 1984; Zimmerman 1992). But, in claiming that American federalism is not a zero-sum system, these authors and others usually offer ad hoc explanations rather than a powerful set of theoretical concepts that can explain how the system helps to set federal and state agendas.

The perspectives and approaches of agenda setting scholars also contribute to the limited integration between these fields, something that some have recognized for several years (Walker 1977, 424; Nelson 1984). Kingdon (1995, 229–30) suggests as much in the update to his original seminal work, but he also admits that "federalism complicates an analysis of agenda-setting, because there are multiple agendas possible for the same subject matter at a given time." In particular, the agenda setting literature contains two limits that are worth considering here.

First, major studies of agenda setting have typically not explicitly examined the influence that state officials and other subnational actors can play in setting the federal agenda. The authors in Riker's (1993) edited volume ignore the states completely and Light's (1999) study of the president's agenda does not identify the states as a possible source of ideas.[4] Kingdon (1995) barely mentions the states in his classic study. In their book on agendas and national policy change, Baumgartner and Jones (1993) do include a chapter on federalism; however, they tend to emphasize a zero-sum view of the system, which I described earlier, where federal officials can use grants to change the priorities of state and local governments.

Beyond those authors, Berkman (1993) comes closest to articulating a careful theory that gets beyond the popular, but sometimes problematic, metaphor of states as laboratories for national policy innovation.[5] Focusing on the years from 1978 to 1986, he explains how the tax agenda of the U.S. Congress emerged as legislators drew upon their experience with the politics of economic development in their home states. Those experiences affected members' attitudes and the party coalitions in Congress that were essential to changing the nation's tax laws. Thus, Berkman develops a bottom-up theory of agenda setting, what he calls the state-roots model, by exploring the "impact on national politics of subnational political change" (Berkman 1993, 5).

Berkman's (1993) work is a useful departure from previous studies of agenda setting that I have just described. Given the nature of its research design, it still leaves many opportunities for other researchers interested in federalism and agenda setting. For one thing, Berkman focuses on the U.S. Congress rather than multiple institutions of state and national government, which Baumgartner and Jones (1993) argue are important to consider. Additionally, and perhaps more importantly, even though his model posits a dynamic process that allows state and federal agendas to influence one another, because he focuses his empirical work on congressional policymaking, he only conjectures briefly about these feedbacks in his concluding chapter (Berkman 1993, 142–48). By concluding with these possibilities, however, it is clear he hoped that future work would consider feedback processes more deeply and explain how state and federal agendas can influence each other through time.

A second feature to note about agenda setting studies, and much federalism research, too, is how scholars have described how policy advocates take advantage of multiple policy venues in the United States. Venues are institutions that possess the authority to act on behalf of all citizens in a particular political jurisdiction (Baumgartner and Jones 1993). Because many governments and hundreds of state and federal agencies comprise the American federal system, policy entrepreneurs have numerous institutional venues where they can agitate for their interests. The availability of multiple venues has become more important since the 1960s as governments have become increasingly interdependent across policy areas (Chubb 1985b; Fesler and Kettl 1996).

Multiple venues are useful for policy advocates because if they find doors closed in one place, they might have more luck opening them elsewhere (Grodzins 1966; Anton 1989; Baumgartner and Jones 1993, 31–35; Burns 1994; Gray and Lowery 2000). This process of venue shopping is important to consider. But it is incomplete because it omits that officials at one level of government may seek advantages at another level not as an alternative to but as a complement for acting in their own. Baumgartner and Jones (1993, 232) briefly allude to this idea by noting that "the multiple venues of the states and the federal government sometimes coalesce into a single system of positive-feedback, each encouraging the other to enact stronger reforms than might otherwise occur." Those authors tend to stress how policy entrepreneurs shift their battles from venue to venue. The research does not illuminate the mechanisms that can enable these entrepreneurs to promote agendas at a particular level of government by leveraging opportunities that exist elsewhere in the system.

Identifiable mechanisms are crucial, though, because, without them, it is impossible to explain how ties between multiple venues in the American federal system help to set government agendas. Focusing on American federalism's centralizing tendencies has perhaps distracted scholars from such a search (Nathan 1990; Walker 1995; Conlan 1998). Admittedly, it is hard to dispute that the federal government has grown much stronger since the New Deal (Derthick 2001, chapter 10). However, if the American federal system tends toward centralization, emphasizing that feature downplays much of the system's variation. Note, for example, that states have become more professional and capable policy actors during the same period that the gravitational pull toward Washington, DC, has increased. Explicitly recognizing these growing state capabilities can help explain how activity in state venues can affect the federal agenda (Anton 1989; Posner 1998; Beamer 1999; Gormley 2001).

The rest of this chapter develops a theory to address the two primary research questions that chapter 1 introduced. My borrowing strength model of agenda setting incorporates a handful of key concepts and processes that integrate major findings from the literature on federalism and agenda setting. In the process, it offers the kind of crisp conceptualization that authors such as Anton (1989) and Kingdon (1995) have urged scholars to pursue.

CONCEPTUAL BUILDING BLOCKS

Building on the introductory discussion in chapter 1, this section describes in more detail three key concepts—policy entrepreneurs, license, and capacity—that I use to explain a government's level of interest and involvement in a policy area.[6] The ensuing section develops a theoretical model that relates them to the process of borrowing strength. Together, these ideas and the model explain how federalism influences agenda setting.

Policy Entrepreneurs

Policy entrepreneurs help to set the political and policy agendas of government. They can be elected politicians, government employees, or workers in the idea communities of think tanks, universities, and interest groups (Walker 1977; Polsby 1984; Smith 1991; Mintrom 2000; Sheingate 2003). In Kingdon's model of agenda setting these entrepreneurs play a key role. The critical linking of problems, policies, and politics, which he argues must precede policy change, does not occur by chance, but when "entrepreneurs perform the function for the system of coupling the previously separate streams" (Kingdon 1995, 182). By implication, these entrepreneurs are not mere bystanders but advocates who fight to push their ideas onto the agenda or defend their turf against other rising concerns.

The best policy entrepreneurs do not limit their sights only on the immediate contexts where they work. True, a member of the U.S. Senate may try to influence the legislative agenda from inside a committee, the chamber, or the Congress as a whole. A Washington lobbyist may spend time with executive branch officials or in meetings with House and Senate committee staff. But entrepreneurs might also influence the federal agenda by capitalizing on opportunities that exist elsewhere in the American compound republic.

Since the early 1980s, especially, several governors known as education reformers have assumed high posts in the federal government. A short list of the most well-known officials includes former education secretaries Richard Riley and Lamar Alexander (who subsequently became a U.S. Senator), and presidents Bill Clinton and George W. Bush. Seeking a greater federal role in K–12 education, but recognizing Washington's inherent limitations in this policy area, these leaders and others have attempted to leverage the license and capacity of state governments to build federal education agendas. That does not mean that federal policy entrepreneurs, even those with state experience, always accurately assess what states can offer; nor do these entrepreneurs always protect state prerogatives (Posner 1998).

State leaders have been equally entrepreneurial in developing their own political and policy agendas. For example, while unfunded federal mandates are sometimes cast as great burdens on subnational units of government, Posner (1998, 217–18) argues they have "also served a political function for state and local governments in gaining leverage—in policy struggles within their own governments." He continues by noting that in some cases "state and local officials found mandates to be a useful tool to accomplish their own policy agendas in the face of recalcitrant local political actors." During the 1980s, for example, many governors developed license to expand their reach over their state education systems by invoking the principles contained in the federal report *A Nation at Risk*.

These examples underscore two important points about agenda setting in a federal system. First, policy entrepreneurs are key players in the agenda setting process. Ultimately, it is people, not faceless government institutions, that produce government agendas. Second, as entrepreneurs develop their agendas, they can seek advantages by leveraging the rhetorical arguments and capabilities (what I call license and capacity) that emanate from other governments.

License to Act

License refers to the strength of the arguments available to justify government action. Where do policy entrepreneurs find the license they need to support their proposals?Four main sources exist. First, and perhaps most generally, license resides in the wells of political capital that politicians cultivate, conserve, and spend at important moments in time. Second are the frames that entrepreneurs impose on issues that link them to other concerns, as when state administrative issues regarding drivers' licenses become connected to national security concerns about fighting terrorism. A third way to justify action is to draw on constitutional or statutory language that grants control over a policy area to a certain level of government. A final source of license is a track record of past policymaking that has withstood challenge over time. If a government has acted previously and rebutted serious criticism, this past experience may justify future efforts along the same, or a similar, path.

In sum, policy entrepreneurs, especially elected officials, are on the strongest ground when they can identify formal sources of license. Statutory or constitutional provisions that identify formal powers, or a track record of persistent policy action, can be quite persuasive. License is important because typically politicians must offer justifications when they assert their power. Scholars of agenda setting and federalism have addressed this general idea both directly and indirectly. Consider these examples from the literature.

Agenda setting scholars have argued that perceived crises can justify government action (Birkland 1997). Policymakers tend to agree and sometimes even assert that governments are essentially hamstrung unless a crisis exists (Kingdon 1995, 95). At least initially, as people turn to public officials for help, crises can boost a leader's stock of political capital and provide compelling frames to justify action. Examples of this phenomenon include the security upgrades at public buildings after the Oklahoma City bombing in 1995; the heightened concerns over nuclear power after the Three Mile Island accident in 1979; the range of school safety measures introduced after the tragedy at Columbine High School in 1999; and the expansion of anti-terrorism activities following the September 11 attacks on the United States in 2001.

Crises may increase the potential for a government to expand its interest and involvement in a policy area, but they do not guarantee it. In crisis and noncrisis situations alike, policy entrepreneurs are most persuasive when they offer a narrative about a problem's causes and the probable effects of policy responses. One of the best explicit treatments of this topic is Stone's (1989, 1997) work on causal stories. She argues that issues only become problems when policy entrepreneurs convince others that problems are amenable to government action. Baumgartner and Jones (1993, 25–30) discuss this idea and note how policy entrepreneurs craft "policy images," which the authors describe as the "way that policy is understood and discussed."[7] Relevant stakeholders and the public need to believe there exists a lever the government can pull to create positive results (Weiss 1998; Majone 1989). Similarly, Polsby (1984, 2) alludes to the importance of license, without actually using that word, by arguing that because needs are essentially ubiquitous— all people feel like they need something—there must also exist "a doctrine, or theory, or idea, or notion, or attitude, or custom, that legitimates governmental activity with respect to this need." Developing these causal stories can be especially challenging when problems are unfamiliar or multidimensional.

Sometimes a federal policy entrepreneur becomes interested in expanding the federal government's role onto the turf of state governments. This complicates the narrative and search for license even more. Not only does the entrepreneur need to link the problem to positive government action, but she must also justify why the federal government should undertake this effort at all. Indirectly, work on federalism has addressed the latter part of this entrepreneur's challenge in discussing how to justify the allocation of policy responsibilities in a federal system.

Using a functional approach, federalism scholars sometimes divide policy into two broad categories: developmental and redistributive (Peterson 1995; Peterson, Rabe, and Wong 1986). Developmental policies are designed to improve the quality of life of particular communities and most frequently focus on economic issues. For example, infrastructure enhancements, such as bridge and road construction, would be developmental activities. Redistributive policies try to benefit needy groups including the poor, unemployed, elderly, or disabled. Welfare and other social service programs are examples in this category.

Scholars using this classification system reason that levels of government closer to citizens have greater license to design and administer developmental policies, while higher levels of government can more easily justify redistribution. State and local governments are more attuned to their own particular economic needs, so the argument goes, and therefore are best able to assess what developmental policies they should enact. The federal government, conversely, should target redistributive policies. Burdening state or local governments with redistribution would force them to raise taxes, which can harm their overall development and undermine their attractiveness compared to other jurisdictions (Tiebout 1956; Hirschman 1970).

In applying this typology, it is sometimes hard to distinguish between developmental and redistributive policies.[8] Education policy provides a case in point. On one hand, it is clearly developmental. Mayors, governors, and industry leaders regularly argue that state and local economies depend on well-educated work forces to attract high-wage employers (Goldberg and Traiman 2001). In addition, businesses often court potential employees by describing how strong the public schools are in the communities where their firms reside. On the other hand, education policy also has redistributive elements. One of the original and ongoing missions of the ESEA Title I program has been to channel resources to communities with large concentrations of poor children in order to improve their life prospects (Jennings 2001). Advocates of school vouchers or charter schools make a parallel point when they argue that school choice already exists in the United States for children of affluent families but not for poor ones. A way to remedy that inequity, they argue, is to provide impoverished families with access to schools of their choice, which, over time, can help disadvantaged students escape poverty (Peterson and Hassel 1998).

Deciding whether education is a developmental or redistributive policy area may tie federalism scholars in analytical knots. But its ambiguity can help federal policymakers to develop license as they attempt to extend Washington's role in America's schools. It can also empower state officials who simultaneously call on the federal government to stay off their turf in some areas of education but beg Washington for help in others. Put another way, because education is both developmental and redistributive, it offers creative policy entrepreneurs opportunities to develop license to act regardless of formal statutory or constitutional provisions that, on their face, appear to demarcate authority over the nation's schools.

Capacity to Act

Capacity refers to the ability to act once policymakers decide they want to act. Concretely, it includes the human, budgetary, and institutional resources or infrastructure that governments possess. Simply because policy entrepreneurs can muster license to justify government involvement in an area does not necessarily mean the government can act and be effective. Capacity is therefore a key variable contributing to the development of government agendas.

Sometimes, low capacity is related to dwindling tax revenues due to a slow economy. For instance, nearly all state budgets were pinched in 2001 and 2002 as the national economic expansion of the 1990s ended (National Conference of State Legislatures 2001b). At other times, politicians may purposefully create a capacity deficit as a strategy to restrain government activity. That line of argument appeared frequently during the 2000 American election season as some candidates called for tax cuts as the best way to use the (apparent) federal budget surplus. When money stays in Washington, they claimed, politicians will undoubtedly spend it on programs. Finally, the structure of ongoing government commitments can also affect capacity. From a local perspective, once school districts pay employee salaries and benefits, maintain the physical infrastructure of school buildings, and put gas in their buses, there is usually little money available for other initiatives.

The presence of government capacity can increase the probability that jarring events will expand government involvement in a policy area. Budgetary expansion of a relevant agency is one example that Nelson (1984, 44) provides in her book about the rise of child abuse as a public concern. "The [Children's] Bureau was able to give so much attention to child protection, physical abuse, and ultimately child neglect," she argues, "because the problems emerged on the agenda exactly, and fortuitously, at the same time that the Bureau was infused with resources for research."

In addition to money, capacity also depends on the quality of a government's workforce and its bureaucratic structures. Improvements in these areas have enabled state governments to become vital players in the American policy system (Hedge 1998; Van Horn 1996). At least up until the 1960s, their ranks lacked professionalization. Legislative and gubernatorial staff members tended to possess minimal knowledge and lacked policy analysis skills. The modernization of the states led the U.S. Advisory Commission on Intergovernmental Relations to remark in a 1985 report, which Nathan (1990, 242) quotes, that "state governments have been transformed in almost every facet of their structure and operations." In addition to better political staff and institutions, state administrators in executive departments have become increasingly skilled, which better positions states to respond to policy challenges (Bowling and Wright 1998).

One can portray the relationship between federal and state capacity as a one-way street that runs either in a federal-to-state or a state-to-federal direction. The former approach characterizes some of the principal-agent analyses of federalism that I noted earlier in which national policymakers attempt to leverage state capabilities and even change state priorities. The second version of the federal-state relationship portrays the federal government as copying ideas from the states and incorporating them into federal law. That bottom-up model reflects the view that states can be laboratories that test diverse solutions to the problems confronting the country.

These top-down and bottom-up perspectives capture some elements of the relationship between federal and state capacity, but they are incomplete. Federal-state interactions are rarely just top-down or bottom-up. At any point in time within a policy area federal and state entrepreneurs may interact in both fashions. Thinking dynamically, federal policy that may appear driven by ambitions of changing state priorities at one moment may in fact develop and unleash forces that foster greater independent state capacity in later periods. State capacity, in turn, can create feedbacks that then promote or retard the development of future federal license or capacity. These interactive dynamics in the American federal system have implications for how policy and political agendas develop. Thus, a model that adopts this dynamism as its central organizing principle will be better able to describe and explain changes in government agendas than the top-down and bottom-up views working together or alone.[9]

SETTING THE AGENDA IN A FEDERAL SYSTEM

When policy entrepreneurs mobilize license and capacity, they can promote government interest and involvement in a policy area. In this section, I develop a general model that relates those concepts. I then embed the model in a federal context to explain how policy entrepreneurs can borrow strength from elsewhere in the system to overcome license or capacity deficits that may otherwise block the development of their agendas.

The Borrowing Strength Model of Agenda Setting

Figure 2.1 presents a simple model of agenda formation that relates the key concepts I have discussed so far. The arrows create three pathways that represent the activities policy entrepreneurs engage in when they want to develop a government's agenda.

The top path shows entrepreneurs leveraging government license to craft the persuasive arguments that can justify action. The bottom path shows entrepreneurs mustering pre-existing government capacity that can produce concrete policy. The middle path illustrates how policy entrepreneurs use an ongoing strategy known as "softening up" (Kingdon 1995) to promote their agendas. By definition, entrepreneurs are passionate policy advocates. Thus, they do not abandon their goals if a government lacks license and capacity. Nor do they stop test marketing and refining their proposals with key policy players and groups even when license and capacity are high. That constant promotion helps them to hone their ideas. Overall, then, considering these three paths, one could state the model as $L + C + S \rightarrow A$, which means the entrepreneur's efforts to combine license (L) and capacity

FIGURE 2.1
A model of agenda formation
Note: This figure corresponds to the following symbolic representation
$L + C + S \rightarrow A$, which appears in the chapter text.

(C) and the effects of softening up (S) generate a government's agenda (A) in some policy area.

Figure 2.2 presents a typology characterizing the scenarios policy entrepreneurs would face given different configurations of license and capacity at their particular level of government. License is on the horizontal dimension and capacity on the vertical. Even though the figure creates four combinations, which I discuss here, each dimension really varies continuously. Further, given that entrepreneurs are passionate and persistent advocates, I assume that softening up is present in all four scenarios even though it does not appear explicitly in the figure.

Predicting a government's level of interest and involvement in a policy area is perhaps not difficult for situations falling into quadrants I and III. The former depicts government possessing high license and high capacity to act in some area. In other words, the arguments for government action are clear and the capabilities adequate. Government officials can strive to expand their interest and involvement because they can provide a solid rationale and they possess adequate resources to act. Symbolically, $L_1 + C_1 + S_1 \rightarrow A_I$, where the capital letters represent high license (L), high capacity (C), and the ongoing softening-up strategy (S). The subscripted number "1" signals a focus on a particular level of government and the subscripted numeral "I" indicates that the government's agenda scenario re-

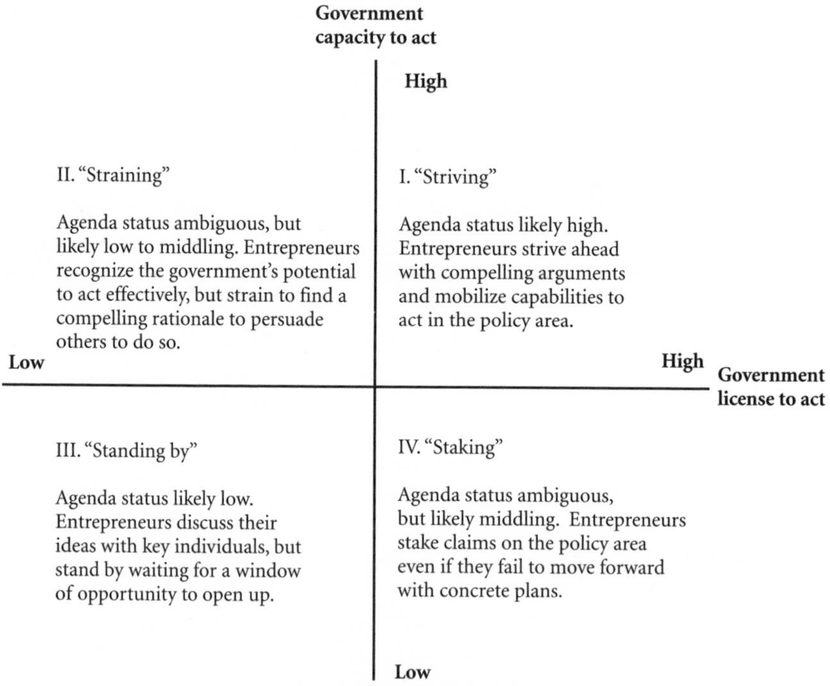

Government
capacity to act

High

II. "Straining"

Agenda status ambiguous, but
likely low to middling. Entrepreneurs
recognize the government's potential
to act effectively, but strain to find a
compelling rationale to persuade
others to do so.

I. "Striving"

Agenda status likely high.
Entrepreneurs strive ahead
with compelling arguments
and mobilize capabilities to
act in the policy area.

Low   High
                                                                          Government
                                                                          license to act

III. "Standing by"

Agenda status likely low.
Entrepreneurs discuss their
ideas with key individuals, but
stand by waiting for a window
of opportunity to open up.

IV. "Staking"

Agenda status ambiguous,
but likely middling. Entrepreneurs
stake claims on the policy area
even if they fail to move forward
with concrete plans.

Low

FIGURE 2.2
Predicting agenda status of a policy area based on a government's license and capacity to act in that area

sembles quadrant I from figure 2.2. An example of this is the American military response in Afghanistan to the events of September 11. Few people would deny that a nation has the right to defend itself when attacked. License to act was clear. And, despite some concerns about Afghanistan's climate and terrain, nearly all American officials and the general public were confident that the American military possessed the capacity to oust the Taliban regime, which had provided Al Qaeda with a safe haven for its operations.

Quadrant III illustrates the opposite scenario. Here, both license and capacity are low. One would predict that policy entrepreneurs would be unlikely to increase a government's interest and involvement in a policy area of this sort. Amidst the range of potential issues that might make the government agenda, policy entrepreneurs would tend to continue softening up potential supporters for their ideas but would largely be in standby mode in this case. If the government lacks license to justify action and the capacity to carry it out, it would make little sense for an entrepreneur to expend resources to mount a significant effort beyond the softening up strategy that I described earlier. In symbolic terms, $l_1 + c_1 + S_1 \rightarrow A_{III}$, where the lowercase letters represent low license and low capacity. Continuing with the September 11 example, a city council could pass a war resolution supporting or opposing a military response to the attacks in New York, Washington, DC, and Pennsylvania. While some city governments may have created a small amount of agenda space for such a symbolic gesture, it is highly unlikely that city officials spent many weeks or months discussing its official position on how to respond overseas. Local governments have no formal say over the conduct of U.S. foreign policy primarily because the U.S. Constitution provides the national government with overwhelming power in this area. Thus, other than expressing sympathy for the victims of the attacks and supporting the nation's troops, city governments lacked license to develop military strategy and tactics for overseas interventions. Furthermore, because city governments do not have the money, military forces, or diplomatic corps needed to prosecute a foreign war, their capacity to act in anything but a symbolic way was extremely limited.[10]

More ambiguous cases occur in quadrant II and quadrant IV. In the former, license is low and capacity high ($l_1 + C_1 + S_1 \rightarrow A_{II}$), whereas the latter illustrates high license and low capacity ($L_1 + c_1 + S_1 \rightarrow A_{IV}$). If policy entrepreneurs need license and capacity to promote interest and involvement, then what would the government's agenda look like in these cases?

In quadrant IV, high license may allow policy entrepreneurs to stake a clear claim that the policy is important and resides in the government's domain. The intersection of license and capacity in quadrant IV implies there is a good chance government officials will at least discuss the issue, regardless of whether they eventually act. Quadrant II represents a scenario where capacity is high but license is low. Simply because capacity exists does not mean entrepreneurs can mobilize it to accomplish any imaginable objective. That may frustrate policy entrepreneurs who strain to identify persuasive arguments to justify action, which they believe the government is fully capable of executing.

Depending on the particular intersection of license and capacity, the probability that a government would demonstrate interest and involvement in some policy area might resemble the possibilities described in figure 2.2. However, those predictions only serve as a convenient starting point. The reason is that so far I have not incorporated into my discussion the possibility that policy entrepreneurs may borrow strength from other governments in the nation's federal system to ameliorate their own deficits in license or capacity. The quadrant in figure 2.2 where a policy entrepreneur ultimately finds himself, then, depends in part on the stock of license and capacity at the entrepreneur's level of government. Crucially, it also depends on the entrepreneur's ability to mobilize license and capacity that resides elsewhere in the American federal system. For creative individuals, federalism thus opens up additional agenda building possibilities.

Stated concretely, federal interest and involvement in an area does not depend only on what license and capacity are available to federal officials. Policy entrepreneurs at the federal level may seek license or capacity from other levels of the nation's compound republic to help them build policy agendas in Washington. Similarly, limits on license and capacity at the state level may minimize a state government's agenda, but state policy entrepreneurs can overcome this problem by seeking these ingredients from the federal level. Borrowing strength is the mechanism that characterizes these efforts.

Figure 2.3 extends the model from figure 2.1 by incorporating the process of borrowing strength. This adjustment shows how policy entrepreneurs working at one level of government can convert the agenda scenarios in quadrant II ("straining") or IV ("staking") into scenarios more like quadrant I ("striving"). Part A of figure 2.3 presents a case where Government 1 possesses high capacity and low license to act. The thick arrow shows how a creative policy entrepreneur working at this level of government can sidestep Government 1's license problem by borrowing license from Government 2. In so doing, the entrepreneur can promote Government 1's interest and involvement in the area, rather than straining to do so as quadrant II of figure 2.2 predicts. Stated symbolically, $(l_1 + L_2) + C_1 + S_1 \rightarrow A_I$.

As an example, consider the case where a state acts as Government 1 and the federal government plays the role of Government 2. A governor might possess low license to justify a particular school reform agenda, which may prevent her from persuading constituents and other state officials to endorse her idea. However, the governor can attempt to leverage license from federal officials who may be considering a similar course for the entire nation. Presidents or members of Congress investing political capital like this become valuable resources for an enterprising governor seeking license to expand her own agenda. "If it's good for the nation, why isn't it good enough for our state?" a governor might argue. One could imagine other examples, too, with the states assuming the Government 2 role and the federal level becoming Government 1. In that case, policy entrepreneurs in Washington, DC, could adapt state arguments for their own purposes. Borrowing license would help them push federal interest and involvement in their favored policy area.

Part B of figure 2.3 shows a situation where entrepreneurs are borrowing capacity. In this case, the equation $L_1 + (c_1 + C_2) + S_1 \rightarrow A_I$ captures the borrowing process. For an example, imagine federal entrepreneurs, acting as Government 1, who lack the capacity to reform the nation's schools on their own. They can overcome that barrier by developing laws that leverage state efforts already underway. In the process of borrowing state capacity, they can ensconce their own interests and priorities on the federal agenda.[11]

It is possible that a policy entrepreneur stuck with quadrant III of figure 2.2 might borrow license and capacity to promote a government's interest and involvement in some policy area. The logic of this final borrowing scenario is not present in figure 2.3 but can be stated symbolically as $(l_1 + L_2) + (c_1 + C_2) + S_1 \rightarrow A_I$. In practice, it is doubtful that policy entrepreneurs would have much luck converting the agenda scenario in quadrant III into the one that quadrant I represents. That effort would represent a massive attempt at borrowing strength and

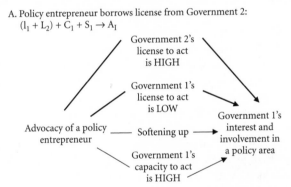

A. Policy entrepreneur borrows license from Government 2:
   $(l_1 + L_2) + C_1 + S_1 \rightarrow A_I$

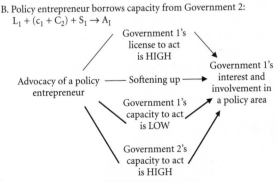

B. Policy entrepreneur borrows capacity from Government 2:
   $L_1 + (c_1 + C_2) + S_1 \rightarrow A_I$

FIGURE 2.3
A policy entrepreneur borrowing strength to promote Government I's agenda

the demands on the policy entrepreneur would simply be too great. "Standing by," as quadrant III predicts, appears to be the most likely outcome.

Borrowing Strength and Policy Feedbacks

Notice that both parts of figure 2.3 represent the process of borrowing strength from the perspective of one level of government at a particular moment in time. Without sketching a new diagram, it is also possible to imagine policy entrepreneurs at federal and state levels attempting to borrow strength from each other simultaneously and across time. As those relationships unfold, much like a strategic dance between federal and state actors, feedback effects become apparent and agendas take shape.

Activities at one level of government that drive political and policy agendas in another illustrate how feedback mechanisms can influence agenda setting. Scholars have generally characterized feedbacks in two ways (Baumgartner and Jones 1993, 2002a). Positive feedback accelerates trends already in motion and can produce bandwagon effects when an idea becomes popular and spreads. The literature on policy diffusion in the states offers examples of this process (Walker 1969; Gray 1973; Mintrom and Vergari 1998). Conversely, negative feedback processes promote stability. To borrow examples from Baumgartner and Jones (2002a, 9), negative feedback works much like a thermostat that kicks out heat when a room drops below a specified temperature, the Federal Reserve that attempts to jumpstart a sluggish economy by lowering interest rates, or a social service agency whose budget expands when unemployment rises.

Scholars of federalism and even casual observers of American government often emphasize the power of negative feedback by arguing that federalism tends to frustrate rather than promote policy action. Anton (1989, 8) identifies this scholarly tendency, which Derthick (2001, 39) describes this way: "Fragmentation of authority in the federal system is often portrayed, at least in academic literature, as a severe handicap to the federal government's pursuit of its goals." Arguably, this is what James Madison and the other founders had in mind. In Madison's view, dividing control between the states and the national capital would prevent any one elected official or small group from consolidating power. As long as leadership of the nation's policymaking institutions remained dispersed, the nation's citizens could rest assured that tyrants would not trample on their rights. This was the advantage of what Madison, in *Federalist No. 51*, called the nation's compound republic.

A slightly different version of the founders' view is implicit in functional theories of federalism, which I outlined earlier, that claim the federal government should handle distributive policies and governments closer to the people should stress developmental ones. If a government's agenda were based only on the capabilities at its immediate disposal, then that might be a reasonable approach (assuming one could identify policies as clearly distributive or clearly developmental). But, because policy entrepreneurs can reach across the federal system to leverage other levels of government, the developmental-redistributive allocation framework is too limiting.

Focusing on federalism's arresting tendencies understates how the compound republic can facilitate policy action. Conceptualizing negative feedback and positive feedback processes in a theoretical model with clearly stated mechanisms is needed to overcome the disconnects between current scholarship on federalism and agenda setting. The borrowing strength model of agenda setting is my attempt to do just that. As policy entrepreneurs in Washington, DC, and the states leverage their own supplies of license and capacity and also borrow strength from one another, they set feedback processes into motion that can increase their chances of successfully building their agendas. License or capacity that exists at one point in time may produce interest and involvement, which, over many years, helps to promote subsequent license and capacity to expand agendas even more. Modeling that process is theoretically tractable as long as one carefully considers the timing and sequencing of events (Pierson 2000a, 2000b).

Overall, the dynamics of positive and negative feedback essentially capture one of E. E. Schattschneider's (1935) classic insights, that new policies create new politics. Considering how policy feedbacks play out in the American federal system is an essential component of explaining agenda development across time (Skocpol 1994). In education specifically, feedbacks have influenced the scope of federal and state agendas since 1965. During the last two decades in particular, positive feedback from state education reforms has expanded the ability of federal policymakers to leverage change. State actions have allowed federal officials to extend their reach over the nation's schools in new and unexpected ways. Simultaneously, though, assertive states have also beaten back the federal hand or redirected its reach in other areas more consistent with state prerogatives. Over time, federal policy dating to the first ESEA has cultivated in states the very capabilities that have allowed states to expand their own reform agendas while challenging Washington officials who seek greater involvement in schoolrooms across America. Many of these positive and negative feedback processes in education will become more concrete in later chapters. For now, consider the following general expectations that my borrowing strength model suggests.

Expected Agenda Dynamics in a Federal System

The processes presented in figures 2.1, 2.2, and 2.3 suggest several predictions about how governments in a federal system build their agendas. I discuss those predictions here, and, for the reader's convenience, I reproduce them in table 5.1 of chapter 5 where I explore them in further detail. The first expectation articulates the basic relationship between policy entrepreneurs, license and capacity, and government interest and involvement in a policy area.

1. Policy entrepreneurs operating with high license and high capacity will tend to promote a government's interest and involvement in a policy area.

These next two expectations describe how borrowing strength can promote positive feedback processes, which can help entrepreneurs to build government agendas. They also underscore a point that Anton (1989), Kingdon (1995), and others have made: policy agendas emerge when individuals, not simply abstract government institutions, make choices and then act. In my terms, that means that borrowing strength occurs when policy entrepreneurs make strategic choices to increase government interest and involvement in particular areas.

> 2. Lacking license or capacity, policy entrepreneurs may bolster either or both, and thus develop their government's interest and involvement in a policy area, by borrowing strength from another level of government.

> 3. Policy entrepreneurs will be more likely to borrow strength to promote agendas when they think it will help them achieve political gains and make good policy.

The borrowing strength model produces a third set of expectations that considers some of the consequences occurring when federal officials attempt to borrow strength from the states. These statements illustrate how borrowing apparent strengths can produce negative feedback processes and subsequent adjustments to federal agendas. These statements also underscore the interactive qualities of the American federal system. States are not passive agents who simply respond to the wishes of domineering federal principals. Rather, they can use federal interest or involvement in policy matters to promote their own agendas.

> 4. Federal officials who borrow strength from states will be more likely to enjoy political and policy success if they accurately assess the license and capacity of state governments.

> 5. State officials will attempt to extract concessions from federal officials if they think that, in borrowing strength, federal officials have overestimated state license or capacity.

> 6. Federal officials will modify policies that depend on borrowed strength if they are persuaded they have overestimated state license or capacity.

These final expectations emphasize that borrowing strength is neither easy nor costless. Federal officials, in particular, cannot simply copy the arguments that governors or state legislators develop and then apply them to federal efforts in a related area. They must adapt. Similarly, and perhaps more challenging still, is that these federal officials need to assess accurately the strengths that states possess. Overestimating state capabilities, and thus attempting to borrow license or capacity that seems to exist but actually does not, can generate federal policies that overburden state governments and distort their priorities. That can produce outcries from disgruntled state policymakers while simultaneously undercutting the effectiveness of federal policy. Furthermore, overestimating state license or capacity can have devastating political consequences for federal officials who were hoping to make good policy and score political points by seeking this leverage in the first place. Future chapters will describe some of these ill-fated attempts at borrowing and how states have responded. These chapters will also show, however, that states themselves have sometimes been guilty of encouraging these behaviors. By promoting their own successes and maneuvering to borrow strength from the federal government, states sometimes foster conditions that encourage federal officials to overreach.

Overall, the borrowing strength model of agenda setting provides an appealing way to study agenda development in the American federal system. The mechanism of borrowing strength is a powerful analytical tool that forges a conceptual link between the federalism and agenda setting literatures. The overall model uses a handful of powerful concepts to capture federalism's fluid and dynamic nature and, in the process, to relate the institution of federalism to the process of agenda setting.

The model outlined in this chapter is especially useful for addressing the two main research questions introduced in chapter 1. Despite an apparent creeping federalization in education that has supposedly minimized state power, my analysis will show how state leaders have also leveraged the federal government to promote their own education agendas, sometimes with great success. Because these interactions are necessarily back-and-forth, it becomes clear that approaches considering primarily top-down or bottom-up relationships will omit much of the story. Empirically, then, the "protean" reality of American federalism, to use Derthick's (2001) term again, makes the borrowing strength model of agenda setting a strong tool for explaining changes in education agendas in Washington and the states.

The theoretical and empirical approaches that guide future chapters also align well with one of Baumgartner and Jones's (1993, 40) primary contentions; namely, that to understand an issue's agenda status, one needs to consider many different agendas across time. On that point in particular, the borrowing strength model is attractive because it allows analysts to consider policy and political agendas across issues, time, and levels of government. The model can reveal links between federal and state agendas in specific aspects of K–12 education and show how those relationships have unfolded. By considering the diverse menu of state and federal education policies that have developed since the 1960s, and by remaining sensitive to the timing of key events, the borrowing strength model enables me to describe and explain the "patterned disorder" (Orren and Skowronek 1994, 330) that has characterized the evolution of American education policy during the last four decades.

STUDYING THE EVOLVING AMERICAN EDUCATION AGENDA

This book uses a political development approach to describe and explain how federalism has affected the nation's education agenda. The study aligns most closely with the work of political development scholars who have emphasized how feedbacks influence policy change. Whether those feedbacks spawn opportunities or constraints depends much on the creativity of policy entrepreneurs.

Especially in the context of American federalism, the condition of past federal and state policies at particular moments can limit the future choices of officials at either level of government. However, because policies have unintended consequences, those limits may not prevail over the long term and may actually become opportunities as creative policy entrepreneurs discover how to use old policies in new ways. Thus, even though prevailing paths may limit where most policymakers dare to tread, policy entrepreneurs often find ways to shift agendas onto new trajectories. Borrowing strength is one strategy they can use to produce this result. In short, paths channel action but they do not absolutely constrain it. Nor is change simply the product of broad sweeping forces that remain present and relatively constant across time (Orren and Skowronek 1994; Pierson 2000b; Thelen 2002).

Beyond considering policy feedbacks, the political development approach also possesses some general strengths that are ideal for addressing this book's key questions. First, the development approach encourages scholars to consider contextual factors that contribute to policy change. Accounting for and learning from the details of history helps make comprehensible the array of forces that may be cross-pressuring or confusing policymakers who struggle to understand complicated policy processes (Lowi 1994; Orren and Skowronek 1994). Second, the approach can accommodate developments that include both incremental and rapid change (Baumgartner and Jones 1993). This is crucial in education policy, especially, where federal and state agendas can develop at different speeds, sometimes in concert and sometimes not. Breakthroughs at one level can be both leading and lagging indicators of more incremental activity elsewhere and may not even become completely apparent until many years after they have occurred.[12] Finally, the development approach emphasizes that in analyzing political change, scholars need to study carefully the timing and sequencing of events (Pierson 1994, 2000b; Baumgartner and Jones 1993, 2002b; Skocpol 1994).The evidence in this project will show that education analysts and pundits have been insensitive to some of these dynamics because they have allocated greater causal weight to major events that are breakthroughs in conventionally understood ways but may actually be more revealing for other reasons.

Overall, the political development approach is well-suited for investigating changes in the American education agenda since the 1960s. It is very supple methodologically and amenable to many empirical techniques and sources of evidence. To leverage that strength, and to study the multiple agendas that Baumgartner and Jones (1993) have reminded scholars to consider, my analysis draws on several quantitative and qualitative sources. I describe these sources here briefly and provide additional details in the appendix.

The quantitative data include content analyses of major presidential speeches, congressional hearings, and public laws. Public opinion and election-related sources include the biennial National Election Studies and two databases on political advertising, one that focuses on presidential ads across time and another that provides comprehensive coverage of the presidential race in 2000. Other quantitative measures are from the annual *Digest of Education Statistics* and various other government publications. I also analyze qualitatively these same presidential speeches, hearings, and public laws to provide key contextual details regarding particular events or policy decisions. This analysis draws on the work of historians who have compiled accounts of major events in education policymaking.

Sixty elite interviews with members of the education policy community in Washington, DC, which I conducted from April 2001 through May 2002, also inform my analysis. They include current and former congressional staff members (both personal and committee staff); current and former appointees and career officials from the executive branch of the federal government; lobbyists who represent the states and other governmental and nongovernmental organizations; analysts from think tanks that study education; and members of the trade press and popular media who cover education issues. These interviews serve many purposes. They provide an important validity check on my broad theoretical arguments and claims that emerge primarily from other sources of evidence. My interview respondents have also helped me understand the details of federal and state policy change that are central to this analysis but are not often present in published sources.

THIS CHAPTER HAS DEVELOPED A THEORY TO EXPLAIN HOW FEDERALISM AFfects government agendas. As policy entrepreneurs mobilize license and capacity, and borrow strength to ameliorate their shortcomings, they can expand government interest and involvement in their favored policy areas. The borrowing strength model of agenda setting offers a conceptually tight way to unify scholarship on federalism and agenda setting and simultaneously to generate predictions about how government agendas in a federal system are likely to unfold. The next four chapters use this model to describe and explain the development of the American education agenda since the 1960s.

NOTES

1. Nelson (1984) builds on this approach in her work on child abuse as a public agenda item.
2. Elazar (1991, 69) noted as much in arguing that the "'marble cake' is not a theory. Grodzins never used it as a theory but only as a metaphor."
3. A popular normative perspective on federalism, which I discuss later in the chapter, appears in Peterson, Rabe, and Wong (1986) and Peterson (1995). Those authors argue that the national government should assume responsibility for "redistributive functions" and lower levels of government should take on "developmental functions." See also Anton (1989, chapter 2), who argues why federalism research focusing on fiscal federalism, hierarchy, and public choice is also an essentially normative approach to the subject.
4. That is not entirely true. Riker's own substantive chapter in this volume does explore federalism; namely, the debates over the topic that occurred during the ratification of the U.S. Constitution. However, his analysis does not explore how the institution of

federalism affects the process of agenda setting. Rather he studies how the debate over federalism reveals insights about what he calls the Dominance Principle and the Dispersion Principle, two concepts he uses to explain the dynamics of agenda formation.

5. The laboratories of innovation metaphor suffers from many of the same limits as the metaphors of federalism that I just reviewed. In particular, it is short on identifying clear mechanisms and causal processes. Put another way, if states are indeed laboratories of policy innovation, how is it that some of their innovations become ensconced into federal law and others do not? The laboratory metaphor itself does not tackle that question head on.

6. It is worth noting that Anton's (1989, 101) terms "authority" and "power" loosely parallel my notions of license and capacity.

7. To use one of Baumgartner and Jones's (1993) running examples, if citizens associate pesticides with an image that evokes agricultural production and the maintenance of an abundant food supply, then they will tend to favor more lenient approaches to pesticide regulation and use. Alternatively, if policy entrepreneurs frequently discuss how pesticides cause toxic runoff that pollutes streams and leads to birth defects, then this new policy image will likely produce public support for stricter regulatory strategies.

8. Anton (1989, 23) makes a parallel point about research on fiscal federalism in which scholars assume one can cleanly distinguish between allocation, distribution, and stabilization functions of government. The problem, he argues, is that the real world rarely fits neatly into this framework.

9. Other examples of that focus on dynamic relationships include Gormley (2001), who writes from the federal perspective, and Beamer (1999), who considers these issues from the perspective of state governments.

10. That does not mean local governments did not spend time discussing ways to prevent future attacks. Local law enforcement agencies are directly related to securing the homeland; however, conversations about foreign policy and war fighting are different domains altogether.

11. The logic of borrowing capacity parallels Salamon's (2002) discussion of how policymakers often use indirect tools of government when they lack "automaticity" to accomplish their objectives.

12. Jones-Correa (2000–2001) describes this idea in the context of state-level racial restrictive covenants.

PART II

EVIDENCE AND EXPLANATIONS

3

Patterns of Federal Interest in Education

IN THE FIRST TWO CHAPTERS, I DEVELOPED A THEORY TO EXPLAIN HOW GOV-ernment agendas unfold in a federal system. Considering the concepts of license, capacity, and borrowing strength offers a compelling yet concise way to explain how the nation's education agenda has taken shape. Before I can use my theoretical model to explain these changes, though, I first need to describe the changes that have occurred. Thus, in this chapter and the next, I focus primarily on my two other key concepts, interest and involvement, in order to map out variation in the nation's education agenda since the 1960s.

This chapter focuses on one part of the federal education agenda. It uses several data sources to describe how federal interest in education has varied during the last half of the twentieth century. Recall my definition of the agenda from chapters 1 and 2. There, I explained that agendas are comprised of a government's level of interest and involvement in a policy area. By exploring federal interest in this chapter, I begin to answer important descriptive questions such as: Do federal policymakers talk about education very much? Do their conversations probe the topic in detail or do they typically dwell on generalities? Have their interests shifted or have some dimensions of education consistently captured their attention across time?

The chapter proceeds in three sections. The first examines congressional interest in education by exploring the presence of education as a topic at hearings and in celebratory declarations that Congress passes as symbolic public laws. The second focuses on presidential interest, in particular the interest of presidential candidates on the campaign trail and also the interest that presidents themselves demonstrate in their inaugural and State of the Union speeches. The final section examines the education content of the Republican and Democratic Parties' national platforms.

CONGRESSIONAL INTEREST IN EDUCATION

In this section, I focus on the presence of education issues in congressional hearings and in the symbolic public laws that the national legislature adopts each year. I chart both of these measures from 1950 until 2000.

The content of legislative hearings is a strong indicator of congressional inter-ests in a policy area. Sometimes hearings address pending legislation even though that is not always their main or even most valuable purpose. Oleszek (1996, 109) quotes former Senator Albert Gore Jr. to that effect. As a Democratic senator from Tennessee, Gore once noted, "Legislation need not always be the answer. In many areas, the most important missing ingredient is attention, and an elevated aware-ness of the problem can be a very successful outcome of hearings." Regarding their agenda setting function, Smith and Deering (1990, 142) explain that hearings can "serve as platforms to publicize a cause" and that "they can be important tools in building majority coalitions for or against legislation." When committee leaders schedule a hearing, it means they have determined that time, their most scarce re-source, is worth devoting to some specific issue. As a measure of congressional in-terest, then, the number of hearings devoted to education is strong.

Figure 3.1 plots the annual number of hearings addressing K–12 education from 1950 to 2000. The data points for each year, which include House, Senate, and joint hearings, show that members of Congress have become more interested in K–12 education since the 1950s. From 1950 to 1964, the number of hearings re-mained essentially flat, averaging roughly fifteen per year. A noticeable increase begins after the first ESEA became law in 1965. However, congressional interest in education did not rise at a constant rate after that year. The increasing trajectory after 1965 tapers off for most years between 1974 and 1980, with 1977 being a no-table exception. The pace of hearings increases after 1980, with a particularly large spike in 1983. That increasing interest persists into the early 1990s, a trend that levels off and dips somewhat during the middle part of the decade before increas-ing to relatively high levels near the end of the series.

Two other patterns exist in this overall trajectory of development. First, the number of hearings tends to fall during election years. Across the entire period presented in figure 3.1, there are fewer hearings in even- than odd-numbered years. Presidential and mid-term election years produce an average of twenty-five hearings, while non-election years generate thirty-six. Six of the ten lowest totals occur in presidential election years, and none of the ten years achieving the high-est totals feature a presidential contest. Those differences likely exist because the pressure to campaign at home creates fewer days for members of Congress to hold hearings in Washington.

Examining the content of these hearings allows a second pattern to emerge. When members of Congress have a hearing on education, what kinds of issues in-terest them? Given the sweep of time and the number of hearings considered here, I am not able to systematically report the full range of topics that Congress has ex-plored. Hearings sometimes stray onto tangents that their formal descriptions do not capture. However, looking anecdotally at hearing titles, abstracts, and wit-nesses who appeared does reveal some information about the shifting menu of topics that the hearings have contained.

Some areas have consistently interested representatives and senators; these topics include antisocial or destructive student behaviors such as violence and

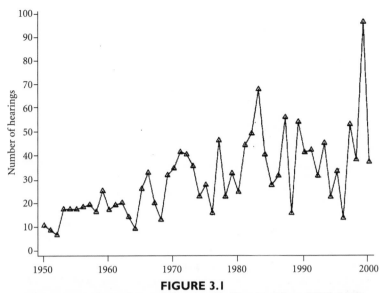

FIGURE 3.1
Congressional hearings addressing K–12 education, 1950–2000
Source: **Author's coding of data from the Policy Agendas Project.**

drug use in school. Other topics have become less popular and others more so. For example, the federal school breakfast and lunch program was a popular item that used to attract noticeable attention, but during the 1990s, it was the subject of only five hearings. Also, compared to earlier periods, hearings from the 1980s and 1990s reveal increasing congressional interest in school reform issues that affect all students. During those decades, one would be more likely to witness hearings dealing with general state and local reform efforts and some of the specific state reforms that I described in chapter 1 including accountability, charter schools, testing, and teaching in subjects such as math and science.

In short, since the early 1980s, members of Congress have begun to pay increasing attention to educational quality. Prior to that period, hearings placed much more emphasis on relatively narrow categorical programs or other efforts designed to benefit specific student groups. The brief burst of interest in educational excellence reflected in the 1950s, immediately after Sputnik, became a more regular topic for discussion during the 1980s and 1990s. That emphasis on excellence is also present in the ESEA reauthorization hearings of 1994 and 1999, which included much talk of reforming American schools. Other ESEA reauthorization years focused more exclusively on specific programs and their beneficiaries.

Beyond hearings, another way to measure congressional interest in education is to examine the commemorative or symbolic public laws that Congress has produced since the 1950s. To clarify, the definition of interest that I offered in chapter 2 excluded public laws, which I argued more accurately capture federal involvement. Commemorative public laws are an exception to this general rule. Unlike a

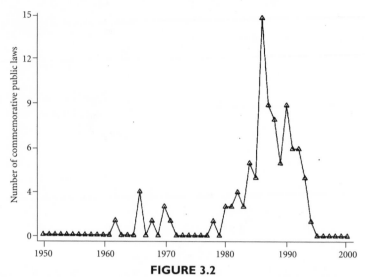

FIGURE 3.2
Commemorative public laws addressing K–12 education, 1950–2000
Source: Author's coding of data from the Policy Agendas Project for years 1950–98 and author's coding of public laws catalogued on the Thomas website, http://thomas.loc.gov/, for 1999 and 2000

substantive law that may result in a new program or program authorization, commemorative laws are symbolic gestures. They allow members of Congress to highlight important national issues, but nothing more because commemorative laws do not create new agencies, establish funding streams, or initiate other substantive action. For that reason, they are a better measure of federal interest than involvement.

Commemorative laws often declare that a specific day, year, or month is somehow special. Figure 3.2 shows a remarkably clear picture of such declarations since the 1950s. Most years in the series contain zero symbolic public laws addressing K–12 education. The strongest burst of congressional interest is evident during a roughly fifteen-year period beginning in 1980. Looking more precisely at the trend line, almost all of the symbolic measures in the figure became law between 1980 and 1993. In 1986 alone, fifteen pieces of commemorative legislation were passed. Those included P.L. 99-480, which designated 1986 as the National Year of the Teacher, and P.L. 99-259, which proclaimed March 1986 to be Music in Our Schools Month.

PRESIDENTIAL INTEREST IN EDUCATION

This section tracks presidential interest in education since the 1960s. I start by looking at how education has appeared in presidential campaigns. Next, I consider the way that presidents have used their inaugural messages and State of the Union addresses to talk about education policy.

Presidential Campaigns

Despite some popular stereotypes that presidential campaigns are more about personalities than substance, many citizens study these campaigns for their issue content. Voters often have issues that most concern them, and how candidates address those topics can influence how citizens vote. This is a consistent finding across time and electoral contexts (Campbell et al. 1960; Nie, Verba, and Petrocik 1976; Fiorina 1981; Krosnick 1990; Aldrich, Sullivan, and Borgida 1993; Miller and Shanks 1996; Iyengar and Simon 2000; Weisberg and Wilcox 2004). Even though this research also suggests that other factors, such as a person's party identification, more strongly predict people's choices, issues can have noticeable impacts on electoral outcomes.

Education policy did not begin to play a consistently large role in presidential elections until the 1990s. In addition to anecdotal evidence documented in secondary sources (Moore, Preimesberger, and Tarr 2001; Abramson, Aldrich, and Rohde 2002, chapter 6), one way to see the break toward education in the 1990s is to examine how presidential candidates, working in concert with their national party organizations, have used education in televised presidential campaign advertisements since the 1960s. The content of political advertising provides a nice barometer of candidate interest in education. Among other things, television advertisements are one of the few types of campaign communications, other than speeches on the stump or televised debates, where candidates can present themselves as they see fit. Because advertisements cost money to produce and air, one can reasonably conclude that candidates will focus their advertising on topics they believe will produce electoral success.[1]

Figure 3.3 reports the proportion of presidential campaign advertisements that were produced from 1960 to 1996 that contained some K–12 education content (I will take up the 2000 election shortly using a more complete data source). Two conclusions emerge and support the overall argument that education did not appear to be a major campaign issue until the 1990s. First, it was not until 1992 that a presidential campaign occurred in which more than 10 percent of the advertisements created for each major party candidate addressed education. In a few campaigns before that year, one side but not the other appeared to emphasize education (Democrats in 1960 and 1968; Republicans in 1972). But in those contests, the issue did not capture the interest of both candidates, which suggests it was not a central point of discussion in the campaign (Abramson, Aldrich, and Rhode 2002, 131).

Second, the period from 1976 through 1988 reveals an overall lack of interest from candidates of both parties. Interestingly, presidential candidates appeared to give education policy little attention during this period as figure 3.3 illustrates. Despite the popularity of A Nation at Risk and increasing presidential interest in

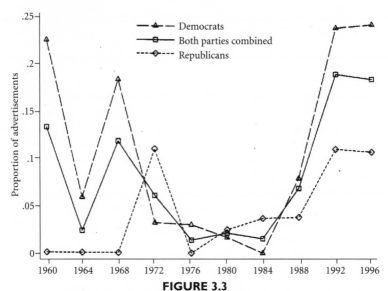

FIGURE 3.3
Education in presidential campaign advertisements,
1960–96 general elections

Note: Each data point represents a proportion based on the number of unique ads produced, not the proportion of ad airings.
Source: Author's coding of presidential advertising data from John Geer.

education after 1983, which I will demonstrate shortly, education policy possessed a relatively low profile in the 1984 and 1988 campaigns.

President Ronald Reagan certainly took credit for *A Nation at Risk*, incorrectly calling it a "presidential commission" in his 1984 State of the Union message (it was actually a commission that his secretary of education, Terrell Bell, created after the White House refused to sponsor it). Reagan's Democratic opponent that year, Walter Mondale, even complimented the president on his education efforts in one of their debates. However, issues such as Mondale's liberalism and proposals to raise taxes, Reagan's deficits, the state of the economy, and the Cold War were much more significant factors in the campaign (Abramson, Aldrich, and Rohde 2002). Even in 1988, with then Vice President George H. W. Bush aspiring to be the nation's "education president," the education policy debate during that contest was anemic at best. It typically involved Bush issuing symbolic attacks on his Democratic opponent, Governor Michael Dukakis of Massachusetts, who had vetoed a bill that would have required his state's students to say the Pledge of Allegiance in public school classrooms (Moore, Preimesberger, and Tarr 2001). After 1988, education policy started to assume a larger, more consistent presence in presidential campaigns. Figure 3.3 shows that in 1992 and 1996, for example, Bill Clinton's focus on education exceeded that of all other presidential contenders since 1960. Notice that two of the three highest proportions for Republicans appeared in 1992 and 1996, as well.

Due to the emergence of more advanced data collection techniques, which track the number of ad airings rather than simply the number of unique ads produced, I am able to provide a more detailed picture of presidential candidate advertising during the 2000 election. During that campaign, education arrived on the national political stage like never before. Table 3.1 provides the details. This table presents evidence from a comprehensive database of presidential advertisements from the 2000 campaign. The data show the emphasis that Republican candidate George W. Bush and Democratic candidate Albert Gore placed on education. The first two columns describe the 144 unique advertisements that the candidates (or the major parties on their behalf) produced and aired. Those columns are roughly comparable to the advertising data presented in figure 3.3. The second two columns take full advantage of the data by examining systematically all 223,572 airings of these 144 unique ads.

At least two key substantive conclusions emerge from table 3.1. First, ads favoring Bush emphasized education much more than those supporting Gore. This is somewhat surprising given that elected officials and scholars typically have considered education to be a Democratic issue (Petrocik 1996; Iyengar and Simon 2000). Among the unique Bush ads, roughly 48 percent included education in some way, while only 34 percent of Gore's ads did. The gap favoring Bush widens when one considers individual ad airings: 50 percent of his spots (over 60,000 airings) mentioned education in some way compared to just under 32 percent for Gore. Considering airings of ads that were completely about education, the "stand alone" category from table 3.1, the number of Bush spots (over 29,400) outnumbered the Gore spots (nearly 8,500) by a wide margin.

The second major conclusion emerging from table 3.1 is that relative to Gore, Bush's advertisements mainly addressed K–12 education. Looking at the ad airings numbers specifically, nearly 44 percent of Bush's ads focused on elementary and secondary education, which was twice the emphasis that Gore's ads, at 21 percent, devoted to the topic. While a plurality of Gore airings addressed K–12 education, Gore's message was not as focused as Bush's. Gore appeared to be splitting his efforts between K–12 and college education, while Bush focused primarily on K–12 or general statements about the nation's education system, which, I should note, frequently implied or explicitly addressed concerns about America's elementary and secondary schools.

Presidential Speeches

How have winning presidential candidates discussed education once they assume office? This section traces presidential interest by examining the inaugural messages and State of the Union addresses of presidents from John Kennedy through Clinton.[2] The data in this section describe the level and nature of presidential interest in the nation's schools.

I chose to analyze inaugurals and State of the Unions because they are excellent indicators of a president's policy interests. Unlike a campaign stump speech or

TABLE 3.1

Attention to education in presidential campaign advertisements, 2000 general election

Content of advertisement	Proportions among unique advertisements[a]		Proportions among advertisements aired[a]	
	Bush	Gore	Bush	Gore
Emphasis on education[b]				
None	.519	.667	.499	.686
Allusion	.185	.244	.258	.232
Stand alone	.296	.089	.242	.083
Level of education mentioned[c]				
General	.093	.067	.086	.012
Pre-K	.019	.022	.019	.008
K–12	.407	.200	.435	.212
College	.019	.078	.001	.121
N	(54)	(90)	(121,554)	(102,018)

[a]The proportions in the first two columns are derived from the 54 and 90 unique advertisements that were produced and aired by either the Bush or Gore campaign or the Democratic National Committee or Republican National Committee on behalf of their respective candidate. The proportions in the last two columns account for the number of times each of these 144 unique advertisements was aired.

[b]"None" means that education was not mentioned at all; "allusion" means that it was mentioned along with other non-education topics; "stand-alone" means that the advertisement was completely about education.

[c]Ads in the "level of education" section could be coded in multiple categories if they addressed more than one level of education.

Source: Author's coding of data from the Wisconsin Advertising Project.

even a press conference, presidents have rare opportunities during these two major speeches to address the entire nation. With the exception of unique events such as a declaration of war (i.e., Franklin Roosevelt's Pearl Harbor speech) or an unfolding scandal (i.e., Clinton's contrition address regarding Monica Lewinski), if citizens hear a president deliver a speech, it will likely be an inaugural or a State of the Union. Furthermore, the latter is a strong indicator of presidential interest in education because presidents and their allies typically consider State of the Union addresses as "*the* statement of legislative priorities" (Light 1999, 160).[3] Given limited time, presidents typically will not dwell on trivial matters in these annual addresses. If education appears, it means the president and his advisers possess significant interest in this topic relative to others. Their high profile, then, makes inaugural messages and State of the Union addresses excellent sources for discovering presidential interest in education.

Table 3.2 begins my analysis of these speeches. That table presents the results of a coding procedure that used the sentence as the unit of analysis to identify the policy agents that presidents mentioned. A sentence received an agent code if it identified some entity that is involved in the development, production, or execution of education policy. If a sentence included an agent, I also noted whether the president mentioned the agent positively, negatively, or in neutral terms. A single sentence could also receive multiple agent codes if it contained more than one agent.

Table 3.2 summarizes the sentences in which a president identified an agent in a positive way. Two substantive conclusions emerge. First, given that states and localities are the primary stewards of education in the United States, it seems remarkable that all presidents mention the federal government so often in a positive way. That appears especially counterintuitive for Reagan who was known as a harsh critic of Washington's role in the nation's schools. Across his two terms, even he identified the federal government positively in 67 and then 50 percent of the sentences where any agent appears in a positive way. Then again, Reagan's behavior is perhaps not surprising given that time is limited and presidents prefer to articulate a legislative program or celebrate successes in these speeches (Light 1999, 160). In short, they tend not to dwell on negatives. In fact, a separate analysis of agents appearing in these speeches revealed that only three presidents in the series—Richard Nixon, Reagan, and Clinton—spoke negatively of any agent whatsoever; and those assessments appeared quite infrequently.[4]

The second substantive finding that table 3.2 shows is that presidents more consistently began to identify the states as policy actors starting with Reagan's first term. Democrats Kennedy, Lyndon Johnson, and Jimmy Carter failed to mention them positively at all, while Republicans Nixon, Gerald Ford, Reagan, and Bush did. Democrat Clinton is the lone exception to this partisan split, mentioning the states positively in 7 percent of these statements in his first term and 14 percent in his second.

Perhaps more striking than the partisan continuity among the Republican presidents is how the positions of states and local governments have varied relative to each other. Specifically, Nixon and Ford mentioned local governments more frequently or just as often as the states. That pattern reverses during both of Reagan's terms and Bush's one term. States received more positive attention than local governments across that twelve year period of Republican control. Local governments climbed ahead of the states during Clinton's two terms, but unlike his Democratic predecessors he devoted much more time to the states, especially during his second term. The increasing state presence in these speeches is related to my larger story about how federal policymakers borrowed strength from states to develop their education agendas. I elaborate that point in chapter 5, but for now I turn to a different issue.

How often and at what level of detail do presidents discuss the substance of education policy, not simply the actors that produce or deliver it? A second round of coding addressed this question. In this part of the analysis, I identified individual sentences that mentioned some specific aspect of education policy. As with the

TABLE 3.2

Agents that should act in K–12 education policy mentioned in major presidential addresses, 1961–2000

Agent				*Proportion of sentences mentioning specific agents in a positive way*						
	Kennedy	Johnson	Nixon	Ford	Carter	Reagan I	Reagan II	Bush	Clinton I	Clinton II
Governmental										
Government in general	—	—	—	—	—	—	—	—	.04	.01
Federal government	.86	.88	.76	1.00	1.00	.67	.50	.58	.64	.58
State government	—	—	.19	.33	—	.17	.10	.14	.07	.14
Local government	—	.04	.33	.33	—	.11	.05	.06	.20	.20
Nongovernmental										
Parents	—	—	—	—	—	.11	.10	.03	.04	.02
Private sector	—	—	—	—	—	.06	.05	—	.09	.01
Nonprofit sector	—	—	—	—	—	.06	—	—	.02	.02
Local community	—	—	.05	—	—	.11	.05	.06	.02	.02
General ("we" or "whole nation")	.14	.13	.19	—	—	.22	.40	.25	.13	.27
N	(7)	(24)	(21)	(3)	(5)	(18)	(20)	(36)	(45)	(116)

Note: "—" indicates < .01. N corresponding to each column equals the total number of sentences mentioning an agent in a positive way. Columns may sum to greater than 1.00 because sentences could receive multiple agent codes if they mentioned more than one agent in a positive way.

Source: Author's analysis of presidential inaugural addresses and State of the Union messages. See the appendix for a couple of exceptions.

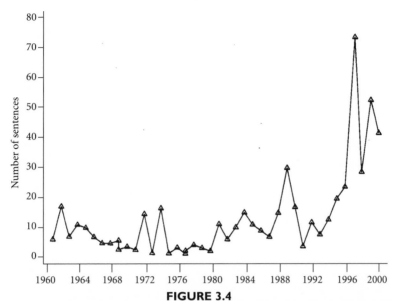

FIGURE 3.4
Count of sentences about K–12 education in major presidential addresses, 1961–2000
Source: Author's analysis of presidential inaugural addresses and State of the Union messages. See the appendix for a couple of exceptions.

agent coding, a sentence could receive multiple codes if it addressed more than one policy area.

Before examining these details, it is useful to consider figure 3.4, which presents the overall count of these sentences about policy for each year. With a few exceptions, nearly all years before the early 1980s produce totals hovering around five sentences per year. After the early 1980s, presidents typically include at least ten or more sentences, oftentimes many more. Perhaps the most striking aspect of the figure is the level of interest that Clinton demonstrated in his second term. The period from 1997 to 2000 produced the three largest annual totals across the entire time series.

Table 3.3 breaks these annual counts into specific policy areas. The clearest result from the table is that presidential interest in education policy intensified as the 1980s began. The number of policy areas presidents discussed, including those earning relatively in-depth coverage, increased dramatically and generally persisted beginning with Reagan's first term. Some topics, such as federal funding for education, have been mainstays since 1961. Similarly, the second to last row shows that all presidents from Kennedy to Clinton have used their bully pulpit to make general statements about improving the quality of schooling that the nation's young people receive.

Prior to Reagan, though, presidents rarely explored many topics in depth. Judging by table 3.3, the nation's chief executives appeared to be uninterested in

TABLE 3.3

Aspects of K–12 education policy mentioned in major presidential addresses, 1961–2000

Policy area		Kennedy	Johnson	Nixon	Ford	Carter	Reagan I	Reagan II	Bush	Clinton I	Clinton II
		Proportion of sentences mentioning each policy area									
Academics and teaching											
Curriculum		—	.03	—	—	—	.11	.15	.15	.07	**.09**
Standards and accountability		—	.03	—	—	—	.08	—	.08	.09	**.12**
Testing		—	—	—	—	—	.03	.12	.02	—	**.09**
Social promotion		—	—	—	—	—	—	—	—	—	.07
Teaching method		—	.03	—	—	—	—	.06	.06	.07	.02
Teachers		**.25**	**.23**	—	—	—	**.08**	**.09**	**.13**	.02	**.12**
Choice											
School choice (general)		—	—	—	—	—	—	—	**.10**	.04	.02
Competition		—	—	—	—	—	**.06**	—	—	—	.01
Vouchers		—	—	—	—	—	—	.03	—	—	—
Charter schools		—	—	—	—	—	—	—	—	.04	**.05**
Issues and programs											
Administration		—	—	—	—	.33	.06	—	.04	.02	—
At-risk students		.05	—	—	—	—	—	—	**.08**	.04	.01
Bilingual education		—	—	—	—	—	—	—	—	—	—

	(20)	(31)	(28)	(5)	(6)	(36)	(34)	(52)	(56)	(182)
Class size	—	—	—	—	—	—	—	—	—	.05
Facilities and equipment	.30	.06	—	—	—	—	—	—	.09	.14
Finance of schools	.05	.13	.64	.40	.17	.25	.15	.08	.09	.08
Finance for parents and students	.05	.03	—	—	—	.06	—	.02	.07	.02
Job-related or school-to-work	.05	—	—	—	—	.08	—	—	.05	—
Nutrition programs	.05	—	—	—	.50	.06	—	—	.02	—
Opportunity or civil rights	.15	.42	.11	—	—	—	.09	—	.16	.11
Parental involvement	—	—	—	—	—	.08	.06	.13	.11	.04
Preschool (linked to K–12)	—	—	—	—	—	—	—	—	.04	.01
School culture	—	—	—	—	—	.11	.32	.04	.07	.06
Other										
General improvement or policy	.30	.42	.36	.60	.50	.22	.24	.29	.23	.10
Other policy areas	.10	.10	—	—	—	—	.09	.04	.04	.04
N	(20)	(31)	(28)	(5)	(6)	(36)	(34)	(52)	(56)	(182)

Note: "—" indicates <.01. Row N corresponding to each column equals the number of sentences addressing K-12 education and mentioning a policy area. Areas mentioned at a rate of .05 or greater are in boldface, with the exception of the "other policy areas" category. Columns may sum to greater than 1.00 because sentences could receive multiple codes if they mentioned more than one policy area.

Source: Author's analysis of presidential inaugural addresses and State of the Union messages. See the appendix for a couple of exceptions.

education during the 1970s, a claim that Finn (1977) supports. That finding is still somewhat surprising given that the U.S. Department of Education was created during Carter's administration. In fact, during his entire term, Carter mentioned the idea of a department only one time in these major speeches. Even that lone mention came in the context of broader concerns about government organization and efficiency, not as a springboard for exploring substantive educational issues.

Only after the 1970s did presidents express detailed interest in education policy in their major addresses. Among sentences that mention some policy area, the number of specific policy areas that appear at least 5 percent of the time (flagged in bold in the table) jumps with Reagan's first term and continues through Clinton's tenure. Not including the "other policy areas" category, which acts as a grab bag of unrelated topics, no president prior to Reagan, with the exception of Kennedy, mentioned more than six policy areas in 5 percent or more of these statements. In contrast, all presidents after Carter identified no fewer than nine areas at this same rate.

Looking anecdotally at these speeches reveals how presidents have adapted their rhetoric within specific categories to offer their own perspective on timely issues. For example, Kennedy's and Johnson's concerns over facilities and equipment included much detail about school construction, while Clinton's interest also involved high-tech topics such as wiring schools to the Internet and developing school computer networks. Similarly, Reagan's concerns over school prayer frequently animated his interest in school culture, while later presidents focused on culture by discussing violence on school campuses.

NATIONAL PARTISAN INTEREST IN EDUCATION

In this final section, I examine the education content of the Republican and Democratic party platforms from 1960 to 2000. My analysis here parallels the work that generated table 3.3 in which I focused on specific aspects of policy in presidential speeches.[5]

The major party platforms play many key roles in American politics. Most generally, they aim to coalesce diverse interests under a common banner. In the process, they provide interest groups and party constituencies across the country with opportunities to influence a party's programmatic direction. That give-and-take process is perhaps as or more important than the actual platform language that results (Herring 1965, 230–37). Substantively, that means platforms represent one measure of federal interest in education because federal officials and presidential nominees can wield much influence over the crafting of party platforms. But because the platform-writing process brings together people from across the country, one should remember that platforms can represent much more than a Washington Beltway perspective on issues (Geer 1998b; Maisel 1994).

More than simply symbolic statements, platforms can sometimes even predict the policy positions that Republicans and Democrats take in national governing institutions, such as the U.S. Congress or the White House (Budge and Hofferbert 1990; Wolbrecht 2000). Interest groups also recognize this and see platforms as an important place to assert their influence (Maisel 1987). Even though races for national offices are becoming more candidate- rather than party-centered, the platforms' content still matters a great deal to national partisans.[6] Hence, these documents provide another window for measuring the development of federal interest in education policy. Tables 3.4 and 3.5 summarize the content of the Democratic and Republican platforms since 1960 using the same coding rules that produced table 3.3.

Compared to major presidential speeches, both parties have tended to address more specific K–12 education areas across all years. This difference is especially clear during the 1970s when education was essentially absent from presidential State of the Union and inaugural speeches. Unlike those speeches, platforms provide parties with more opportunities to take positions on many issues, in large part because length is not a major constraint on a platform's content. Televised speeches must fit into a relatively short time frame, but platforms can run on for several dozen pages. With that flexibility, the parties can use platform language to clarify their views and appeal to different groups.

Like presidential speeches, platforms do exhibit some continuity across time. For example, both the Republican and Democratic platforms consistently stress a general need to improve the nation's education system or general education programs. With the exception of Republican platforms in 1960 and 1964, that general concern, reported in the second to last row in each table, has always comprised at least 5 percent of all sentences about education policy; in most platform years, the total hovers around 15 percent. Education spending is another consistently popular area. Across both parties and in all years (with the lone exception of the Republicans in 1992), the topic of school funding has appeared in at least 5 percent of all sentences mentioning some policy area. In some years, finance has been a dominant concern as in the Democratic platforms of 1964 and 1988, and the Republican platforms of 1964 and 1976.

Change is also apparent in tables 3.4 and 3.5. Areas such as bilingual education and student nutrition have become less popular platform topics across time; after 1988, especially, both platforms mention them infrequently. Conversely, sentences about setting higher standards and holding schools and teachers accountable for results have increased in Republican platforms since 1980 and Democratic platforms since 1992. The change is most apparent for Democrats given that those topics barely appeared until after 1988 but then were prominently featured in 1992 (10 percent of sentences mentioning a policy area), 1996 (10 percent), and 2000 (21 percent).

Two specific areas illustrate some of the policy differences between the two major parties. The first is facilities and equipment, which includes such topics as

TABLE 3.4
Aspects of K–12 education policy mentioned in Democratic Party platforms, 1960–2000

Policy area	Proportion of sentences mentioning each policy area										
	1960	1964	1968	1972	1976	1980	1984	1988	1992	1996	2000
Academics and teaching											
Curriculum	.03	—	**.05**	**.08**	—	.01	**.06**	**.25**	**.10**	**.10**	**.09**
Standards and accountability	—	—	—	—	—	—	.02	—	**.10**	**.10**	**.21**
Testing	—	—	—	.01	—	.01	—	—	.03	—	.02
Social promotion	—	—	—	—	—	—	—	—	—	—	.01
Teaching method	—	—	.05	.02	—	—	.02	—	—	.01	.01
Teachers	**.08**	—	.07	.04	—	**.06**	**.06**	**.08**	**.10**	**.11**	**.18**
Choice											
School choice (general)	—	—	—	—	.02	—	—	—	.03	.01	.01
Competition	—	—	—	—	—	—	—	—	—	—	.01
Vouchers	—	—	—	—	—	—	—	—	.03	—	.02
Charter schools	—	—	—	—	—	—	—	—	—	.01	.03
Issues and programs											
Administration	.03	**.10**	.02	.01	.02	.03	—	—	.03	.04	—
At-risk students	—	—	—	.02	—	.01	.03	—	.03	.01	.01
Bilingual education	—	—	.02	**.08**	.02	.02	.02	.04	—	—	.01

	(36)	(10)	(41)	(104)	(41)	(109)	(90)	(24)	(29)	(79)	(154)
Class size	.03	—	—	—	—	—	—	—	—	.01	.02
Facilities and equipment	**.14**	**.10**	**.05**	.02	—	.01	**.08**	—	.03	**.05**	**.05**
Finance of schools	**.14**	**.40**	**.12**	**.16**	**.29**	**.19**	**.08**	**.33**	**.14**	.01	**.08**
Finance for parents and students	**.14**	**.20**	**.10**	.04	**.10**	**.10**	.04	**.08**	**.17**	**.19**	**.06**
Job-related or school-to-work	**.06**	**.10**	**.07**	**.11**	.07	**.06**	**.12**	.04	**.07**	**.06**	.03
Nutrition programs	.03	**.10**	**.05**	.01	.02	.04	.02	—	—	.03	—
Opportunity or civil rights	**.22**	—	—	**.18**	**.22**	**.14**	**.14**	.04	—	.01	.02
Parental involvement	—	—	—	—	—	.02	.02	—	.03	.03	**.05**
Preschool (linked to K–12)	—	—	**.05**	**.07**	.02	.02	—	**.17**	.03	.04	.03
School culture	—	—	—	.02	—	—	.02	.04	**.07**	**.16**	**.06**
Other											
General improvement	**.06**	**.10**	**.32**	**.10**	**.17**	**.23**	**.22**	**.08**	**.14**	**.13**	**.10**
Other policy areas	.19	—	.15	.13	.15	.17	.18	—	.03	.06	.06
	(36)	(10)	(41)	(104)	(41)	(109)	(90)	(24)	(29)	(79)	(154)

N

Note: "—" indicates < .01. *N* corresponding to each column equals the number of sentences addressing K–12 education and mentioning a policy area. Areas mentioned at a rate of .05 or greater are in boldface, with the exception of the "other policy areas" category. Columns may sum to greater than 1.00 because sentences could receive multiple codes if they mentioned more than one policy area.

Source: Author's analysis of party platforms.

TABLE 3.5

Aspects of K–12 education policy mentioned in Republican Party platforms, 1960–2000

Policy area	Proportion of sentences mentioning each policy area										
	1960	1964	1968	1972	1976	1980	1984	1988	1992	1996	2000
Academics and teaching											
Curriculum	.02	—	—	**.05**	.02	**.05**	**.16**	**.18**	**.07**	**.15**	**.10**
Standards and accountability	—	—	—	.02	—	.03	**.08**	.03	**.06**	**.07**	**.06**
Testing	—	—	—	—	—	—	.01	.01	.04	—	.01
Social promotion	—	—	—	—	—	—	—	—	—	—	—
Teaching method	.02	—	**.06**	.02	—	.02	.04	.01	**.09**	.04	.01
Teachers	**.07**	—	—	.02	—	**.14**	**.11**	**.06**	**.06**	**.07**	**.10**
Choice											
School choice (general)	—	—	—	.01	—	.02	.01	.04	**.08**	**.11**	**.05**
Competition	—	—	—	—	—	—	.01	.02	.01	—	.02
Vouchers	—	—	—	—	—	—	.02	.01	—	.04	.01
Charter schools	—	—	—	—	—	—	—	—	—	.01	.02
Issues and programs											
Administration	**.14**	**.30**	—	.03	**.20**	**.14**	**.08**	**.05**	.04	**.15**	.04
At-risk students	—	—	—	—	—	—	—	**.07**	—	.01	.02

	(42)	(10)	(18)	(93)	(50)	(58)	(99)	(120)	(103)	(72)	(110)
Bilingual education	—	—	**.06**	.02	.04	.02	—	—	—	.01	.01
Class size	—	—	—	—	—	—	.01	—	—	—	—
Facilities and equipment	**.17**	—	**.06**	.01	—	—	.01	.02	—	—	—
Finance of schools	**.14**	**.30**	**.11**	**.12**	**.20**	**.10**	**.05**	**.05**	.02	**.07**	**.10**
Finance for parents and students	**.07**	**.40**	**.22**	**.12**	**.10**	**.05**	.04	.04	.04	**.11**	**.16**
Job-related or school-to-work	.02	**.10**	**.17**	**.12**	.02	**.09**	**.06**	**.08**	**.07**	.01	.01
Nutrition programs	**.05**	—	**.06**	.02	.04	—	.01	—	—	—	—
Opportunity or civil rights	**.29**	**.20**	—	**.19**	**.20**	**.17**	**.09**	.03	—	.03	**.05**
Parental involvement	—	—	—	—	**.06**	**.07**	.03	.04	**.07**	**.07**	.03
Preschool (linked to K–12)	—	—	**.11**	**.05**	—	—	—	.03	.02	—	.03
School culture	—	—	—	.04	**.06**	.03	.03	**.08**	.04	**.11**	**.14**
Other											
General improvement	—	—	**.17**	**.16**	**.06**	**.09**	**.20**	**.20**	**.28**	**.15**	**.15**
Other policy areas	**.12**	**.10**	**.06**	**.13**	**.08**	**.12**	**.13**	**.11**	**.13**	**.11**	**.15**
N	(42)	(10)	(18)	(93)	(50)	(58)	(99)	(120)	(103)	(72)	(110)

Note: "—" indicates < .01. *N* corresponding to each column equals the number of sentences addressing K–12 education and mentioning a policy area. Areas mentioned at a rate of .05 or greater are in boldface, with the exception of the "other policy areas" category. Columns may sum to greater than 1.00 because sentences could receive multiple codes if they mentioned more than one policy area.

Source: Author's analysis of party platforms.

upgrading outdated buildings or purchasing new microscopes for science labs. Democrats emphasized these areas a great deal in their 1960 and 1964 platforms. And even though they have not sustained that interest across the platforms for all years, the topic does recur with some regularity through 2000. That contrasts sharply with Republicans who appeared to lose interest after 1968. On various aspects of school choice, including charter schools and vouchers, the relative levels of interest are reversed. Republicans began addressing choice with greater regularity and growing interest during the 1980s and 1990s. They were especially popular in their 1992 and 1996 platforms before dropping off somewhat in 2000. Democrats have tended to downplay the choice issue altogether.

OVERALL, THIS CHAPTER HAS USED SEVERAL DATA SOURCES TO DESCRIBE changes in federal interest in education. The evidence illustrates that members of Congress, presidential candidates and presidents, and the major political parties became more concerned about K–12 education in the last half of the twentieth century. The years after 1980 are especially important. During the 1980s and 1990s, federal leaders and the nation's political parties devoted more time to education while simultaneously expanding the number of education-related topics on their agendas. Put another way, federal interest in education became wider and deeper after the early 1980s. How federal policymakers developed license and capacity to expand their interests in this way is the subject of chapter 5.

In describing how federal interest in education has varied, I have tried to foreshadow some of the connections between the federal government and the states that chapter 5 will also develop. It is no accident that federal education agendas have expanded into areas where, according to my overview in chapter 1, the states have also established priorities. The issue of standards and accountability is one example. Using that information to infer that federal agenda change proceeds in a bottom-up fashion explains only part of the story. State agendas themselves have sometimes taken their cues from the federal government. Influence has occurred simultaneously as policy entrepreneurs working in federal or state venues have attempted to borrow license and capacity from one another to expand their agendas. My theoretical burden is to show how the borrowing strength model of agenda setting accounts for these dynamics better than other competing explanations. Before confronting that task head on in chapter 5, however, in chapter 4 I continue describing the agenda changes that have occurred. The present chapter described variability in federal interest in education. In the next chapter, I consider federal involvement, the book's other key dependent variable.

NOTES

1. Two experts in the field have noted the increasing importance of advertising by arguing that "televised political advertising is the main way that modern campaigns communicate with voters" (Goldstein and Ridout 2004, 205).

2. I note a couple of exceptions in the appendix.

3. Emphasis appears in the original.

4. Only two of Nixon's sentences, both referring to local governments, negatively identified an agent. Reagan criticized the federal government in five sentences during his first term. In his second term, he used one sentence to criticize government in general and one more to criticize the federal government. Clinton remained positive in his first term but in his second criticized the federal government in one sentence and local communities in another. These exceptions illustrate the otherwise general rule that presidents tend to discuss agents in a positive way in their inaugural messages and State of the Union speeches.

5. Given the ubiquitous references in the platforms to the pronoun "we," and the often vague or undefined antecedents that accompany the word, it was impossible to reliably code the agents as I did for presidential speeches in table 3.2.

6. One example from 2000 illustrates this idea. Upon learning that conservative groups, such as the Family Research Council, were planning to oppose the education language that Republican nominee George W. Bush wanted in the GOP platform, he dispatched advisers to help settle the argument in his favor. Interviews with Chester Finn and a congressional staffer confirmed this account.

4

Patterns of Federal Involvement in Education

The previous chapter showed that members of Congress, presidential candidates and presidents, and the nation's major parties have demonstrated greater interest in education since the 1960s. This chapter continues describing changes in the federal education agenda. In it, I focus on federal involvement and consider whether concrete federal action has accompanied all the talk that chapter 3 described. Simply because policymakers discuss issues more often or in greater depth does not necessarily mean they commit public resources to address them. It makes sense, then, to consider interest and involvement as separate components of a government's overall agenda.

The two sections in this chapter focus on different aspects of federal involvement in education. The first section maps the trajectory of federal education spending and the substantive public laws that address the nation's schools. The second section examines some of the major institutions that federal officials have constructed to help them develop, produce, and implement federal education policy. Paralleling chapter 3, both sections also begin to foreshadow important connections between the federal government and state education agendas. Those links will become more explicit in chapter 5, where I use the borrowing strength model to explain the variation described in this chapter and the previous one.

FEDERAL MONEY, LAWS, AND PROGRAMS FOR EDUCATION

Since the 1960s, the federal role in K–12 education finance has remained relatively stable and small when compared to spending from other levels of government. Recall figure 1.2, which documented the percent of education revenues coming from localities, states, and the federal government. According to that figure, the federal contribution increased during the mid-1960s from approximately 4.5 to 8 percent, then, after hovering between 8 and 10 percent for the latter half of the 1960s and all of the 1970s, the federal proportion actually dropped to between 6

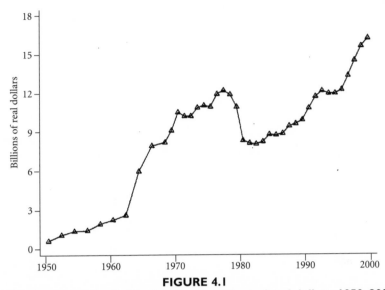

FIGURE 4.1
Federal revenues for K–12 education in billions of real dollars, 1950–2000
Note: Years correspond to the beginning of a school term (i.e., 1950 = 1950–51 school term).
Data are not available for even-numbered years from 1950 to 1968.
Source: Author's calculation from National Center for Education Statistics (2004, tables 35 and
156) using 1982–84 as the base years.

and 7 percent, where it has remained ever since. States and localities have always
paid the lion's share of the nation's education bill.

The stable pattern of federal spending that figure 1.2 documents does mask one
underlying source of variation. The federal role looks steady relative to state and
local contributions, but the amount of federal funding for K–12 education has
changed over time. Figure 4.1 plots federal education spending in real dollars
from 1950 to 2000. The jump coinciding with the first ESEA is quite noticeable.
Spending more than doubled between 1963–64 ($2.9 billion), the full school year
before the ESEA became law, and 1965–66 ($6.3 billion), the first academic period
that benefited from the law's funding authorization. Spending continued to increase after that, though at a slower pace. It peaked in 1978–79 and then declined
sharply after cutbacks and program consolidations during Ronald Reagan's first
term. The decline was short-lived, however, and spending began to increase once
again, albeit quite slowly, after the 1983–84 school year. Growth accelerated in the
last half of the 1980s and into the early 1990s. After a lull during the middle of the
1990s, spending again increased in 1996 and continued upward through the year
2000.

Beyond finances, tracing the production of education laws is another way to
examine how federal involvement in education has varied. To analyze trends in
federal lawmaking, I examined public laws from 1950 to 2000. I considered a law

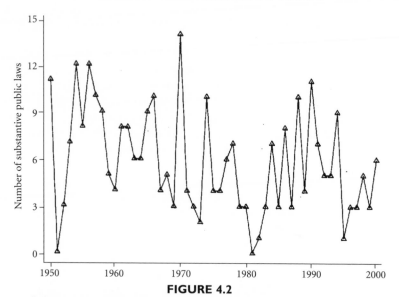

FIGURE 4.2
Substantive public laws addressing K–12 education, 1950–2000
Source: Author's coding of data from the Policy Agendas Project for years 1950 to 1998,
and author's coding of public laws catalogued on the Thomas website,
http://thomas.loc.gov/, for 1999 and 2000.

relevant to K–12 education if it exclusively affected elementary or secondary education or if it affected multiple levels of education but included K–12 schooling as a co-equal or major component.

Counting public laws to ascertain federal involvement in education provides insights about the changing federal education agenda, but this technique has limits. For one thing, it omits education provisions present in large catch-all laws, known as omnibus legislation, that have become increasingly popular (Krutz 2002). Another limit is that counting education laws omits amendments about education that are attached to bills primarily addressing other subjects. Consequently, without scanning the complete text of all omnibus legislation and amendments to all other non-education measures (both Herculean tasks given the sweep of time considered here), my counting method likely produces a conservative estimate of federal involvement. The analysis is useful nonetheless, especially when combined with anecdotal evidence from the laws themselves.

Figure 4.2 presents a count by year of these substantive federal laws. Over time, no dominant upward or downward trend emerges. The essentially erratic pattern does not seem to suggest any systematic changes in federal involvement over time. Scanning the substantive issues these laws address is one way to move beyond the relatively blunt measure of involvement that figure 4.2 provides. Another way is to examine the content of the ESEA, the nation's principal law for K-12 education. Both of these perspectives, which the rest of this section presents, offer added nuance that helps to describe the evolution of federal involvement in the nation's schools.

Since 1950, the federal government has produced many laws that please relatively narrow interests and do not represent broad forays into K–12 education. In nearly every year since 1950, for example, federal involvement has materialized with laws similar to P.L. 84-30, which authorized the Vineland (California) School District to use certain federal lands; with laws that promoted nutrition for poor students through the free and reduced cost milk, breakfast, and school lunch programs; and with legislation that addressed the education of Native Americans and the nation's disabled youngsters.

Laws fostering the development of curriculum and teaching methods in particular subject areas appeared periodically from the 1950s through the 1980s. Examples include the National Defense Education Act of 1958 (P.L. 85-864), which supported math, science, and foreign language instruction at all levels; P.L. 91-516 (1970), which focused on environmental education; and P.L. 98-377 (1984), which appeared after *A Nation at Risk* and authorized funds to upgrade instruction in math, science, technology, and foreign languages from elementary through graduate levels. The latter is an exception to the generally symbolic or hands-off nature of federal education policy that persisted during most of the 1980s.

Federal involvement demonstrates no consistent interest in broad educational reform until the 1990s. During that decade, laws emerged that established a National Commission on a Longer School Year (1991, P.L. 102-110); extended the National Commission on Time and Learning (1992, P.L. 102-359); established a national framework to link school and work (1994, P.L. 103-239); codified national education goals and aimed to improve learning and teaching through a national framework for education reform (1994, P.L. 103-227); amended previous federal efforts from 1994 to support charter schools by passing a specific law to improve and expand federal support for this reform model (1998, P.L. 105-278); and provided all states with new flexibility as they implemented federal education laws and pursued their own reform efforts (1999, P.L. 106-25). In short, substantive federal involvement in the nation's schools appears to have increased, notwithstanding the erratic pattern that figure 4.2 suggests.

One way to see this increasing involvement is to examine the cornerstone of federal efforts to help the educationally disadvantaged, which is Title I of the ESEA (Jennings 2001). As I noted in chapter 1, Title I is easily the most important component of the nation's principal K–12 education law. Studying Title I's symbolic and substantive features illustrates how policymakers have periodically adjusted this part of the ESEA to promote educational equity and, increasingly, to increase student performance. Given the overall importance of Title I, being able to explain its variation is a crucial test for the borrowing strength model of agenda setting. Chapter 5 uses the model to explain how changes in Title I have increased federal involvement in the nation's schools. For now, I use the next few pages to describe the changes that have occurred.

Title I received a rather cumbersome substantive name in the original ESEA of 1965.[1] In the law itself, members of Congress declared that the purpose of Title I was "to provide financial assistance . . . to local educational agencies serving areas with concentrations of children from low-income families to expand and improve their educational programs by various means (including preschool programs) which contribute particularly to meeting the special educational needs of educationally deprived children" (P.L. 89-10, Title I, Sec. 201).

Before examining that statement in detail, it is worth underscoring that statements describing a law's purpose do have important substantive impacts on policy implementation, even though a casual glance might suggest they are merely symbolic in nature. In stating the law's purpose, Congress helps to establish its intent, which can provide useful guidance to program managers in the federal bureaucracy. Statements of purpose can help these managers to field questions from state and local governments who frequently inquire about what they can and cannot do as they implement federal law.[2]

Two things about Title I's original statement of purpose are notable. First, the focus on disadvantaged students was clear and consistent with the goal of promoting equity. Second, the law would assist disadvantaged young people with specific educational programs to meet their "special educational needs." That language showed how Congress saw these students as a group distinct from the broader school population. The substantive provisions of Title I reflected this programmatic focus.

The overall approach of Title I and its substantive name remained the same in the 1967, 1970, and 1974 ESEA reauthorizations. In 1978 (P.L. 95-561), Congress gave the title a more general overall label, calling it "Financial Assistance to Meet Special Educational Needs of Children." The opening half of Title I's declaration of policy appended a new sentence to the 1965 language, recognizing other "special educational needs of children" in addition to poverty. Section 101 reinforced and extended distinctions between these students and others by identifying additional needy groups including children of certain migrant parents, Indian children, and handicapped, neglected, and delinquent children. This version of the law basically elaborated Title I's equity mission and remained organized around auditable programs that required local jurisdictions to document how they were helping disadvantaged students.

Even though it was not an explicit reauthorization of the ESEA, Title V, Subtitle D of the Omnibus Budget Reconciliation Act of 1981 (P.L. 97-35), introduced educational block grants and began to refocus Title I, now technically called Chapter 1 (but frequently still identified in the literature as Title I, a name that would officially return in the 1988 ESEA reauthorization), ever so slightly. While the title's overall name changed from the 1978 version, its purpose and substance continued to focus on the disadvantaged (identifying only low-income students specifically, however).[3]

The statement of purpose also included two changes in 1981. It stressed the need to decrease red tape that often accompanied federal programs and it identified the states as a new agent, in addition to school districts, that would support the law's aims. This was the first time the states had appeared specifically in Title I's statement of purpose. Their inclusion, however, reflected a governing philosophy that was consistent with the overall state-centered approach of Reagan's block grants (Anton 1989, 219) rather than a specific policy vision for education reform.

From 1965 through most of the 1980s, then, Title I and the regulations that accompanied it constructed various channels through which federal resources would flow to the nation's poorest school districts. Throughout these years, the law focused on educational inputs, such as the size of program authorizations and number of children served, rather than on outputs, such as student achievement (Jennings 2001). By and large, federal involvement meant tending to and often expanding the number of programs that would serve these students.

The ESEA reauthorization of 1988 (P.L. 100-297) began to reflect the increasing importance of states as educational reformers. In that law, Congress also resurrected earlier language by identifying specific types of disadvantaged students, in addition to low-income children, in Title I's statement of purpose. Not only did the states appear explicitly in the title's statement of policy, but the law also began to link academic performance of Title I students to state-defined achievement levels as a way to identify poorly performing schools (Jennings 2001).[4]

Congress also reframed the purpose of Title I programs in 1988. While they would still meet the particular needs of disadvantaged children, they also served the generic aim "to improve the educational opportunities of educationally deprived children by helping such children succeed in the regular program of the local educational agency, attain grade-level proficiency, and improve achievement in basic and more advanced skills" (P.L. 100-297, Title I, Chapter 1, Sec. 1001(b)). Previously, Title I's rationale had never mentioned academic achievement of disadvantaged students nor had it identified them as members of their schools' regular academic programs. Past versions had focused on these students' particular educational needs and the specific programs that could address them. Furthermore, in 1988, the law recognized that programs targeting entire schools, rather than disadvantaged populations alone, could be suitable for achieving Title I's aims.

Substantively, the law reflected this new purpose of Title I. It included provisions to increase accountability for the success of disadvantaged students and it added flexibility to help schools meet that goal (Jennings 2001, 1988). Specific provisions required states to define academic achievement levels that students in schools receiving Title I funds were required to attain. States had to identify, by name, schools not producing significant student progress. To increase flexibility, the law also allowed schools in which at least 75 percent of their student populations were eligible for Title I funding to bundle those funds and create schoolwide programs. These changes in Title I's approach began to shift the law away from the audit- and input-oriented mindsets that had driven the law since its earliest days. Last, and certainly not least, the 1988 update to the ESEA increased the program's authorization by more than $500 million, something that veteran House education staffer Jack Jennings (1988, 62) called "the chief characteristic of the new law."

Despite these changes in 1988, some features remained the same. Title I continued to single out disadvantaged students from general school populations. By that, I mean that the educational standards and achievement levels described in the previous paragraph applied only to disadvantaged students served by Title I. Federal policymakers still considered students eligible for Title I as a distinct group.

The focus on achievement and the increase in reliance on the states intensified in 1994. In that year, Congress reauthorized the ESEA yet again. It's new official name was the IASA, which I briefly introduced in this book's opening chapter, but policymakers and analysts would sometimes continue to call it the ESEA in their discussions and publications (Smith, Scoll, and Plisko 1995; Manno 1995; Jennings 1998; Farkas and Hall 2000). In this version, officially known as P.L. 103-382, the adjustments to Title I were profound and created an important shift for the borrowing strength model to explain. The influence of the state standards movement, which had been brewing since the 1980s and had accelerated in the 1990s, became quite explicit. Congress renamed Title I "Helping Disadvantaged Children Meet High Standards." Its opening general statement of policy encompassed all students, not just the disadvantaged as the 1988 law had done.[5] That deepened federal involvement and implied federal policy should properly consider more than the educational needs of the disadvantaged as a particular isolated group.

After beginning Title I with this general frame, Congress continued in Section 1001(b) with a "recognition of need" that highlighted some of the educational difficulties facing students of particular disadvantaged groups. First among these problems was the "sizable gap" in educational achievement between the disadvantaged and other children. Section 1001(c) elaborated on what the nation had learned about education since the last ESEA reauthorization in 1988 and opened with a statement that all students, including those whom Title I served, could meet high expectations (P.L. 103-382, Title I, Sec. 1001(c)(1)). Also apparent from educational research was that supplemental programs for the disadvantaged could be helpful, but that these students also needed access to "effective high-quality regular school programs" (P.L. 103-382, Title I, Sec. 1001(c)(4)).

With those developments in 1994, Congress made Title I's new mission explicit in its statement of policy, again highlighting the role of the states: "The purpose of this title is to enable schools to provide opportunities for children served to acquire the knowledge and skills contained in the challenging State content standards and to meet the challenging State performance standards developed for all children" (P.L. 103-382, Title I, Sec. 1001(d)). That final part of Title I's opening section elaborated in nine specific points how to accomplish this purpose. Testing, through state assessment systems, was an explicit part of this overall strategy and would measure "how well children served under this title are achieving challenging State student performance standards expected of all children" (P.L. 103-382, Title I, Sec. 1001(d)(8)).

These changes in the law reflected the reform framework that the Clinton administration articulated in the Goals 2000: Educate America Act of 1994 (P.L. 103-227). The link between Title I and high standards became ironclad, as the IASA's version of Title I required states participating in the program to develop academic standards that all students, not just those served by Title I, needed to meet. This provision about achievement obliterated the distinction between the Title I and non-Title I student populations. As Thomas Payzant and Jessica Levin (1995, 62–63), education officials in the Clinton administration, put it, "The new Title I makes a powerful break with past practice by replacing minimum standards for some children with challenging standards for all."

Whereas the accountability provisions in the 1988 law addressed achievement, they affected at most only 20 percent of the nation's students (the Title I-eligible population). The federal government also did not implement the 1988 provisions very aggressively. In 1994, with Goals 2000 and the newly reauthorized ESEA the federal reach expanded significantly because it required Title I students to meet the same standards as all other students. The accountability provisions that accompanied Title I's changes in 1994 required states to test students no less than one time in grades three through five, six through nine, and ten through twelve. Rather than testing everyone, though, the law allowed states to measure progress by testing samples of students and it gave states five years to phase in these activities.[6]

The 1994 ESEA also expanded flexibility in two main ways. It allowed individual schools to implement schoolwide Title I programs if their low-income student populations exceeded 50 percent, which was lower than the 75 percent level from the 1988 reauthorization.[7] Also, it gave the secretary of the U.S. Department of Education power to waive certain federal requirements that hindered students from achieving at high levels.

This new direction for Title I continued unabated when the ESEA was reauthorized, and renamed yet again, as NCLB in 2001 (P.L. 107-110). In chapter 6, I consider that law in detail. Briefly, though, Title I received a new substantive name once again with NCLB, but it still kept the same spirit that the 1994 ESEA had articulated.[8] Its statement of purpose paralleled the 1994 law; with NCLB, Title I would "ensure that all children have a fair, equal, and significant opportunity to obtain a high-quality education and reach, at a minimum, proficiency on challenging State academic achievement standards, and state academic assessments" (P.L. 107-110, Title I, Sec. 1001). Among the twelve specific points following that general statement, many carried over from the 1994 ESEA.

Alex Medler, acting director of the public charter schools program at the U.S. Department of Education, attested to the substantive continuity in the 1994 and 2001 versions of the ESEA. In a personal interview, he described to me the connection between the two reauthorizations this way: "When [Clinton education secretary Richard] Riley and [acting undersecretary] Mike Smith were around you could have called the Department of Education the 'Department of High Standards and Forty Other Ideas.' What has followed has built on that. All of the things that have come along are moving in the same direction."

EVOLVING INSTITUTIONAL ARENAS AND THE FEDERAL ROLE IN EDUCATION

Examining the organizations that federal officials have designed to help them create, manage, and implement policy also sheds light on how federal involvement in education has changed. This section focuses on four institutions in particular: the Gardner Education Task Force of 1964; the U.S. Department of Education, formed in the late 1970s; the NCEE, which produced the famous 1983 report, *A Nation at Risk;* and the National Education Goals Panel (NEGP), formed after the first national education summit in 1989. The character of these institutions and the issues they have addressed provide insights about the changing federal role in education. They also reveal that the federal-state relationship in education has changed dramatically since the 1960s.

The Gardner Education Task Force

During the summer of 1964, incumbent Lyndon Johnson was anticipating a November victory over Republican presidential opponent Barry Goldwater. In July of that summer, LBJ announced to his cabinet that he was creating fourteen policy task forces to help him build on his Great Society speech that he had delivered on May 22 at the University of Michigan's commencement. The task forces would operate in secret, develop ideas for the president's domestic and international agenda, and report their findings to the president no later than November 10. John Gardner, president of the Carnegie Corporation, chaired the president's task force on education. Overall, its members included three federal, one state, and two local officials; six academics; and two members each from the private and nonprofit sectors.

The relatively low profile of the states, with their lone representative in the group, was consistent with general feelings that existed inside the Johnson administration and on the task force itself. As former Johnson adviser Samuel Halperin described to me in a personal interview, "The people who you could call the Kennedy and Johnson elites—I don't use that term negatively—didn't think that we could get educational justice from the states. Some of them said that the states were actually the problem." In his oral history, which is available at the LBJ presidential library, U.S. Commissioner of Education Francis Keppel, a member of the task force, said many of its members "felt that the state departments of education were the feeblest bunch of second-rate, or fifth-rate, educators who combined educational incompetence with bureaucratic immovability" (Graham 1984, 63).

Despite this criticism, Keppel also recognized the Johnson education program could not succeed without state government capacity. "Having sat on that educational bureaucracy in Washington," he said, "the last thing in the world I wanted was all those 25,000 school districts coming in with plans with my bureaucrats deciding whether to approve them or not. I wanted that stuff done out in the states. And to make it work in the states, you have to improve the state departments in making grants" (Graham 1984, 63). My interviews with Halperin and Gordon Ambach, a veteran of federal and state policy arenas dating to the 1950s, confirmed this view. Comments from both illustrated how important Keppel saw the states' role even as these governments remained marginalized during the actual development of the first ESEA.[9]

By late September 1964, Gardner summarized the group's top priorities in a memo to task force members. The memo stressed an overall antipoverty theme and included proposals for supplementary educational centers, educational research and development labs, and higher education. Gardner's memo reflected Keppel's view that state departments of education were too weak at the time and that the U.S. Office of Education, which Keppel headed, would likely not be able to effectively manage the new Johnson education program. To address that potential problem, the Gardner memo proposed removing the Office of Education from the Department of Health, Education, and Welfare, and creating a stand-alone federal education department instead (Graham 1984, 66).

On November 15, Johnson received the task force's final report. It was a much expanded but essentially unchanged version of Gardner's memo and it provided the basis for titles I, III, IV, and V of the first ESEA. The president reportedly read the report from cover to cover and was pleased with its contents. Shortly after Thanksgiving, he met with his advisers and instructed them to press on with a legislative program for education based on the Gardner task force report (Graham 1984, 70–71). The first ESEA became law roughly five months later.

The U.S. Department of Education

Even though a federal education department did not emerge in 1965, the Gardner group's recommendation for one was actually not new. During the first half of the twentieth century, members of Congress had introduced more than fifty bills that would have established such a department and given education cabinet-level status (Radin and Hawley 1988, 23). The vision for a department finally became reality when, on October 17, 1979, President Jimmy Carter signed into law the Department of Education Organization Act (P.L. 96-88).

Creating the department was a notable legislative accomplishment. But in substantive terms, it is perhaps a less significant achievement than passage of the first ESEA and, by implication, the work of the Gardner task force. That is because the ESEA of 1965 represented a major break with past federal education policy and overcame persistent concerns about race, religion, and federal intrusion that had torpedoed past proposals for greater federal involvement in the nation's schools. The Carter initiative that created the Department of Education, while certainly criticized for unduly increasing federal control, did not represent this kind of substantive breakthrough. Exploring the rationale that motivated Carter's advocacy for the department reveals why.

Carter and his allies offered reasons for creating the new department but neither overhauling the nation's education system nor altering the major substantive

thrust of federal programs was part of their rationale. In short, an education reform agenda did not animate their efforts. In an interview with Arthur Wise, a former Carter administration official whose "pen wrote most of the legislation [to
create the department], at least the first drafts," Wise said this about the early
stages of the process: "Other than saying that we should have an education department, the president and others behind it hadn't given much thought to what that
actually meant." Perhaps that lack of foresight is one reason why White House
groups assigned to develop the original proposal basically ignored the issue of federal-state relations (Radin and Hawley 1988, 77). Wise continued in our discussion by noting that most people in the White House who worked on the initiative
"had a very unsophisticated approach. Many of them argued that what needed to
be done was to gather up everything remotely related to education and put it in
the department."

As the effort unfolded, the primary rationale that emerged was a perceived
need for bureaucratic reorganization. Much evidence supports this conclusion.
First, Carter's team lodged its effort to create the department in a broader initiative called the President's Reorganization Project, which was designed to improve
the work of many government agencies. Education was but one part of this overall
reorganization effort (Radin and Hawley 1988).[10] Second, despite his remarks at
the signing ceremony for P.L. 96-88, both during the legislative process and after
leaving office, Carter emphasized organizational concerns when focusing on why
the nation needed the department (Stephens 1983–84, 647; Carter 1982, 76).
Finally, some of the department's supporters and members of Congress actually
argued that this new federal agency would produce little policy change. To minimize fears of growing federal control, the Senate committee that considered the
bill in 1979 stated in its report, somewhat remarkably, that the new department
"should not directly . . . improve American education. It is not intended to do so
because that is really the province and duty of the States and localities" (Stephens
1983–84, 654).[11]

The U.S. Department of Education opened its doors on May 4, 1980. Less than
one year later, Ronald Reagan entered the White House with promises to abolish
the fledgling department. Despite Reagan's animosity, the institution survived
and created an effective bully pulpit for his own and subsequent education secretaries. Perhaps one of the most effective uses of the department's platform was by
Terrell "Ted" Bell who served as its secretary during Reagan's first term.

The National Commission on Excellence in Education

In 1981, Bell faced a nearly impossible task when he resigned as commissioner and
chief executive officer of the Utah System of Higher Education to become the nation's second education secretary. In his memoirs, he described his job as captain-
ing a ship called Reagan's Titanic. His pessimism was due to the president's
campaign promise to eliminate the new department and pull back the federal role
in education (Bell 1988).

Bell's feelings proved prescient when he proposed that Reagan rally the American people by naming a presidential commission on education. Reagan's top advisers rejected the idea. But Bell and others remained convinced that many of the economic and social problems that confronted the nation were intimately linked to the quality of American schools. So, even though the White House may have agreed with Bell's diagnosis, Reagan's people rejected the secretary's proposal. After licking his wounds, Bell pressed on undeterred and appointed his own departmental commission. Though a cabinet-level effort, rather than one operating with the White House's imprimatur, would not pack the punch Bell desired, in his mind it was better than not acting at all.

On August 26, 1981, Bell created the NCEE—the National Commission on Excellence in Education. David P. Gardner, president of the University of Utah and president-elect of the University of California, chaired the commission. Bell gave Gardner and seventeen other commission members eighteen months to examine the condition of American education—with a particular focus on high schools— and to offer practical suggestions for improvements. Half of the NCEE's appointees came from either state (three members) or local (six members) governments; six were academics; two represented the private sector; and one was from the non-profit sector. Notably, unlike LBJ's education task force, the NCEE contained no federal officials.[12]

When the NCEE presented its findings in April 1983, its tone and recommendations landed the document on newspaper front pages across the country. In what some observers criticized as inaccurate overstatement, the commission's report, titled *A Nation at Risk,* began in military-like terms: "If an unfriendly foreign power had attempted to impose on America the mediocre educational performance that exists today, we might well have viewed it as an act of war. . . . We have, in effect, been committing an act of unthinking, unilateral educational disarmament" (National Commission on Excellence in Education 1983).

The commission continued by detailing what it believed were national educational shortcomings in four broad areas: school curriculum, expectations for students, the use of time in American schools, and teachers and teaching. It recommended reforms including strengthening graduation requirements by increasing the number of required courses in core subjects; adopting more rigorous expectations and standards in classrooms at all levels; increasing the hours of the school day; improving teacher preparation and prestige; and encouraging citizens and parents across the country to demand that elected officials exercise leadership and provide adequate financial resources to help implement the report's recommendations. As part of that leadership effort, the NCEE identified key roles for principals, superintendents, school board members, governors, state legislators, and federal officials. In so doing, it assigned to the federal government "the primary responsibility to identify the national interest in education. It should also help fund and support efforts to protect and promote that interest" (National Commission on Excellence in Education 1983).

The report's immediate impact on the federal government was more important for symbolic than policy reasons. Arguably, *A Nation at Risk* may have saved the Department of Education from Reagan's ax, which ironically preserved a bully pulpit that the president's subsequent education secretary, William Bennett, would use quite effectively.[13] But if the NCEE piqued federal interest in education and provided it with license to act, it did not have the same effect on federal involvement during most of the 1980s. As figure 4.1 shows, inflation-adjusted federal spending on education continued to stagnate, although it never actually decreased, for the rest of Reagan's tenure. Rather than heeding the NCEE's call to provide policy leadership and funding, by and large the federal government eschewed that role and relied upon states to sustain the reform momentum. More intense federal involvement would come in the 1990s. Why those changes occurred later rather than sooner has as much to do with the capacity challenges that Washington faced in the 1980s as it does with the policy preferences of Reagan and his allies. Borrowing capacity from the states to overcome these challenges was a relatively limited option for several reasons that the next chapter will explain.

The National Education Goals Panel

While both the Gardner Task Force of 1964 and the NCEE were ad hoc institutions and the Department of Education was a permanent government agency, the National Education Goals Panel (NEGP) amounted to something in between. It operated for more than a decade, from 1990 to 2001, and thus outlived LBJ's group and the NCEE. Unlike those two institutions and the federal education department, state officials—in particular governors—were the key players on the NEGP. Their impact reflected the burgeoning influence they possessed in the 1990s as educational reformers. That reputation and their role on the NEGP also helped to shape federal involvement in the nation's schools.

The idea for national education goals, and in turn the NEGP, emerged from the September 1989 national education summit in Charlottesville, Virginia. In calling that meeting, President George H. W. Bush summoned the nation's fifty governors to discuss American schools and to keep his campaign promise to become the education president. Dating back to 1983, when the NCEE released *A Nation at Risk,* then Vice President Bush had recognized the potentially important role that states could play in improving the nation's schools. In his memoirs, Bell (1988, 134–36) attested to Bush's thoughts on this subject, as did the executive director of the NCEE, Milton Goldberg, in a personal interview with me.

At Charlottesville, Bush aspired to convene the states' chief executives to share education success stories and exchange ideas. The governors found the summit idea attractive but they and their aides at the National Governors' Association (NGA) resisted Bush's approach, which they found redundant. They had already discussed these topics at other meetings and preferred to use the summit as a platform to develop a list of national education goals. Ultimately, as published sources and my interview respondents with experience at the summit told me, they persuaded Bush to go along (Vinovskis 1999c). The president and the governors left the summit promising to begin a process to develop such a list, which they completed shortly thereafter.[14]

During their meetings after the summit, Bush and the governors realized that national education goals would be meaningless unless a group existed to monitor the country's progress toward achieving them. Thus, they invented the NEGP to address that need. After creating it, Bush and the state's chief executives issued a joint statement that identified the panel's overall purpose, which was to "oversee the development and implementation of a national education progress reporting system" (Vinovskis 1999a, 8).[15]

The joint statement continued and described specific responsibilities for the panel, which included monitoring indicators to chart overall educational progress of the nation and individual states; producing an annual report to document that progress; soliciting input from experts to analyze the most promising educational practices; and disseminating the results of these commissioned studies to interested parties across the country. Completing these and other tasks would serve to "fulfill those responsibilities set forth in the Federal-state partnership at Charlottesville" (Vinovskis 1999a, 9).

Overall, the NEGP extended the federal bully pulpit in education, but it did so with an important twist. Federal officials had a new platform to promote their own interest and involvement in education, to highlight American educational performance, and to encourage reform. Simultaneously, states had great influence over the panel's work. During the negotiations with the White House that developed the NEGP's structure, the governors pushed hard to prevent federal representatives from dominating its membership (Vinovskis 1999a). The final agreement from July 1990 reflected those preferences: governors occupied six of the panel's fourteen seats and the NGA would appoint the panel's chair. Of the eight federal representatives, four were members of Congress and four were executive branch officials. During its first four years, the panel's official power was derived from the Federal Advisory Committee Act; the Office of Policy Development in the Executive Office of the President provided its administrative support. In 1994, the NEGP grew to eighteen members and was codified, along with a slightly expanded set of national education goals, in the Goals 2000: Educate America Act.[16] The revision gave state officials an even larger role with eight governors and six state legislators on the panel; the other six slots were occupied by two members each from the U.S. House, the Senate, and the executive branch.

During the 1990s, the panel performed important substantive and symbolic functions. There is no question that the research it commissioned and its outreach efforts helped to keep education a top priority for governments at all levels (Vinovskis 1999b). It enabled the governors and the federal government to more easily focus the nation's attention on education. From the governors' perspective, this was important for continuing to secure federal support for their reform initiatives. It also helped them to repel critics who claimed that states were usurping local power over the nation's schools.

From the federal government's vantage point, the NEGP and the national education goals provided a lever to hold states to their promises. That was not a minor point and illustrated the lingering suspicion that federal officials harbored about the states' willingness to improve education. Even though federal officials recognized the states' critical role, they also understood that states would require future prodding to keep them on course. The executive director of the NEGP, Ken Nelson, made this point implicitly in his testimony before a House committee in 1996. In reacting to one committee member's suggestion that the states fund the NEGP, Nelson replied, "To provide annual reports for each of ten years requires secure and predictable funding, which could be jeopardized by relying on the states. . . . In addition, some states are more interested than others and if some withdrew support others might find it difficult to continue" (Vinovskis 1999b, 43).

Despite the NEGP's successes, Congress dissolved the panel in 2001. There were substantive and political reasons for that outcome. Some opponents reasonably argued that the panel's purpose was to monitor the country's progress toward meeting the national education goals by the year 2000. After the new century arrived, that specific task was complete and these critics argued that the NEGP should close its doors. At the same time, Republicans in the House were anxious to excise from federal law any education policies that had the word "goals" in their name, given the direct link between that term and President Clinton's Goals 2000 initiative from 1994. These forces combined to shut down the panel without much fanfare. As John Barth, acting executive director of the NEGP during its final days, remarked to me in an interview: "Overall, the panel's problem isn't from a crowd of loud critics, but from a dearth of passionate friends."

THIS CHAPTER AND THE PREVIOUS ONE HAVE DESCRIBED VARIATION IN FEDeral interest and involvement in K–12 education during the last half of the twentieth century. In recapping the central trend of the present chapter, I restate that, since the 1960s, federal involvement in the nation's schools has grown but in a sometimes irregular pattern. Beginning in the late 1980s and especially the early 1990s, federal involvement increased and became more substantively coherent. Through developments in Title I of the ESEA and institutions like the NEGP, federal officials began supporting standards-based reforms that affected all the nation's students, not just the disadvantaged or those with particular educational needs.

Trends in federal involvement are not unrelated to agenda changes in the states. Since the 1960s, the states have increased their role in education finance; they have adopted an expanded menu of reforms to improve educational quality that includes promoting educational standards that were so critical to revisions of the ESEA in 1994 and 2001; and they have been political and policy leaders at high profile events such as the Charlottesville education summit and in important institutions such as the NEGP.

Having described sources of variation in federal interest and involvement in education and having identified crucial turning points along the way, I now return to the borrowing strength model to explain how these changes have occurred. The next chapter will show how federalism has created opportunities for policy entrepreneurs in Washington and the states to develop their education agendas. Changes across these venues have been related, and the mechanism of borrowing strength shows how. More than simply offering another version of cooperative federalism or states as laboratories of policy innovation, the analysis in chapter 5 will show how entrepreneurs working at federal and state levels have leveraged their own license and capacity and strategically borrowed strengths from one another to ameliorate their shortcomings. Overall, the borrowing strength model provides a compelling theoretical and empirical perspective. It integrates the research literatures on federalism and agenda setting with a tight collection of key concepts. It also accounts for changes in federal and state education agendas that have unfolded since the 1960s.

NOTES

1. It was called "Title I Financial Assistance to Local Educational Agencies for the Education of Children of Low-Income Families and Extension of Public Law 874, Eighty-First Congress."

2. Consider the following example of how a law's statement of purpose can influence implementation. In a letter from 2004, the U.S. Department of Education responded to a school district's questions about how to interpret the collective bargaining provisions of NCLB. After identifying the relevant provision in the statute, the letter began its reply with the following passage: "This provision must be implemented *in concert with the purpose of Title I*, which is quite clear: 'to ensure that all children have a fair, equal, and significant opportunity to obtain a high-quality education and reach, at a minimum, proficiency on challenging state academic achievement standards and State academic assessment.' *The statement of purpose further declares that this purpose can be accomplished*, in part, by 'significantly elevating the quality of instruction' and by 'holding schools, local educational agencies, and States accountable for improving the academic achievement of all students . . .'" (emphasis mine). Many thanks to Michael Petrilli of the U.S. Department of Education who provided me with a copy of this letter.

3. The name now read "Chapter 1—Financial Assistance to Meet Special Educational Needs of Disadvantaged Students." That adjustment replaced the word "children" from P.L. 95-561 with "disadvantaged students."

4. In part, the Congress declared "it to be the policy of the United States to provide financial assistance to State and local educational agencies to meet the special needs of such educationally deprived children at the preschool, elementary, and secondary levels." See P.L. 100-297, Title I, Chapter 1, Sec. 1001(a)(2)(A).

5. That section (emphasis mine) reads as follows: "The Congress declares it to be the policy of the United States that a high-quality education *for all individuals* and a fair and

equal opportunity to obtain that education are a societal good, are a moral imperative, and improve the life of every individual, because the quality of our individual lives ultimately depends on the quality of the lives of others" (P.L. 103-382, Title I, Sec. 1001(a)(1)).

6. I would like to acknowledge Jack Jennings for help in clarifying the changes between the 1988 and 1994 versions of Title I.

7. See Farkas and Hall (2000, 76–77) for data on the expansion of schoolwide Title I programs after the 1994 reforms.

8. It was now called "Improving the Academic Achievement of the Disadvantaged."

9. Halperin told me that "Keppel was a strong believer in [Title V of the ESEA]. He pushed the idea that the states needed to be built up." In my interview with Ambach, he reflected on his work in the Kennedy administration from 1961 to 1964 and recalled that Keppel used to say that the order of the ESEA titles was essentially backwards—Title V should have come earlier—because creating state capacity was such an important feature of the law.

10. My interview with Arthur Wise also confirmed that bureaucratic reorganization was the driving factor. "So you are right in your general characterization that it was mainly nothing but a rearranging of the boxes," he told me.

11. See also Radin (1988, 218) and Elmore and McLaughlin (1983, 328).

12. One member, Albert Quie, did have past federal experience. He had been a member of Congress before becoming governor of Minnesota from 1979 to 1983.

13. Two of my interview respondents, Arthur Wise and Milton Goldberg, concurred with that assessment. Wise attributed the department's survival to "Bell's skillful use of *Nation at Risk*." Goldberg, who was executive director of the NCEE noted, "I can tell you that after the report was released some people said to me 'You just saved my job.'"

14. The six goals that the president and the governors agreed to were: (1) All children in America will start school ready to learn. (2) The high school graduation rate will increase to at least 90 percent. (3) All students will leave grades 4, 8, and 12 having demonstrated competency over challenging subject matter including English, mathematics, science, foreign languages, civics and government, economics, arts, history, and geography, and every school in America will ensure that all students learn to use their minds well, so they may be prepared for responsible citizenship, further learning, and productive employment in our Nation's modern economy. (4) The United States students will be the first in the world in mathematics and science achievement. (5) Every adult American will be literate and will possess the knowledge and skills necessary to compete in a global economy and exercise the rights and responsibilities of citizenship. (6) Every school in the United States will be free of drugs, violence, and the unauthorized presence of firearms and alcohol, and will offer a disciplined environment conducive to learning. Cited at the NEGP web site, http://www.negp.gov/page3-1.htm (accessed various dates, Spring and Summer 2002), which is now archived at http://govinfo.library.unt.edu/negp/page3-1.htm.

15. The panel's eventual mission statement interpreted this to mean that it would "catalyze fundamental change in schools, communities, states and the nation in order to achieve the National Education Goals." Cited at the NEGP website, http://www.negp.gov/page1-11.htm (accessed various dates, Spring and Summer 2002), which is now archived at http://govinfo.library.unt.edu/negp/page1-11.htm.

16. The two additional education goals to be accomplished by 2000 were: (1) The Nation's teaching force will have access to programs for the continued improvement of their

professional skills and the opportunity to acquire the knowledge and skills needed to instruct and prepare all American students for the next century. (2) Every school will promote partnerships that will increase parental involvement and participation in promoting the social, emotional, and academic growth of children. Cited at the NEGP website, http://www.negp.gov/page1-11.htm (accessed various dates, Spring and Summer 2002), which is now archived at http://govinfo.library.unt.edu/negp/page1-11.htm.

5

Borrowing Strength, Federalism, and Education Agendas

In the last two chapters, I have described changes in the federal education agenda over long periods of time. In this chapter, I explain how those changes have occurred by incorporating a more explicit discussion of state education agendas and by returning to the borrowing strength model of agenda setting. I build my discussion in this chapter around the six expectations about federalism and agenda setting that I advanced in chapter 2. For the reader's convenience, I have reproduced those expectations in table 5.1. Substantively, this chapter shows how the interactive nature of American federalism can simultaneously accelerate and attenuate the development of agendas in Washington, DC, and the nation's fifty states. In defending that claim, I will also argue that the borrowing strength model offers a compelling theoretical approach that builds on past research while simultaneously generating several new insights about how federalism influences agenda setting.

This chapter contains three sections. The first explains the license and capacity challenges that nearly always confront policy entrepreneurs working in Washington, DC, who wish to influence the federal education agenda. The second section explains how borrowing strength can generate positive feedback that enables state and federal agendas to expand. The third section considers an opposing dynamic that occurs when attempts at borrowing strength set off negative feedback processes that can attenuate the ambitions of policy entrepreneurs as they seek to develop their agendas. Across all sections I note the importance of attending to the timing and sequencing of events.

WASHINGTON'S AGENDA CHALLENGES IN EDUCATION

Policy entrepreneurs hoping to build agendas would prefer to command high license and high capacity to act. They enjoy perhaps the greatest likelihood of increasing the agenda status of their favored initiatives when the government possesses a strong warrant and robust capabilities. The first expectation from chapter 2 and table 5.1 states this idea: *Policy entrepreneurs operating with high license and high capacity will tend to promote a government's interest and involvement*

TABLE 5.1
Expectations about agenda dynamics in a federal system

1. Policy entrepreneurs operating with high license and high capacity will tend to promote a government's interest and involvement in a policy area.

2. Lacking license or capacity, policy entrepreneurs may bolster either or both, and thus develop their government's interest and involvement in a policy area, by borrowing strength from another level of government.

3. Policy entrepreneurs will be more likely to borrow strength to promote agendas when they think it will help them achieve political gains and make good policy.

4. Federal officials who borrow strength from states will be more likely to enjoy political and policy success if they accurately assess the license and capacity of state governments.

5. State officials will attempt to extract concessions from federal officials if they think that, in borrowing strength, federal officials have overestimated state license or capacity.

6. Federal officials will modify policies that depend on borrowed strength if they are persuaded they have overestimated state license or capacity.

Note: These expectations originally appeared in chapter 2 under the subheading "Expected Agenda Dynamics in a Federal System" and are reproduced here for the reader's convenience.

in a policy area. One point to address at the outset of this chapter is that policy entrepreneurs in Washington, DC, rarely enjoy high license and high capacity to act in education. This brief section explains why borrowing strength is essentially always required for federal policy entrepreneurs who work in this area.

Compared to building agendas for national defense or immigration, for example, policy entrepreneurs who care about American schooling face a more difficult challenge when they attempt to expand Washington's agenda in K–12 education. Certainly, federal license and capacity to act in education have increased since the first ESEA became law in 1965. The dynamic relationship between interest and involvement and license and capacity is one reason why. Recall from chapter 2 that interest and involvement at one point in time may produce license and capacity in later periods. Still, even as federal license and capacity to act have increased, entrepreneurs have had to overcome high hurdles as they have sought to expand the federal role into core functions of the nation's schools—functions such as supporting standards and accountability for student achievement—that reach beyond programmatic efforts that target more narrowly defined and typically disadvantaged student groups.

Consider license, specifically. Despite growing public support for federal involvement in education, citizens still generally prefer state and local control of schools. They also worry that too much federal activity will undermine the efforts of classroom teachers and principals. Some of the negative reactions to NCLB, which I describe in the next chapter, illustrate as much. Policy entrepreneurs and elected officials in Washington frequently walk on tightropes as they attempt to expand their education agendas while simultaneously rebutting claims that they aspire to become a de facto national school board.

Federal license to act has sometimes expanded when entrepreneurs have linked education to other goals such as national defense, civil rights, or the reduction of poverty. Still, celebrated instances, including the Soviet Union's Sputnik launch in 1957 and efforts from the 1960s and 1970s to promote equality, have typically only justified limited support in specific areas (i.e., promoting math and science education for talented students) or for particular student groups (i.e., the poor, limited English proficient, or disabled). For much of its history, federal education policy has remained peripheral to the teaching and learning in American schools that involves all students (Kaestle and Smith 1982, 400, 405; Hill 2000). A shortage of license has tended to limit the federal role to programmatic or niche areas. As Schwartz and Robinson (2000, 178) have argued, it is often difficult to justify federal leadership in K–12 education, "especially when the focus shifts from programs targeted to specific groups of students in need of federal protection to a strategy aimed at raising the achievement of all children."

Finding capacity to act has also challenged federal policy entrepreneurs for two institutional reasons. First, the fiscal federalism of American education and limited bureaucratic capacity in Washington constrain the federal role. Because the federal government supplies only a small portion of the nation's K–12 education dollars, its leverage over the conduct of schooling across the nation is necessarily limited. In a personal interview with me, Gerald Tirozzi, a former state education chief and education official in the Clinton administration, described this fact in colorful terms. He noted how the federal role is limited due to the golden rule that says, "He who has the gold makes the rules." Federalism scholars will recognize that federal policymakers often attempt to parlay that logic when they use grant programs to influence state priorities. Even that approach is not a panacea, however, given the license and capacity barriers that Washington policymakers must overcome when they use the carrot of federal grants to alter state education agendas.

A second enduring limitation on federal capacity exists due to the relatively weak bureaucratic structures and policy expertise the federal government possesses in education. For most of its history, the federal education bureaucracy has been comprised of compliance-oriented positions with staff who are primarily responsible for keeping federal dollars flowing to states and school districts. Several of my veteran interview respondents—Jack Jennings and Christopher Cross, for example—as well as others who have recent experience working in the federal bureaucracy—like Alex Medler—noted to me how federal capacity in education has tended to be organized around this banking function rather than in substantive areas such as curriculum development and testing. These features of limited federal capacity in education produce a situation where policymakers in Washington nearly always rely on other levels of government to make their education initiatives work.

Any compelling explanation of how the federal education agenda has expanded must deal directly with the license and capacity barriers that federal policy entrepreneurs confront. The explanation must also flow from a theory that embraces American federalism's dynamic qualities. Much work on cooperative federalism or principal-agent studies of federal grant programs do a reasonably good job of considering dynamics. However, work in both areas tends to focus on the dynamics of implementation after agendas have formed. Thus, they tend not to explore how federalism influences the dynamics that allow agendas to form in the first place and how those agendas then unfold over time. The borrowing strength model accounts for both kinds of dynamics and therefore represents an improvement over these current approaches.

POSITIVE FEEDBACK, BORROWING STRENGTH, AND THE DYNAMICS OF THE AMERICAN EDUCATION AGENDA

One of my key arguments is that federal policy entrepreneurs have been able to expand the federal education agenda by borrowing strength from state governments. Borrowing allows creative federal entrepreneurs to make up for their own weaknesses and expand their agendas. Frequently, this borrowing has coalesced with federal education initiatives designed to build capacity at lower levels of government. This combination has produced positive feedbacks that have enabled future federal policymakers to borrow capacities that previous federal policy, working in concert with state officials, has helped to create. That logic based on borrowing and building strength was central to the first ESEA.

Borrowing and Building State Capacity with the First ESEA

By 1965, President Lyndon Johnson's Gardner Education Task Force and other LBJ advisers recognized the federal government's then feeble ability to affect meaningful change in education. As they crafted the first ESEA, license to promote LBJ's education agenda came from a few main sources. One source was Johnson's own cache of political capital, which his landslide victory and long coattails from the 1964 election had provided. Another was the linkage of the ESEA to the broader civil rights goals that were driving the entire Great Society. Published authors have recognized that connection (Kaestle 2001, 30; Hartle and Holland 1983, 419; Halperin 1975, 10), as did Samuel Halperin in my personal interview with him. Promoting educational equity for poor and disadvantaged children, an idea that extended the logic of the U.S. Supreme Court's 1954 decision in *Brown v. Board of Education*, became the explicit mantra of the federal government's primary education law.

Focusing on the disadvantaged also assured critics that the ESEA would not attempt to change the core functions of American schools. That point helps to underscore a theoretical difference between the borrowing strength model and other work on agenda setting that has discussed how windows of opportunity can produce punctuated change (Kingdon 1995; Baumgartner and Jones 1993). The intersection of Johnson's landslide in 1964, President John Kennedy's assassination, which was still fresh in many citizens' minds at the time, and the burgeoning civil rights movement produced a powerful window for LBJ to push his education agenda. Even though the window was wide open, he really only possessed license to help the nation's underserved students, not to use federal power to fundamentally alter the nation's schools. There would be no national curriculum as is common in other nations, for example. Considering how license figures into the development of policy agendas helps to clarify the limits that policy entrepreneurs face even when they enjoy windows of opportunity to push for major change. When windows open up, policy entrepreneurs do not necessarily possess unlimited license to act, which can constrain their ambitions even as they extend their agendas.

If Johnson's license to act in education was growing (but still limited), he faced capacity problems that were quite severe. The federal government lacked capacity to manage the greater assistance for disadvantaged student groups that the Gardner Education Task Force had in mind. That was true even though the president and like-minded policy entrepreneurs could appeal to equity concerns to justify the original ESEA. In the language of figure 2.2, Johnson and his allies could stake their claim for greater federal action, but they still needed to find the capacity to make it happen.

In the mid-1960s, the U.S. Office of Education was a smallish operation inside the Department of Health, Education, and Welfare. Federal education laws, such as the Impact Aid Program, did exist and provided some federal capacity to draw upon. However, to affect the changes the Johnson people desired required much, much more. Borrowing capacity was an absolute necessity given Commissioner of Education Francis Keppel's firm arguments against overburdening the already limited federal education bureaucracy. Johnson adviser Samuel Halperin (1975, 15) explained Keppel's unique contribution on this point: "Almost single-handedly, Commissioner Keppel convinced the executive branch that Washington's educational bureaucracy could not and should not be the operating focus for most federal programs." Rather, Keppel preferred to have federal officials work through state governments, which, in turn, would coordinate with local school districts.

Borrowing state capacity was a way out of the potential boondoggle that Keppel predicted would occur if Washington tried to deal directly with local districts. Borrowing capacity from the states created problems of its own, though. During the 1960s, state education departments and state governments in general were nearly as weak as (and often weaker than) the federal education bureaucracy. Keppel and other federal policy entrepreneurs found themselves in a double bind: They needed to borrow and create state capacity essentially simultaneously. How would they accomplish that feat?

The key component of their capacity-building strategy was Title V of the first ESEA, which Johnson's advisers designed to assist state education departments. In short, Title V was more than simply a crass way to buy off state support for new federal initiatives. Rather, it would help to lay institutional foundations that would enable federal policy to succeed (Elmore and McLaughlin 1982, 165; Berke and Kirst 1972, 377). The evidence suggests that Title V did meet this objective during the ESEA's first decade. In my interview with Halperin, he said this part of the law "was consciously and deliberately a capacity building program." That echoed his own written remarks from the mid-1970s in which he summarized some of Title V's achievements. At that time, Halperin quoted a state leader who claimed "virtually every innovation we have undertaken in the past decade was either launched with or supported by Title V" (Halperin 1975, 11).[1]

The buildup of state education agencies through the mid-1970s, which Title V supported, created positive feedbacks and promoted subsequent federal interest and involvement in education. The emerging state education agencies supplied a continuing source of bureaucratic capacity from which future federal policymakers could borrow. During the 1960s and 1970s, those agencies provided a conduit for subsequent federal efforts. The widening of Title I's definition of "disadvantaged students," the growing number of ESEA programs, and the annual increases in real federal education spending, all detailed in chapter 4, illustrate this pattern.

Using the concepts of license and capacity, so far I have been able to explain the challenges that federal policy entrepreneurs confronted as they crafted the original ESEA. Considering American federalism and relating license, capacity, and the mechanism of borrowing strength allow me to explain in a theoretically tight way how federal and state policy entrepreneurs have expanded their education agendas since 1965. That represents an improvement over the relatively disconnected literatures on federalism and agenda setting that I reviewed in chapter 2. The rest of this section continues that theoretical integration and improvement by explaining how borrowing strength can produce positive feedbacks that expand federal and state agendas.

Borrowing Strength and National Interest in Education

I have framed this subsection and the next as an explanation of changes in the national (not simply federal) education agenda. That orientation underscores my goal of using the borrowing strength model to analyze simultaneously the relationship between federal and state education agendas that has unfolded since the 1960s. I begin by returning to the variation in federal interest that chapter 3 describes.

An overall result from chapter 3 is that federal interest in education began expanding in the early 1980s. That is consistent with a top-down storyline that the 1983 release of *A Nation at Risk* prompted presidents, other federal officials, and even state policymakers to attend more closely to American schools. One could see the Charlottesville education summit of 1989 in a similar light. In the language of the borrowing strength model of agenda setting, then, 1983 and 1989 could be considered key years from Washington's perspective because they provided federal policymakers with added license to expand their interest in education. But, as I will show, expanded federal license to act was intimately related to changes underway in the states before 1983 and 1989. *A Nation at Risk* and the Charlottesville summit have influenced federal and state interest in education—that much is certain. The borrowing strength model provides a more complete explanation of that influence, though, than the top-down perspective I just summarized. The evidence is consistent with my second prediction about agenda dynamics that I outlined in chapter 2 and table 5.1: *Lacking license or capacity, policy entrepreneurs may bolster either or both, and thus develop their government's interest and involvement in a policy area, by borrowing strength from another level of government.*

Despite the lore accompanying *A Nation at Risk* and the Charlottesville summit, quantitative analyses of their impact on presidential and congressional interest in education do not exist. One way to assess these two events and the development of the federal education agenda is to examine more rigorously the education references in presidential speeches and congressional hearings that appear in chapter 3. Exploring changes in those measures of federal interest while accounting for other relevant factors is one way to isolate the extent to which 1983 and 1989 were important turning points. Tables 5.2 and 5.3, which present statistical analyses of the presidential and congressional data, offer the first systematic look at the influence of *A Nation at Risk* and Charlottesville on federal interest in education.

Table 5.2 contains results from three regression analyses of the education sentences, which I presented in figure 3.4, that appear in major presidential speeches from 1961 to 2000. These statistical procedures are designed to identify the factors that explain the number of presidential statements about education. The dependent variable in each model is the annual number of sentences about K-12 education that appear in a president's inaugural message and State of the Union address. (If a president delivered both of these speeches in a single year, I sum the number of sentences about K-12 education from each speech to arrive at the relevant total.) Because this variable is an annual count, substantive and technical reasons move me to employ negative binomial regression in this part of my analysis.[2]

If the years 1983 and 1989 were important shift points that signaled increasing presidential interest in education, then indicator variables associated with the periods 1983–2000 and 1989–2000 (coded 1 if the year fell into these periods and 0 if not) should be positively signed and statistically significant even while accounting for other factors that might drive presidential interest in education. Those other factors that I incorporate into the regressions include a measure of real federal spending on K-12 education in the prior year, the president's party, whether presidents were speaking in an election year, and overall speech length.

In model 1 from table 5.2, the indicator variable for the time period 1965–2000 fails to reach statistical significance. That result suggests the adoption of the first ESEA did not boost presidential interest relative to the period 1961–64. Model 2 illustrates that *A Nation at Risk* does appear to have the predicted impact. The coefficient accompanying the indicator for years 1983–2000 is highly significant sta-

TABLE 5.2
Negative binomial regressions predicting yearly count of sentences about K–12 education in major presidential addresses, 1961–2000

Independent variables	Model 1	Model 2	Model 3
Year is 1965 to 2000	−0.65		
	(0.65)		
Year is 1983 to 2000		0.94**	1.14**
		(0.26)	(0.25)
Year is 1989 to 2000		0.36	
		(0.24)	
Previous year's federal spending	0.08	−0.04	−0.02
on K–12 education	(0.06)	(0.04)	(0.04)
President is a Democrat	−0.24	0.07	0.16
	(0.27)	(0.24)	(0.23)
Even-numbered (election) year	0.53**	0.50**	0.51**
	(0.24)	(0.20)	(0.20)
Speech length in 1000s of words	0.42**	0.31**	0.32**
	(0.07)	(0.05)	(0.05)
Constant term	−0.55	−0.08	−0.33
	(0.60)	(0.47)	(0.40)
Alpha (dispersion parameter)	.47	.29	.30
Log pseudo-likelihood	−129.94	−121.61	−122.02
Model chi-square	55.38**	98.18**	93.00**
N	42	42	42

Note: $*p < .10$, $**p < .05$, two-tailed tests. The dependent variable in all three models is the yearly count of sentences about K–12 education appearing in presidential State of the Union or inaugural speeches. (See the appendix for a couple of exceptions.) Model coefficients with robust standard errors in parentheses are reported. Estimation completed in Stata v8. Total $N = 42$ rather than 40 because of 2 cases where presidents of different parties gave speeches in the same year; those years were double-counted.

tistically, which means beginning in 1983 presidents were systematically more likely to utter sentences about K–12 education than presidents in the 1961–82 period even while accounting for the other factors in the regression.

Once one includes the influence of *A Nation at Risk,* the results from model 2 show that the Charlottesville summit did not exert an independent effect on presidential speechmaking. The coefficient associated with the 1989–2000 period is sta-

TABLE 5.3
Negative binomial regressions predicting yearly count of congressional hearings addressing K–12 education, 1961–2000

Independent variables	Model 1	Model 2	Model 3
Year is 1965 to 2000	0.52*		
	(0.29)		
Year is 1983 to 2000		0.06	0.13
		(0.21)	(0.14)
Year is 1989 to 2000		0.14	
		(0.24)	
Previous year's real federal spending on K–12 education	0.00	0.05	0.05
	(0.05)	(0.04)	(0.04)
Even-numbered (election) year	–0.26*	-0.34**	–0.33**
	(0.14)	(0.14)	(0.15)
Democrats control House	–0.17	0.36	0.24
	(0.37)	(0.41)	(0.36)
Democrats control Senate	–0.23	–0.38*	–0.32*
	(0.16)	(0.22)	(0.16)
Total number of hearings	0.00	0.00	0.00
	(0.00)	(0.00)	(0.00)
Constant term	2.96**	2.86**	2.88**
	(0.31)	(0.32)	(0.32)
Alpha (dispersion parameter)	.08	.08	.08
Log pseudo-likelihood	–151.06	–151.86	–152.03
Model chi-square	43.99**	30.33**	29.56**
N	40	40	40

Notes: *$p < .10$, **$p < .05$, two-tailed tests. The dependent variable in all three models is the yearly count of congressional hearings addressing K–12 education. Model coefficients with robust standard errors in parentheses are reported. Estimation completed in Stata v8.

tistically insignificant at standard levels, albeit not by much.[3] The influence of the 1983–2000 indicator assumes more weight in model 3, which omits the indicator associated with the Charlottesville summit and its aftermath. Using the results in that final model to generate predicted values of the dependent variable produces a correlation of .70 between the actual number of sentences each year and the number the regression predicts should have occurred. That indicates model 3 provides a useful tool for predicting the yearly number of sentences about education in these major presidential speeches.[4]

One way to see the shift in presidential interest that occurred after 1982 is to use the results in model 3 to generate additional predicted counts of the dependent variable. Using the regression results and varying the time period indicator variable while holding the other variables constant at their means allows one to compute these predicted counts. Performing this procedure reveals a predicted count of annual statements equal to 4.5 in the 1961–82 period and 14.1 in the years 1983–2000. Thus, the time indicator variable is not only statistically significant, but, given the predicted jump of nearly ten statements per year, it is substantively important as well.

Table 5.3 presents analogous regressions for congressional hearings data, but with slightly different control measures given the institutional differences between the executive and legislative branches of the federal government. In these models, the dependent variable is the combined number of House, Senate, or joint hearings addressing K–12 education held each year from 1961 to 2000. Those data come from figure 3.1. Like the presidential statements, the dependent variable in these analyses is also an annual count so I employ the negative binomial regression technique here, too.

On the *Nation at Risk* indicator, the results for congressional hearings in table 5.3 differ sharply from the presidential models in table 5.2. As models 2 and 3 in table 5.3 show, members of Congress were no more or less likely to hold education hearings after *A Nation at Risk* than before. Neither did Charlottesville appear to pique congressional interest. The indicator variables for the 1983–2000 and 1989–2000 periods are statistically insignificant at standard levels.

Model 1 suggests, however, that passage of the first ESEA in 1965 represented an important shift. Compared to the 1961–64 period, members of Congress were systematically more likely to hold hearings addressing K–12 education after that period. The statistically significant result for the indicator variable for 1965–2000 suggests as much. That result remains essentially consistent even when one adds more cases and extends the time line in the model back to 1950.[5] Model 1 in table 5.3 provides strong overall predictive power given that the correlation between the actual and predicted number of hearings equals .75. The shift in congressional interest after 1964 also appears to be substantively significant. Generating predicted counts using the results of model 1 from table 5.3 shows why. Holding other variables in this model at their means and varying the time period indicator, the model predicts a total of 20.5 hearings per year in the 1961–64 period and 34.5 in years from 1964–2000.

Why does congressional interest appear to shift in 1965 and not in 1983, the year presidential interest increased? Two explanations seem plausible given the institutional responsibilities of the president and Congress and the insights from my interview respondents. The first is that increasing congressional interest may be driven by Congress's policy responsibilities regarding program oversight. Recall from chapter 3 that the number of federal education programs expanded after the first ESEA became law. This accumulated track record of involvement and accompanying oversight responsibilities likely provided national legislators with added license to devote more time to education. My interview respondents frequently reminded me that federal education programs typically have a congressional champion who defends the program against potentially hostile interests. Members of Congress thus have greater incentives and more time than presidents to remain attentive to their pet programs. A second explanation is that even though the number of hearings appears unaffected by *A Nation at Risk,* additional evidence suggests the report did stoke congressional interest in other ways. An anecdotal skimming of the hearings does illustrate members of Congress began to discuss an expanded menu of topics after 1983, many associated with educational excellence. Additionally, as figure 3.2 shows, the number of symbolic public laws passed after 1983 appears to be a direct result of the report.

Simply confirming that *A Nation at Risk* increased presidential and, to some extent based on the symbolic laws measure, congressional interest in education begs an obvious question: Why was the report such a breakthrough? Certainly, the recycling bins at the Government Printing Office are stuffed with discarded government commission reports on many topics that never captured a wide audience. What made *A Nation at Risk* different?

As I alluded to earlier, top-down perspectives that attribute increasing federal interest to assertive presidential leadership orient many explanations of the report's influence (Toch 1991, 15; Cibulka 2001, 25; Plank and Ginsberg 1990, 124–25; Boyd 1990, 45). Given how the federal education agenda had unfolded between 1965 and 1982, however, these analyses strain to explain the shift that occurred in 1983. Recall that before that year, federal license and capacity to act in education were limited to promoting interest and involvement that supported educational equity for disadvantaged groups, not excellence for all. Additionally, federal efforts prior to 1983 typically began with strong presumptions against any move that might increase federal influence over core functions of the nation's schools, especially policies to address the academic achievement of all students. Therefore, at face value, it seems implausible that, by virtue of brandishing a short commission report—albeit one with highly charged rhetoric—federal leaders could simply assert that supporting educational excellence for all students had somehow become a legitimate rationale to justify federal interest and involvement in education. Rather, I argue that studying the report alongside evolving state education agendas and considering the mechanism of borrowing strength provides a better way to understand the influence of *A Nation at Risk.* Figure 5.1 presents a time line to illustrate the links between the report, state agendas, and borrowing strength.

During the 1970s, state policy entrepreneurs such as governors, legislators, and business leaders became more interested in education because they recognized it was becoming a key economic development issue for states (Timpane and McNeill 1991). Governors understood more than ever before that a state's ability to provide quality education was crucial for determining whether high-wage employers would find their states attractive. Should those employers locate elsewhere, a double hit would ensue: not only would a state lose opportunities for economic development but any educated young people already in the state would

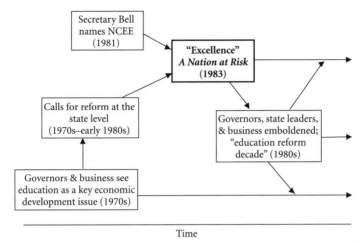

Time

FIGURE 5.1
A Nation at Risk **and increasing federal interest in K–12 education**

likely leave to find better employment elsewhere (Hartle and Holland 1983, 425; Doyle and Hartle 1985, 13; Fuhrman 1987, 154; Ravitch 1995, 3; Schwartz and Robinson 2000, 175).

By the late 1970s and early 1980s, these concerns were particularly salient in the South. Across the political spectrum, southern governors such as Lamar Alexander (Tennessee, 1979–87), Bill Clinton (Arkansas, 1978–80, 1982–92), Robert Graham (Florida, 1978–86), James Hunt (North Carolina, 1977–85, 1993–2001), Charles Robb (Virginia, 1982–86), and William Winter (Mississippi, 1980–84) became more interested in education and set reform efforts in motion (Doyle and Hartle 1985, 13–14). A coalition of states known as the Southern Regional Education Board (SREB) provided a particularly influential forum for pushing reform ideas.[6] In fact, a special task force of the SREB issued its own report in 1981, *The Need for Quality,* two years before *A Nation at Risk* appeared. The SREB's document celebrated the state movement for minimum competency testing, which I described in chapter 1, but cautioned that these expectations were not enough. Rather, the SREB's report argued, "the overall concern must be to challenge all students to attain higher levels of achievement" (Ravitch 1995, 51–52). The Education Commission of the States' Task Force on Education for Economic Growth, founded by Governor Hunt in 1982 (a year before *A Nation at Risk*'s release), concluded similarly in its 1984 report. Fuhrman (1987, 137) describes additional pre-1983 report-writing efforts in the states that produced several reforms.

Incorporating state agendas into the analysis of *A Nation at Risk*'s impact reveals that state interest and involvement in education were already expanding in the 1970s. State education agencies, though far from model organizations, had become more capable due in large part to federal funding, and states had begun to fund a higher proportion of K–12 education expenditures (Kirst 1984, 190; Bacharach 1990, xi; Educational Testing Service Policy Information Center 1990, 26; Kirst 1995, 44). Firestone (1990, 146–47) outlines several reformist items on state education agendas that already existed in 1982. The list includes programs for sharing knowledge with school districts about promising educational techniques (twenty-eight states); local planning for educational improvement (twenty-eight); and parent involvement (fourteen). Additional state efforts "anticipated the excellence movement to varying extents" (Firestone 1990, 146–47) and included curriculum development work (twenty-three states); new teacher certification options (thirteen); mandated teacher proficiency tests (sixteen); and student testing (thirty-six).

Recognizing these changes in state education agendas and considering the mechanism of borrowing strength provides a fresh and more complete explanation of why *A Nation at Risk* had such influence on federal and state education agendas. The report's claim that educational excellence was critical for the national economy paralleled popular rhetoric that state policy entrepreneurs had been using for several years. Federal license to act in education increased in large part because *A Nation at Risk* effectively borrowed strength by incorporating the strong rationales for reform that governors and other policy entrepreneurs in the states had articulated. Perhaps the NCEE's choice of arguments was not surprising given that the commission's membership, as chapter 4 noted, did not contain any federal officials.

Another reason for *A Nation at Risk*'s success was that by supporting reforms already underway, the report failed to stoke ongoing state concerns about intrusive federal involvement in education that might undermine promising state efforts. Recall that previous federal efforts, especially the cornerstone of the ESEA, Title I, had not advocated improving academic achievement for all students or extending Washington's role into the core functions of American schools. Federal policymakers, dating to the original authors of the ESEA's Title VI, who sought to reassure states that Washington's ambitions in education were limited (see chapter 1), recognized this as did federal officials in the 1980s.

Thus, rather than charting a new educational reform course in the American states, *A Nation at Risk* primarily helped to accelerate trends already in motion (Doyle and Hartle 1985, 15; Warren 1990, 57–58). Milton Goldberg, who in 1983 was the executive director of the NCEE, agreed. He told me that the report's rhetoric was powerfully important for conveying its message but also that it "caught a wave. States in the South were already looking at these kinds of concerns." Veteran education lobbyist Bruce Hunter concurred in my interview with him, saying *A Nation at Risk* was important because it and the Charlottesville summit were "symbolic events" that gave "weight to what is going on anyway." He concluded that "the governors already had it figured out before those events." The arguments governors and business leaders had been making about state economic competitiveness were easily adapted to the federal context where national economic competitiveness, a clearly justifiable concern for the federal government, was the issue

(Jennings 1987; Mintrom and Vergari 1997, 166). Doyle and Hartle (1985, 15) note these economic parallels in arguing that "the nation's interest in reversing the sluggish economic growth of the 1970s created a climate that eagerly accepted the commission's [NCEE] strong indictment of the schools."

A Nation at Risk was important, then, not only because it provided federal officials with added license to discuss education. Equally crucial is that it also provided state policy entrepreneurs with opportunities to push their own reform initiatives even harder. When federal leaders called attention to education by echoing what these state officials had been saying since the 1970s, state leaders could borrow license from federal officials to simultaneously increase state-level interest and involvement in education. Theoretically, the relationship between license and borrowing strength allows one to see how federal and state entrepreneurs can assert mutual influence on each other's agendas. As I stated in chapter 2, federalism is not merely a zero-sum system where advances in one government's agenda necessarily signal a decline in another's. The borrowing strength model identifies a specific mechanism that reaches beyond the more general claims about how American federalism is a cooperative system. When policy entrepreneurs seek opportunities by borrowing strength, they can set off positive feedback processes that promote state and federal agendas. Further, the model helps one to understand where ideas come from and not just how governments carry out policies once they are enacted.

So far, this section has explained why 1983 was an important year for understanding federal and state interest in education. I now turn to the Charlottesville education summit of 1989. Like A Nation at Risk, one can best understand Charlottesville's influence by considering it alongside state education agendas that were already taking shape in the 1980s. The events surrounding the summit provide an additional example of how state policy entrepreneurs can borrow strength from the federal government to advance their own priorities. That result is also consistent with the second expectation about agenda setting that appears in table 5.1 and I advanced in chapter 2.

Borrowing Strength and National Involvement in Education

Two words best describe federal involvement in education from 1965 through the early 1990s: programmatic and peripheral. As chapter 4 illustrated, during this time, federal education policy was primarily comprised of specific programs designed to address the particular needs of disadvantaged students. The overall framework of the evolving ESEA illustrates these changes. Between 1965 and the end of the 1970s, the ESEA grew from six titles and roughly a dozen programs to thirteen titles and over 100 program authorizations (Berke and Kirst 1972, 391; Kaestle and Smith 1982, 400–404). Even though cutbacks and consolidations occurred during Ronald Reagan's two terms, a programmatic and peripheral approach still dominated federal education policy up through the early 1990s (Doyle and Hartle 1985, 37).

Federal involvement took this shape largely because limited license and capacity prevented federal policymakers from extending their reach and because opportunities to borrow strength from the states to reach all students were significantly limited. In short, for most of the post-1965 period, federal policymakers could not do much more than reach out to the needy. Certainly, the added license that *A Nation at Risk* provided did attenuate (though not eliminate) presumptions against increased federal involvement. Other reasons, such as the more general policy goals of Reagan administration officials and still limited federal capacity, prevented federal involvement from expanding from 1983 to the early 1990s. That lack of growth in federal involvement is worth underscoring because it illustrates the value in tracking license and capacity as separate concepts that drive agendas. Whereas other federalism research has sometimes assumed that license alone is enough to force concrete action (Anton 1989, 13), policy entrepreneurs who even possess windows of opportunity can be hamstrung unless they can muster capacity to act.

Beginning in the 1990s, though, federal involvement in K–12 education began to touch the core functions of the nation's schools. As chapter 4 illustrated, this shift essentially began in 1994 with the IASA and the Goals 2000 program. Taken together, those laws demanded that states help all students meet challenging state standards. Of course, federal officials did not abandon the programmatic approach entirely. Clearly, though, the move toward promoting educational success for all children was profound. Many of my interview respondents who had worked in education for several years, including Susan Traiman, Michael Resnick, and Gordon Ambach, noted the important shift that occurred in 1994. Traiman, for example, called it "an extraordinary thing." What, though, explains the timing of this shift?

Many experienced observers have attributed these policy changes to top-down federal leadership, in particular the efforts of Presidents George H. W. Bush, Bill Clinton, and George W. Bush.[7] The seminal event in this account is the Charlottesville education summit of 1989. In part, the first President Bush called that event to help keep his promise to be the nation's education president. The summit began a process that eventually produced national education goals, which the president and the nation's governors pledged to work toward achieving by the year 2000. Given his own interest in education and his involvement at Charlottesville, it was no surprise that Clinton, when he became president, pushed for federal involvement grounded in the same ideas about standards-based reform that spawned the national education goals. As the next chapter will explain, President George W. Bush extended the IASA of 1994 and added a more prescriptive set of accountability requirements into what became NCLB. Thus, the narrative associated with Charlottesville often follows a common pattern of identifying strong national leadership as fostering a cooperative relationship between the federal government and the states organized around national education goals and standards.

The top-down view of Charlottesville's impact is overstated, however, because it does not account for the immense barriers that had relegated federal policy to the periphery of American schools for nearly thirty years after 1965. Asserting that presidents claimed this new federal role based on concerns about promoting educational equity and excellence ignores two key considerations. First, despite its growing license to act in education, exactly how federal leaders would translate these rationales into concrete policy was not clear. And second, even if license existed to expand the federal education agenda, federal officials still needed to overcome immense capacity barriers to affect all students.

The development of the national education agenda after Charlottesville is best understood as the product of positive feedbacks flowing from interactions between federal and state agendas. Federal officials borrowed strengths from the states that helped them to gain greater leverage over the nation's schools in the 1990s. Simultaneously, state officials borrowed federal strengths and used growing federal interest and involvement in education to help them advance their own agenda priorities. Figure 5.2 maps out these relationships.

The 1989 national education summit is indeed a critical event in American educational history. It is important, though, for reasons that are rarely considered. Even though President Bush assembled the Charlottesville summit that year, the nation's governors drove its agenda. Schwartz and Robinson (2000, 176) attest to this claim, as did my interview respondents including Michael Cohen, Traiman, and Ambach. Additionally, Milton Goldberg, who in 1989 was a Bush administration official, suggested to me that, "There's no question that the influence of the governors was considerable." The Bush team saw the meeting as an opportunity to gather the governors and to use the president's bully pulpit to trumpet the importance of education. The governors agreed that education was crucial. But for them the summit represented an opportunity to leverage the institutional power of the

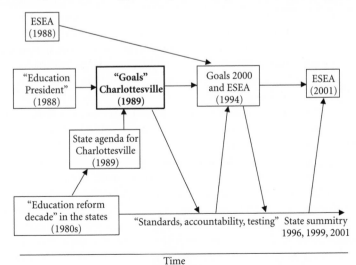

FIGURE 5.2
The Charlottesville summit and increasing federal involvement in K–12 education

presidency—to borrow license as they did after *A Nation at Risk*—to focus the event on identifying national education goals.

The strategy of organizing the summit around goals was outlined in a memo by Cohen, who in 1989 was the top education adviser to the NGA. In part, that memo argued (Vinovskis 1999c, 26):

> The proposal [of focusing at the summit on goals and targets] also has the potential for enormous payoff. For education, it can build and focus public attention and support, and help ensure that existing resources are most effectively utilized. It can help ensure that federal and state policies are appropriately altered along the lines already established by the Governors. *And, it ensures that the governors will remain a dominant force in education policy for the foreseeable future, at both the state and federal levels.*[8]

Evidence that the governors' approach startled members of the Bush education team comes from my interviews with several respondents including Cohen, Ambach, and Goldberg. In particular, Goldberg's reactions strongly suggest that the summit's eventual focus on goals came from outside the White House. In part, he told me, "Given the ideological polarization in the country at the time I couldn't see it [the development of national education goals] happening. . . . I thought it was a crazy idea. And I was as surprised as anybody to see at the education summit—you had George Bush and Bill Clinton there side-by-side."

The governors gambled that pushing for national education goals would help them build license for emerging state reform efforts organized around standards. The 1980s was, after all, the education reform decade in which governors matured as educational leaders. As the decade unfolded, groups such as the SREB and the NGA warmed to the standards-based approach. The latter, for example, devoted its entire 1986 meeting to education. From that event came its report, *Time for Results*, which argued future state reforms needed to include the development of standards that articulated what students should know and be able to do. One author described this meeting "in a sense a trial run for Charlottesville three years later" (Schwartz and Robinson 2000, 176). A 1987 follow-up report from the NGA, *Results in Education*, affirmed this reform trajectory by noting, "states will have to assume larger responsibilities for setting educational goals and defining outcome standards" (Passow 1990, 15).[9]

As Cohen had predicted in his 1989 memo, the governors' success at the summit helped them to influence the federal education agenda to their liking. After Charlottesville—from 1989 to 1994—the governors' prestige as educational leaders continued to increase. The education goals and NEGP, which I described in chapter 4, were important because they created institutional capacity and "an arena where both the federal government and governors could bargain over the national interest in education" (Elmore and Fuhrman 1990, 153). Sometimes, this bargaining revealed itself in concrete ways. Recall that the governors essentially ran the NEGP. Another example involved the National Council on Education Standards and Testing, which a 1991 federal law established to explore the concept of a national test and national education standards. Governors Roy Romer (D-CO) and Carroll Campbell (R-SC) co-chaired the council. In that role, they were able to build momentum for the standards movement while simultaneously guarding against recommendations, which the group published in 1992, that would have extended federal influence in standards and testing farther than many state leaders preferred (Jennings 1998, 20–25; Schwartz and Robinson 2000, 178).

As figure 5.2 shows, President Clinton's efforts in 1994, that linked Title I to state standards, followed on the heels of this state buildup. By the time Congress reauthorized the ESEA as the IASA that year, forty-two states had produced or were working on crafting content standards while thirty were at the same point on performance standards (Jennings 1998, 8). Goals 2000 was a key part of Clinton's strategy in 1994. That initiative illustrates how federal officials not only borrowed strength from the states, but, much like the logic that informed the first ESEA, also how they bolstered state capacity. The idea behind Goals 2000, which actually passed in 1994 before the IASA and provided a framework for that law, was that state capacity was growing but it was not strong enough to fully support the IASA's standards-based agenda.

The linkage between Goals 2000 and the events emerging from the 1989 Charlottesville meeting are clear. Cohen, who in 1994 was a member of the Clinton education team, told me, "We were quite explicit with Goals 2000 to get the feds on the same page as the states. Some of the particulars of Goals 2000, the actual language, came right out of Charlottesville. . . . When we were putting Goals 2000 together, my directions from the president were, 'Remember all of that stuff that we agreed to in Charlottesville? Make sure it gets in there.'" As it turned out, the money Goals 2000 provided, though a small proportion of the overall federal education budget, was important for helping states develop standards and accountability systems. My interview respondents across the political spectrum, including those representing state interests like Ambach and Billie Jo Orr, agreed with this assessment. The General Accounting Office (GAO) also suggested in a 1998 report that the law produced these benefits (Schwartz and Robinson 2000, 186).

While the IASA and Goals 2000 were far from unqualified successes (a topic I take up later in this chapter), these laws and the state-level activities preceding them did generate positive feedback that extended federal and state education agendas for the rest of the 1990s and into the new century. By 2001, forty-nine states had developed content standards in reading and math, forty-eight had assessments in those subjects, and thirty-three had designed accountability systems including student testing and additional measures (Goertz 2001, 52). The quality of these efforts varied, to be sure, and in many cases standards and tests remained unaligned. Nevertheless, these changes represented progress from the systems that existed in most states in the 1980s. Furthermore, as figure 5.2 shows, governors and business leaders continued the tradition of national education summits. This support from these policy entrepreneurs was important given that opponents of federal support for standards-based reform fought hard against the approach (Broder 1995; Jennings 1998, 162–68). By borrowing state license in this area, federal policy entrepreneurs were able to beat back these critics.

The developments in state and federal education agendas that unfolded from 1989 to 1994 nicely illustrate how the American federal system can produce positive feedback that fosters agenda change. Calling this an example of cooperative federalism may be accurate in a general sense; but stopping there misses crucial dynamics and does not clearly identify the mechanisms that foster and shape cooperation. The borrowing strength model reveals cooperation, but it is much more theoretically precise in showing how policy entrepreneurs in Washington and the fifty states can strategically maneuver to expand their agendas. In 1989, the governors recognized that getting the White House to endorse their ideas about standards would provide them with added license to push a standards-based agenda even harder at home. Similarly, by crafting Goals 2000 and the IASA of 1994, which borrowed capacity from the states while also building it, the Clinton administration was able to move the federal education agenda more squarely in line with standards-based reform that the governors had been advancing since the 1980s. These agenda changes provide another illustration of the second expectation about agenda setting and federalism that I outlined in chapter 2 and restated in table 5.1.

Timing and Sequencing of the Nation's Expanding Education Agenda

The evidence from chapters 3 and 4 and the account thus far in this section illustrate that federal interest in education increased in the 1980s, but the deeper substantive involvement that affected core school functions did not emerge until the 1990s. What explains this difference in timing?

The strategic choices of policy entrepreneurs are one reason, which is related to the third expectation from table 5.1 and chapter 2: *Policy entrepreneurs will be more likely to borrow strength to promote agendas when they think it will help them achieve political gains and make good policy.* Perhaps that statement is intuitive. After all, what policy entrepreneur would not want to score political points and advance successful initiatives? Recognizing it explicitly, though, helps to spotlight the role that policy entrepreneurs' preferences can play in setting government agendas. It also underscores the conceptual value in considering interest and involvement as separate variables that chart a government's agenda.

Despite the license to expand the federal role that *A Nation at Risk* provided, Reagan became increasingly interested in education while simultaneously opposing expanded federal involvement. Reagan did mobilize his bully pulpit to expand federal interest and argue that the states, not the federal government, needed to bear the reform burden. The president was thus able to increase education's status on the federal government's political agenda and simultaneously defend his New Federalism principles (Clark and Amiot 1981; Kirst 1984, 190; 1995, 49; Doyle and Hartle 1985, 37–38; Jung and Kirst 1986, 95; Fuhrman 1987, 136; Bell 1988;

Bacharach 1990, 3). Reagan's coolness toward expanded federal involvement in education contrasts with the attitudes of Clinton and George W. Bush, who pushed for federal policy that expanded the federal government's substantive reach into America's classrooms. These examples underscore the idea that the preferences of key entrepreneurs are important because they can help explain why some windows of opportunity, such as the publication of *A Nation at Risk*, create certain changes in a government's agenda, but not others.

A second reason for the ten-year lag between expanded federal interest in education and increased substantive involvement is that limited state capacity created minimal opportunities for borrowing strength and thus hampered federal policymakers in the 1980s. One way to understand this barrier and the gap between increased federal interest in the 1980s and increased involvement in the 1990s is to consider a counterfactual question: If Reagan had wanted to increase substantive federal involvement in education, could he have done it? The likely answer, despite the momentum *A Nation at Risk* created, is no. Insights from the borrowing strength model illustrate why.

Because federal involvement in education depends so much on federal entrepreneurs being able to successfully borrow capacity from the states, any president in the 1980s would have been hard pressed to expand federal involvement in a significant way. It is true that the federal government did possess capacity with the legislative infrastructure of the ESEA, an expanding menu of federal programs, and a budget process that allows it to fund new initiatives even if deficits result.

But to increase involvement in more than peripheral and narrowly programmatic ways would have been next to impossible. Across the 1980s, the federal government's ability to borrow capacity to affect core functions of the nation's schools was severely limited. Recall that during that decade, the states were dramatically expanding their reform agendas and attempting to remake their state education systems. How, in that turbulent environment, federal policymakers could have found a stable leverage point and borrowed strength to expand federal involvement in education in a coherent way would have been difficult to imagine. As one analyst during the 1980s put it, "The modest federal activity is in part the result of an inability to conceptualize an appropriate and meaningful response" (Doyle and Hartle 1985, 38).

It was not until the 1990s and the development of capacity that emerged from the state standards movement that opportunities for substantive expansions of federal involvement would emerge. State standards provided capacity that federal officials could borrow to extend the federal education agenda in ways that affected all students. That capacity simply did not exist in the frenetic reform decade of the 1980s. The borrowing strength model thus suggests why there are limits to cooperation in the American federal system. Even if state and federal policy entrepreneurs had wanted to forge a more coherent partnership in education in the 1980s, it would have been difficult to engineer. Only at the end of the decade, once the standards movement had gotten a foothold and was beginning to take off, did greater cooperation organized around goals and standards emerge.

Also important to note, because it contrasts with a common line of reasoning in analyses of cooperative federalism that begin with Washington's preferences, is that the governors, not federal officials, were the key advocates for cooperation on these terms. That effort benefited state policy entrepreneurs, but it also invited more aggressive federal involvement in the nation's schools. An assertive Washington can benefit the states when it effectively borrows strength. But as federal policy entrepreneurs push their own agendas, deeper federal involvement, which the states were inviting in 1989, can produce challenges that state entrepreneurs would rather do without. The rest of this chapter and portions of the next describe how the dynamics of borrowing strength can foster these frustrations and set negative feedback processes in motion.

NEGATIVE FEEDBACK, ASSERTIVE STATES, AND ADJUSTMENTS TO THE AMERICAN EDUCATION AGENDA

So far, this chapter has focused on how the American federal system can produce positive feedback that helps federal and state entrepreneurs to build their education agendas. The system's interactive nature also allows state policymakers to redirect or slow down federal assertiveness in education. State leaders recognize that their federal counterparts depend on them to make federal education initiatives work. Only rarely, then, can officials in Washington push states in directions inconsistent with the trajectory of state reform agendas. These limits on federal action are especially apparent when the national government attempts to influence the educational experiences of all children and not just to assist narrowly defined student groups.

When federal policymakers overreach, they ignite negative feedback processes that can retard the development of their agendas. Analytically, overreaching is best understood as the result of federal entrepreneurs attempting to borrow strength from the states in ways that overestimate state capabilities. When federal officials accurately assess the limits and strengths the states possess, they are more likely to produce favorable outcomes when they borrow strength. The fourth expectation from chapter 2 and table 5.1 illustrates this idea: *Federal officials who borrow strength from states will be more likely to enjoy political and policy success if they accurately assess the license and capacity of state governments.* Conversely, overreaching often forces federal officials to rethink their agendas, and adjust their levels of interest and involvement in a policy area.

More Powerful but not All-Powerful States

One reason overreaching occurs is because federal officials have become more convinced that states can be capable policy leaders. Overwhelming evidence supports the general claim that states have substantially increased their license and capacity to act in education since the 1960s (Kaestle and Smith 1982, 387; Cohen

1987; Odden and Marsh 1990, 182; Kaestle 2001, 31). However, stronger rationales for state involvement and growing state capabilities have sometimes masked
underlying and persistent state weaknesses, which make federal overreaching a
potential problem. The maturing of states as education policymakers has produced a peculiar outcome, which two education insiders described in the early
1990s: "When the [state education] reforms of the 80s began to unfold, many state
education agencies were still half- or ill-informed organizations. . . . While these
were the conditions in the 80s when the reform movement proliferated and the
important leadership role of the states was particularly trumpeted, the great un-
spoken irony and paradox of inadequately supported state education agencies has
continued into the 90's" (Kaagan and Usdan 1993). Several reasons explain this
paradoxical result.

The first reason is that the original ESEA's Title V never completely realized its
goals. Even though that capacity-building measure produced successes during the
ESEA's first decade, over time, the states failed to support their education departments with sufficient funds. Recall that the architects of the original ESEA believed that after receiving a shot of federal dollars to help state departments
develop, the states themselves would begin contributing more of their own resources to help support this bureaucratic infrastructure. By and large, however,
this did not occur for reasons that I will discuss in chapter 7. Samuel Halperin,
who had celebrated Title V's early successes (Halperin 1975), remarked to me in a
personal interview that in the long run, Title V was probably one of the "biggest
failures" of the first ESEA.

A second major reason why state departments have failed to develop into
highly effective organizations is that for most of their history they have devoted
their resources to compliance-oriented activities. This is partly due to the peripheral and programmatic federal approach to education policy that endured up
through the early 1990s. Until recently, state departments were not asked to develop expertise in areas such as curriculum development and testing. Instead, they
focused on the mundane tasks of monitoring where federal and state dollars
flowed and auditing local school districts to assure those jurisdictions spent funds
appropriately. Thus, even though state departments have become more capable,
they matured with compliance-driven orientations that have compromised their
ability to do strong substantive work on education reform (Elmore and
McLaughlin 1982, 165; Kirst 1984; Fuhrman 1987, 140).

A third reason that explains state capacity gaps is the sheer magnitude of the reforms states have initiated since the early 1980s. These agendas, which pre-date
the passage of NCLB, have included increasing testing requirements for students;
expanding quality control measures for new teachers; adopting standards-based
reform; aligning state curriculum frameworks and state testing systems so state
exams reflect what students learn in class; assisting persistently failing schools and
districts; modernizing data collection systems to monitor the progress of multiple
reforms; and encouraging greater parental choice in education through open-enrollment and charter school policies. Even the most mature and efficiently run or-

ganization would have found these tasks daunting. Bureaucratic capacity has simply not kept pace with the expanding state education agendas.

Ironically, the resulting overload that state departments have experienced is directly related to the general overall increase in capacity that state governments have enjoyed since the 1960s. As one scholar remarked in the early 1980s (a claim that one could repeat today with much accuracy), "Many states are in trouble *because* the reforms designed to modernize and democratize state governments have worked. Their troubles are the unintended offshoots of the reforms. The problems are part of the price of success" (Murphy 1982, 196). In other words, because states have become more capable policy actors, the demands on them have increased but outpaced their capacity to respond effectively.

A final reason explaining the state capacity problem in education is that the research base underlying particular reform agendas or programs is sometimes thin, even nonexistent, or the subject of substantial disagreements. In attempting to implement reforms, state education agencies have had to sift through the mountains of available options (frequently supplied from vendors anxious to profit from state efforts) to decide what would work best in their particular state. The lack of consensus around different policy options and the continuing mismatch between capacity and demands add yet another layer of complexity to the task of implementing reform (Cohen 1987, 2002; Kaagan and Usdan 1993; Goertz 2001).

Overall, even though the states have become more powerful actors in education, they are far from all-powerful. In celebrating state accomplishments and ingenuity, as governors and federal officials have done since the 1980s, many federal and state policy entrepreneurs often neglect this basic reality. State capacity gaps can influence both state and federal agendas in education and produce negative feedback as state policymakers resist federal commands. On this point, it is helpful to reconsider the multiple indicators of capacity that I described in chapters 1 and 2.

Two different aspects of capacity are particularly relevant here. Recall that capacity can increase when a government passes laws and writes regulations to address a substantive policy area. By this measure, it is clear that states have increased their capacity to act in education. The massive number of statutes emerging from the education reform decade of the 1980s and the specific laws and regulations to support standards-based efforts in the 1980s and 1990s are evidence of this. These state laws and regulations are two key places where federal policymakers have reached in attempting to borrow capacity to extend federal involvement in education.

Capacity can also increase when state officials develop knowledge bases and technical expertise in different policy areas. While it is true that personnel in state education departments have improved their technical competencies, as I just noted, those improvements have not kept pace with demands. At the same time, though, governors and state legislatures have increased their own staff expertise in education. "Staffing up" has bolstered capacity in state legislatures and governors' offices and it has allowed state elected officials to demonstrate their bona fides in education policy, which increases their license to act in this area. Put another way, hiring trained staff certainly builds capacity. But over time, these aides help governors and legislators to accumulate a track record of education policy accomplishments, which also bolsters license and helps them to promote their successes.

The intersection of increasing state capacity in the form of laws, regulations, and the staff resources of elected officials with the lagging capacity of state education bureaucracies creates a challenging situation for federal policy entrepreneurs attempting to build education agendas. Since the early 1980s, state elected officials have increased their license to act in education and publicized their capacity building measures even as they have failed to make the critical investments in state education bureaucracies that would be required to make their efforts succeed. Federal officials have often been attuned to the former reality (the trumpeting of state legislative accomplishments) while being less sensitive to the latter (state agencies that struggle to implement these laws successfully). The growing role of state elected officials in organizations such as the NCEE and NEGP along with the increased attention presidents have given states in their major speeches since the 1970s (see table 3.2) are consistent with this assessment. Thus, a federal blind spot of sorts has sometimes led entrepreneurs to extend federal involvement in education by attempting to borrow strength from the states without accurately assessing the strengths that states actually possess.

The result of attempted borrowing where strengths might not exist is what I have called federal overreaching. As federal education laws play out, they often produce complaints from states and the need to adjust federal agendas. In short, overreaching produces negative feedback and state demands for adjustments in federal policy, which the fifth expectation from chapter 2 and table 5.1 illustrates: *State officials will attempt to extract concessions from federal officials if they think that, in borrowing strength, federal officials have overestimated state license or capacity.* Because the success of federal initiatives depends on state support, when federal policymakers elicit these reactions, frequently they adjust their own agendas. The sixth expectation from chapter 2 and table 5.1 describes this common federal response: *Federal officials will modify policies that depend on borrowed strength if they are persuaded they have overestimated state license or capacity.* The rest of this chapter considers how these two expectations have played out during the legislative process and the implementation of federal education laws. Theoretically, the following discussion also shows how the borrowing strength model provides insights about where ideas and policies come from but also about how those policies perform when they are carried out.

Refinements in the Lawmaking Phase that Reflect State Prerogatives

Sometimes, state policy entrepreneurs can influence federal lawmaking and regulation-writing processes and thus head off federal overreaching at the pass. That does not mean that negative feedback from states always produces federal concessions as laws or regulations take shape. However, because federal policy entrepreneurs depend so much on state capacity and because states possess greater license to act in education than the federal government, state leaders have real opportunities to quell or redirect federal ambitions.

Examples of state influence are present in early iterations of the ESEA. Writing in the early 1970s, two authors noted the "immense areas for state discretion that exist in the allocation of most federal programs," which was due partly to "statutory language that permits state development of distributed formulas and procedures" (Berke and Kirst 1972, 401). In fact, state discretion has been an enduring feature of federal education law. In the IASA of 1994, when federal policymakers began increasing their emphasis on student achievement, federal law still conceded critical ground. On the question of standards, states favored federal involvement that encouraged the development of state curriculum standards but voiced concerns over proposed federal requirements that states identify "opportunity-to–learn" standards. Unlike curriculum standards, which define what students should know and be able to do, opportunity-to-learn standards specify the resources that schools should possess (i.e., facilities, staffing, technology) for students to learn. State officials feared spelling out these details given their likely high price tag and the constituent demands they would prompt. Sensing that opportunity-to-learn requirements might torpedo the entire 1994 ESEA reauthorization, the Clinton administration leaned hard on liberal Democrats in Congress to excise these provisions from the legislation (Jennings 1998). That gave states an important policy victory by helping to steer the federal education agenda away from this course.

Even when federal law has directed states to hold students to high curriculum and performance standards, Washington has always relied upon the states to develop these standards and to define what proficiency means. State officials have consistently beaten back federal encroachments in this area. Examples include efforts during President George H. W. Bush's term to support work on national (but not federal) curriculum standards and a provision in the Goals 2000 legislation, which Clinton championed, that would have created a federally sanctioned board to approve state standards. That aspect of Goals 2000 sparked considerable controversy. The result was that no one was ever appointed to the board, and, in an illustration of state power, amendments to the Goals 2000 law in 1996 eliminated the board entirely (Mintrom and Vergari 1997, 154–55; Jennings 1998; Kaestle 2001, 31).

A related development, which also reflected state influence, occurred at the end of the 1990s with the passage of the Education Flexibility Partnership Act, or "Ed-Flex" (P.L. 106-25). That law passed by wide margins in the House (368 to 57) and Senate (98 to 1), and Clinton signed it in April 1999. Ed-Flex expanded a smaller pilot program, which was part of Goals 2000, and granted to all states the authority to waive federal regulations—except those relating to health, safety, and civil rights—that affected their local school districts. In return, districts needed to show progress on plans to assist disadvantaged students and to increase student achievement (*Congressional Quarterly* 2000, 10–12). The NGA strongly supported Ed-Flex, which NGA Chair Thomas Carper (D-DE) and Vice Chair Michael

Leavitt (R-UT) argued, in its pilot form, had "changed the culture in states and in school districts regarding flexibility" (*Congressional Quarterly* 2000, 10–13).

In many ways, Ed-Flex struck a compromise with the states, which were still struggling to implement provisions from the IASA that required them to accelerate the development of curriculum and performance standards. Their challenges of implementing that law combined with the relatively weak record of federal enforcement of its provisions had convinced some people that states needed and deserved the increased control that waivers could provide. Clinton favored the bill and, at its signing ceremony, stated, "This new law will allow states and school districts, not just to save administrative dollars with less headache and red tape, but actually to pool different funds from different sources in the federal government." Clinton noted, though, that federal aid would not be an unrestricted blank check because "by demanding accountability in return, it will make sure states and school districts focus on results" (*Congressional Quarterly* 2000, 10–19).[10]

Even when states appear to lose in the legislative process, they can bounce back in the critical regulation-writing phase, where officials in the U.S. Department of Education devise rules to guide implementation of federal law. Increasing demands on states that materialized in 1994, for example, produced an ESEA with 75 percent fewer regulations. Issuing guidance, rather than regulations, was the department's preferred approach for Goals 2000 and the ESEA reauthorization of that year (Smith, Levin, and Cianci 1997, 211–12; Goertz 2001, 57).

State Resistance and Lax Federal Enforcement

A top-down view of federal education policymaking would predict that states failing to respond to Washington's commands would be subject to penalties of some sort. In reality, sanctions against states rarely occur in education. Even when the law may justify issuing sanctions, because federal policy entrepreneurs rely so heavily on state capacity, they often adjust their own agendas when state reactions produce negative feedback.

With few exceptions, the federal track record of ESEA enforcement has been rather abysmal. In fact, frequently since 1965, states have not complied with specific parts of the law. Still, those noncomplying states have rarely experienced sanctions other than federal admonitions that they should do better. Many of my interview respondents attested to the federal government's inability and frequent unwillingness to enforce the ESEA. Two factors are primarily responsible for this result.

The first factor has received significant coverage already: the federal government depends heavily on borrowed strength from the states to make federal education policy work. Due to its own weaknesses in license and capacity relative to state policymakers, federal officials often reason that if they did sanction or punish states, it is unlikely these actions would produce the ultimate results they desire. It might also prevent these federal policy entrepreneurs from developing their education agendas in the future. The second factor concerns finances. Even though federal funding for K–12 education is not inconsequential, it represents such a small fraction of most state education budgets that threatening to withdraw federal dollars does not spark great fear in most state policymakers (Berke and Kirst 1972, 378–80; Halperin 1975, 18; Elmore and McLaughlin 1982; Goertz 2001; Cohen 2002). Two examples, both relevant to the challenges confronting NCLB (which I will address in detail in the next chapter), illustrate how enforcement can be difficult when federal policy entrepreneurs attempt to borrow strength but overestimate state capabilities.

Consider first the 1965 ESEA debate and the accountability provisions that Senator Robert Kennedy (D-NY) persuaded President Lyndon Johnson's education team to insert into the law (Halperin 1975, 10, 13; Elmore and McLaughlin 1982, 162–65; Guthrie 1983, 676–77). Using a line of reasoning that would animate federal education debates in 2001, Kennedy believed that without adequate monitoring it would be impossible to know if the ESEA were actually helping students to learn. The response from Johnson's advisers and legislative colleagues was to quietly insert a provision into the House and Senate versions of the ESEA bill. That change, which became Title I, Section 205(a)(5), required states to work with local districts to devise "effective procedures, including provision for appropriate objective measurements of educational achievement . . . for evaluating at least annually the effectiveness of the programs in meeting the special educational needs of educationally deprived children."

Johnson's congressional allies kept this change under wraps due to low federal license to demand evaluations of student achievement. Commissioner of Education Francis Keppel agreed with Kennedy that the provision was a good one: "You're damn right I want it," he said. Keppel then admitted, "But I haven't got the nerve to do it on the executive side, because all the educators will scream bloody-murder if anybody measures them" (Graham 1984, 79). The requirement also presumed a great deal of state and local capacity that did not exist. Not only were state education departments supposed to help develop and then approve local testing systems, they were also required to gather data from these systems and report it to the federal government.

In practice, states were unable to carry out this requirement. The data they received from school districts and transferred to Washington were based on a wide range of tests. Some districts reported no results at all. Rather than sanctioning states for their failure, by 1970, "Washington settled for assurances that the [Title I] money would reach schools that enrolled poor children—no performance results required" (Ravitch 2001). Despite the letter of the law, because federal officials possessed low license to demand student achievement results and because they relied upon state capacity to implement Kennedy's proposed accountability measures, it was no wonder that they altered their policy agenda.

A more recent example, also germane to NCLB's prospects for future success, involved provisions from the 1994 ESEA reauthorization that created the IASA. These provisions called on states to develop aligned accountability systems by decade's end. Specifically, by 1998, the IASA required states to have identified content and performance standards for their students. States had to develop student examinations reflecting the scope of these state content standards by 2000–2001. When it became clear that the vast majority of states would not meet these requirements, officials in the U.S. Department of Education chose not to sanction states that had lagged behind. Instead, federal officials waived the law's timetable and held states to the timetables they had designed for themselves. By 2001, as Clinton was leaving office, the department found only eleven states had fully met the standards and testing requirements of the IASA (Citizens' Commission on Civil Rights 2001, 3). Clinton's former undersecretary of education, the ubiquitous Michael Cohen (2002, 44–45), described the reasoning behind this approach:

> The 2000-01 deadline for having a testing system up and running was workable if a state started development work soon after the law [IASA of 1994] was enacted. However, many states delayed the development of assessments for several years. Once that delay occurred, and once a state began good-faith efforts to develop the assessments, there was little either the state or the federal government could do to speed up the process. . . . No sanctions could speed the process at that point. The department's response was to waive the statutory deadline and hold the state to its planned timetable. Some view these decisions as evidence of lax enforcement, but I see it as evidence of the *limits* of the department's enforcement ability.

Thus, states can respond to federal requirements by saying "no" or "we can't." When that happens, federal policy entrepreneurs may become frustrated, but they typically reply "okay" and adjust their own agendas; they recognize they lack the license or capacity to do much more. The logic of the borrowing strength model of agenda setting, which identifies the potential for overreaching and its likely consequences, helps to systematically predict when that backing off is likely to happen.

Bumbling or Leading? Federal Education Agendas and Negative Feedback

Depending on how far they overreach, federal officials can experience political and policy challenges that threaten to undermine their education agendas. Consistent with the last three expectations appearing in table 5.1 and described in chapter 2, these challenges can motivate federal policy entrepreneurs to revise their expectations and reshape federal interest and involvement in the nation's schools. Normatively speaking, it is interesting to consider whether these adjustments are necessarily good or bad.

On one hand, overreaching might represent what critics of an activist federal government would classify as bumbling. It is wishful thinking, so this argument goes, to believe that policy entrepreneurs working in Washington would be able to accurately assess the capabilities of state governments in education and then craft federal legislation to leverage positive change in the fifty states and thousands of school districts across the country. From this point of view, overreaching reveals a certain ineptness, even arrogance, that occurs when federal officials attempt to borrow state strengths that they believe exist but actually do not.

On the other hand, borrowing strength where it is nascent or lacking may also represent an example of federal officials trying to lead the nation in promising new directions. What one person could see as federal bumbling, another might interpret as an attempt to make good policy and accelerate well-conceived state trends that are already in motion. State leaders who complain about onerous federal time lines, unfunded mandates, or requirements that increase federal involvement in education are themselves sometimes culpable for encouraging federal entrepreneurs to borrow strength in ways that can produce overreaching. The outcome of the Charlottesville education summit is a case in point. By persuading federal leaders to join them in supporting national education goals and the need for high standards and then committing themselves to that path, state policy entrepreneurs increased the possibility that federal officials would attempt to build their own future agendas around these same ideas.

Considering what I have called bumbling and leadership as opposite sides of the same coin reveals two larger points about borrowing strength and federalism. Borrowing strength can be extremely difficult to do, for both federal and state policy entrepreneurs. If states appear to be building capacities that support a particular reform trajectory, federal officials who attempt to borrow in those areas are oftentimes making a leap of faith that those developments will actually materialize as promised. If states build capacity in some areas but not in others, then federal borrowing is bound to produce problems. But because states are not simply passive agents, and in reality command much power over the substance and implementation of federal education policy, they can extract concessions from federal leaders and attempt to shift federal interest or involvement in directions they prefer.

An additional point is that when policy entrepreneurs attempt to borrow strength, they should (and often do) expect responses from other levels of government that can influence the trajectory of their agendas. As this section has illustrated, sometimes those adjustments are the result of negative feedback processes that borrowing strength frequently prompts. The interactive and flexible nature of the American federal system and the activities of entrepreneurs who attempt to develop interest and involvement in specific policy areas produce these results.

THIS CHAPTER HAS ILLUSTRATED WHY STUDYING THE OPPORTUNITIES AND CONSTRAINTS embedded in the American federal system is essential for understanding the long-run adjustments in state and federal education agendas since the 1960s. Changes since that time reveal an interactive system where policy entrepreneurs in Washington and state capitals have pushed their education agendas by mobilizing their own license and capacity and by borrowing strength from each other to ameliorate their shortfalls. Put differently, the nation's expanding education agenda did not simply result from a combination of assertive federal policy entrepreneurs and passive state officials who acceded to federal preferences like dutiful agents of Washington. Nor did federal policymakers simply copy the states' ideas in developing their own interest and involvement in education. In short, neither a top-down nor a bottom-up explanation nor a general perspective that relies upon federal-state cooperation will suffice to explain the agenda dynamics that I have explored. In that regard, the borrowing strength model builds on present insights but provides a marked improvement over what the literature on federalism and agenda setting can explain.

The dynamics documented in this chapter and the borrowing strength model of agenda setting also show that zero-sum approaches to federalism are too limited to explain the richness produced when actors across levels of government attempt to develop their agendas. A focus on which level of government is up and which is down misses these dynamics entirely. But rather than just saying that American federalism is something other than a zero-sum arrangement, I have offered a theory that explains why that is the case. Beginning from the premise that policy entrepreneurs can find the American federal system a field ripe with opportunities and not just a briar patch of constraints produces a better understanding of the worlds that state and federal policy entrepreneurs inhabit as they develop their education agendas.

This chapter has illustrated why my notions of license, capacity, and borrowing strength are useful for explaining long-run changes in the American education agenda that have unfolded since the 1960s. Theoretically, I have shown that it is possible to identify a handful of powerful concepts that can integrate scholarly work on federalism and agenda setting. Empirically, I have accounted for variation in education agendas that have transpired at the federal and the state levels over long periods of time. In the next chapter, I turn my attention away from these general patterns of change to take a close-up look at the development and implementation of NCLB. Ideally, a strong theory should be able to account for broad patterns as well as particular cases. Examining NCLB thus provides a rich context for further testing the utility of the borrowing strength model of agenda setting.

NOTES

1. Halperin (1975, 11) continued and described those achievements this way: "Overall, state departments of education have added well over 2,000 needed staff members with the help of federal funds. Such innovations as state planning and evaluation units have been added in 38 states; new educational data systems (26 states); assessment programs (28); training for planners and evaluators (33); improved management-by-objectives systems (13); multi-year educational plans (8); state-wide planning in programming-budgeting systems (7); improved evaluation methodologies (23); etc."

2. Poisson regression is also appropriate for modeling counts. However, because the Poisson specification makes strong assumptions about the characteristics of the dependent variable, namely that its conditional mean and variance are the same, it rarely applies to social processes. The negative binomial relaxes this assumption and also allows observations to be correlated. That latter characteristic is especially useful here, given that presidents serve multiple-year terms. Thus, we might expect that a president's interest in education in one year might affect his interest in the next. In addition to these theo-

retical reasons to choose the negative binomial, one can also reject the Poisson on sta-tistical grounds. The dispersion parameters reported in tables 5.2 and 5.3 test for the appropriateness of the Poisson specification. In all six models, the parameters are dif-ferent from zero and statistically significant, which means that the negative binomial is a better approach. For more on using and interpreting Poisson and negative binomial models, see Long (1997) and King (1998).

3. Regression and other quantitative analyses often consider a variable to be statistically significant if its p-value is less than .05 or .10. In this particular case, the result for the Charlottesville indicator variable is $p < .14$.

4. As a statistical measure, correlations can range from -1.0, which characterizes a perfect negative correlation between two variables, to 1.0, which illustrates a perfect positive correlation.

5. I omit that model here to keep the time frames consistent with regressions analyzing presidential speeches. In the model including cases from 1950 through 2000, though, the indicator variable for 1965–2000 has a coefficient of 0.41 and a robust standard er-ror of 0.27, which is associated with $p < .13$. Other variables in the model are compara-ble to the original model 1 from table 5.3. The only exception is the "Democrats control House" measure. For that variable, the sign flips and the parameter is much smaller (coefficient $= 0.06$), but the result remains statistically insignificant (robust standard error $= 0.21$; $p < .79$).

6. The SREB was founded in 1948. Its members are the states of Alabama, Arkansas, Dela-ware, Florida, Georgia, Kentucky, Louisiana, Maryland, Mississippi, North Carolina, Oklahoma, South Carolina, Tennessee, Texas, Virginia, and West Virginia.

7. My interview with Chester Finn alluded to the role of presidential leadership. Finn ex-plained that, "The first President Bush got this started. There were national education goals, and America 2000. Those things were activist reform generators." Regarding the Clinton administration's efforts specifically, Manno (1995, 43) argued that the ap-proach emerging out of 1994 was "top-down, plain and simple, much like the central-ized education ministries of many European and Asian countries." A *National Journal* reporter, quoted in Jennings (1998, 150–51), claimed that "Clinton has quite simply, set in motion a revolution in public education."

8. Emphasis mine. Gordon Ambach echoed this idea in my interview with him by sug-gesting Bush found himself trapped at the summit given the governors' strategy to as-sert themselves as educational leaders.

9. Other accounts of the general buildup in the 1980s of the state standards movement in-clude Ravitch (1995, 53–56, 160–61), Schwartz and Robinson (2000, 176), Fuhrman (1994, 93), and Passow (1990, 16–17).

10. However, Raphael and McKay (2001) studied the Ed-Flex pilot program and con-cluded that accountability was frequently underemphasized and that it was difficult to link waivers to clear improvements in student achievement.

6

LEAVING NO CHILD BEHIND IN THE AMERICAN FEDERAL SYSTEM

WHEN THE NO CHILD LEFT BEHIND ACT (NCLB) EMERGED FROM CONGRESS IN December 2001, elected officials and other observers hailed the bill's passage as historic. Representative John Boehner (R-OH), chair of the House Committee on Education and the Workforce, called NCLB "the foundation for the most significant education reforms in a generation" (Fletcher 2001b). Clymer and Alvarez (2001) reported, "It will result in the first major change in the Elementary and Secondary Education Act since it was rammed through Congress by President Lyndon B. Johnson in 1965." At a January 8, 2002, ceremony in Boehner's district, President Bush signed the bill and proclaimed the beginning of "a new era, a new time in public education in our country. As of this hour, America's schools will be on a new path of reform, and a new path of results" (White House Office of the Press Secretary 2002).

These reactions to NCLB were somewhat predictable. Leaders had framed past ESEA reauthorizations in similar terms (Kafer 2001), a fact that moved President Bill Clinton's former Secretary of Education Richard Riley to observe, "We called ours sweeping. Whoever passes the next reauthorization will call it sweeping" (Robelen 2002). Still, had Johnson been alive to study NCLB's features, even he probably would have been amazed at how far the federal role in education had come since the first ESEA of 1965.

The three sections in this chapter use the borrowing strength model to explain how NCLB took shape and how it has evolved. The first section discusses how Bush and his team sized up the president's license and capacity needs as they envisioned their plan. The second section focuses on the legislative process of 2001. There, I examine how members of Congress, the Bush administration, and the states approached the ESEA reauthorization of that year. The final section examines NCLB's early implementation by examining how feedback processes affected federal and state education agendas as NCLB moved forward. Across all sections, I relate the evidence to the expectations about agenda setting that I introduced in chapter 2 and summarized in table 5.1. Overall, the current chapter shows that to understand NCLB's origins, features, and the feedback processes it has prompted, one must consider how policy entrepreneurs mobilize license and capacity and frequently borrow strength to advance their agendas.[1]

ENVISIONING NCLB

As the advertising data in table 3.1 show, Bush made education a top priority during the 2000 campaign.[2] As president-elect, he hoped to present an education reform plan shortly after entering the White House. Even though he assembled a transition team to advise him on education, it amounted to a symbolic group: "Window dressing," is how Chester Finn, an education official during the Ronald Reagan era and occasional Bush campaign adviser on education, described it to me.[3] A handful of close aides, headed by Bush's Texas colleague and confidant Sandy Kress, spearheaded the effort (Gorman 2001c). Despite the drama of the Florida recount that dominated much of the Bush transition, the president-elect and his allies managed to lobby three key constituencies between November and January to cultivate support for his education vision.

First were members of Congress. Bush outlined his ideas to Republicans and Democrats at a transition meeting in the Texas Governor's Mansion. The guests invited would be responsible for ushering his ideas through the legislative thicket on Capitol Hill (Gorman 2001a). At the urging of Boehner, who was Bush's key lieutenant in the House, Bush also invited the ranking member of Boehner's committee, longtime education champion and liberal, George Miller (D-CA), to the meeting. That olive branch proved valuable for the president because Miller found Bush sincere and persuasive. This meeting omitted Senator Edward Kennedy (D-MA), ranking member on the Senate education committee, but Bush did invite Kennedy to the White House to discuss education the day before the president announced his plan (Gorman 2001a; Oppel and Schemo 2000). Also absent was Senator Joseph Lieberman (D-CT). Bush did not meet personally with Lieberman due to the awkwardness associated with the Florida recount and Lieberman's position on the Democratic ticket. Still, Bush praised and consulted the plan that Lieberman and other centrist members of his party, who called themselves New Democrats, had offered the previous year during the failed ESEA reauthorization of 2000 (Alvarez 2001a; Manna 2003, chapter 4). Bush's use of the New Democrats' ideas was not particularly surprising, given that Kress was himself a New Democrat.

Recognizing that the federal government lacked the capacity to carry out his plans, Bush also courted a second group, state officials, during the transition. Shortly after New Year's Day, the president-elect convened nineteen Republican governors at his Texas ranch. At that meeting, Bush articulated his view that annual testing based on Texas's model was needed to make sure no child was left behind. Bush promised the states greater flexibility with federal dollars, which he believed would ameliorate concerns that his administration was planning a top-down approach to reforming the ESEA. Shortly after taking office, Bush held a similar meeting that included Republican and Democratic governors (Gorman 2001b; Salzer 2001).

The business community, including leaders who had been active in education issues at the state level, was a final group Bush consulted between November and January. The president-elect's meetings included several members of the Business

Roundtable (BRT), a group of chief executive officers from some of America's largest companies. In an interview, Susan Traiman, director of the Education Initiative at the BRT, told me that Bush encouraged these leaders to support the education plan he and his allies would propose. The CEOs liked Bush's overall message: "It was like the stars had aligned," Traiman told me. Her remarks suggested that state capacity had come a long way and that state reformers could advance their agendas by borrowing license from federal officials espousing a similar message. In her words, "There had been significant change in education at the state level, so we were at a point, then, where federal money and efforts could make a difference. But at the same time there wasn't enough being done at the state level so there needed to be federal leadership." Encouraged by these meetings, corporate leaders at Intel and Texas Instruments sought advice from Milton Goldberg, then executive vice president of the National Alliance of Business (NAB). (Goldberg had earlier helped develop *A Nation at Risk* as executive director of the NCEE.) Those initial conversations spawned the Business Coalition for Excellence in Education (BCEE), an ad hoc organization formed explicitly to influence the upcoming ESEA debate, not simply to cheerlead for Bush's or anyone else's particular approach.[4]

Bush announced his plan at a press conference on January 23, 2001, three days after his inauguration. Substantively, the plan that Bush and Secretary of Education Rod Paige presented was a thirty-page blueprint rather than a formal piece of legislation. It embraced four main principles centered on testing, flexibility, assisting low-performing schools, and choice (Bush 2001). The first principle proposed annual testing in reading and math for students in grades three through eight. Two days later, the president called annual testing "the cornerstone of reform" (Blum 2001). Annual exams were perhaps the only non-negotiable part of the plan. In February, Kress reaffirmed that commitment by describing testing as "central to the President's thinking. . . . His interest in, and support for, all the other initiatives depends on this particular reform being approved" (Gorman 2001b, 549).

The second principle was that local and state leaders needed greater flexibility to innovate. For Bush, that meant shifting authority and accountability to the local level so that schools could not blame their failings on distant educational bureaucracies. If federal money came with fewer strings attached, then the people closest to children and classrooms would have a better chance to improve learning. That proposal extended the logic of Ed-Flex, which, as chapter 5 described, had offered states added flexibility and had passed by wide margins in 1999.

The third and fourth principles guiding Bush's proposal concerned schools in need of improvement. The president recognized that some schools faced difficult circumstances and therefore needed additional help, which the third principle was designed to address. He promised to provide that assistance, but not as a blank check, and he stressed that children should not remain trapped in dysfunctional schools. To provide an out, Bush advanced his fourth principle and proposed that parents should be able to choose their children's schools through vouchers, which would provide greater public and private school choice, if their current public schools did not demonstrate improvement. Vouchers had been a signature Republican proposal during the previous two decades, so it was not surprising that Bush's plan included them. Still, from the outset, they did not appear as crucial to his thinking as mandatory testing and Bush aides conceded in January they would be willing to compromise on vouchers if that helped them to achieve other more important goals (Goldstein and Fletcher 2001). In January, Bush's chief of staff, Andrew Card Jr., said, "vouchers won't be the top priority of this administration" (Alvarez 2001a).

In previous chapters, I have maintained that license and capacity to act are necessary to promote government interest and involvement in a policy area. Recognizing those concepts illustrates that Bush's formulation of his education plan was consistent with what the borrowing strength model would predict. At this policy development stage, the first three expectations that I offered in table 5.1 are particularly relevant.

The president recognized the need to mobilize license and capacity to push the federal education agenda in his preferred direction. Justifying an expansive federal role and demanding much from the states immediately butted up against the reality that Washington's financial contribution to K–12 education amounted to pennies on the dollar. Nonetheless, Bush's plan to leave no child behind benefited from several sources of license. Some had been longtime arguments that federal policy entrepreneurs had used to justify federal interest and involvement in the nation's schools; other sources emerged from the unique circumstances that Bush enjoyed as he took office. Four of those sources stand out.

First, Bush drew on previously accepted notions, which dated to the first ESEA, that the federal government had a responsibility to help remedy educational inequities. At the press conference where he announced his plan, the president said, "We must confront the scandal of illiteracy in America, seen most clearly in high-poverty schools, where nearly 70 percent of fourth-graders are unable to read at a basic level" (Federal News Service 2001). In a personal interview, David Shreve of the National Conference of State Legislatures (NCSL) echoed the importance and long history of this theme, which several of my other respondents noted, as well. Shreve told me that "Title I [of the ESEA] began to address and point out the equity issue explicitly. More than any program or set of programs that the federal government has passed for education, that focus on equity has mattered most." The goal of promoting educational equity remains a powerful source of license to justify federal interest and involvement in education, even as other sources have emerged (Hill 2000).

Bush mobilized two other arguments that together emphasized the need to promote educational excellence. That source of federal license had become more accepted since the 1980s when it joined equity as a substantive rationale for federal interest and involvement in education. Embracing excellence would enhance the nation's economic well-being and would also guarantee that governments used their resources wisely. The president noted that promoting educational excellence in math and science, "the very subjects most likely to affect our future competitiveness," also required reforms to "focus the spending of federal tax dollars on things that work" (Federal News Service 2001). The need to stress results built on a growing consensus that government should not measure success by examining the volume of bureaucratic activities, but by the results those activities produce (Osborne and Gaebler 1992; Light 1997; Kettl 1997). In education, that philosophy implied that improving student achievement—and not just spending more money or increasing the number of children enrolled in education programs—should be the appropriate benchmark for success.

The political environment in January 2001 provided Bush with a final source of license to push his plan. As figure 1.1 and my discussion of presidential campaigning in chapter 3 show, the country emerged from the 2000 election season with education as a top national priority. People were looking to Washington for action and because the ESEA reauthorization was already a year overdue, Bush would be able to make his case with great urgency. Proposing his plan immediately after his inauguration also allowed Bush to leverage the license that often accompanies a president's honeymoon period.

Like all policy entrepreneurs, Bush would have liked to have possessed high license and high capacity to act, which is what the first expectation from table 5.1 and chapter 2 states. But, given my argument in chapter 4, even as federal capacity in education has grown, the federal government still experiences major deficits in this area. Whether the president and other federal policy entrepreneurs would attempt to borrow strength from the states was not an issue. Policymakers and others outside of government, such as the executives at the BRT, NAB, and the BCEE, recognized that a real chance to make good policy and achieve political gains was within reach. As expectation three from table 5.1 and chapter 2 illustrates, borrowing strength is likely to occur in this very situation.

The 1994 ESEA reauthorization relied heavily upon state capacity, and NCLB would be no different. In fact, given NCLB's specific components and broad ambitions, the law's capacity demands on states were arguably even greater. That posed a challenge to federal policymakers who crafted the act. As Bush's term began, several states were still struggling (critics would say *resisting*) to develop the policy infrastructure that the 1994 reauthorization had required and that NCLB would depend upon. In short, state agenda priorities in education presented challenges that federal officials attempted to address in the legislative process of 2001.

CRAFTING AND ADOPTING NCLB

Observers of American party politics would no doubt find much interesting material in probing the partisan forces that enabled conservative George W. Bush to push the federal education agenda into directions that the GOP had resisted during Bill Clinton's two terms in office (Jennings 1998). Several works have explored the politics that swirled around NCLB during the legislative process of 2001 (Manna 2003, 2004; Rudalevige 2003; Gorman 2001a; Broder 2001a). In this section, I sidestep much of that intrigue and instead focus on how federalism and the education agendas of the federal government and the states influenced NCLB's development. In particular, I discuss how federal and state policymakers addressed the capacity challenges that confronted Washington as the ESEA reauthorization unfolded.

It is perhaps an understatement to note that federal officials found difficulty in writing a law that held states more accountable for student achievement while simultaneously recognizing the massive variation in the states' educational systems and student populations. Shortly before the House-Senate conference committee began its work to iron out differences in their respective NCLB bills, Kress characterized the difficulties of mobilizing federal license and capacity to act in education, issues that emerged consistently in my interviews: "What makes this tough is designing something that will work in 50 very different states, and then figuring out how you can leverage change when you're only paying 7 percent of the bill" (Broder 2001b). The areas of testing and measuring adequate yearly progress (AYP) were especially difficult.

On testing, Bush's plan included the cornerstone of annual state tests in math and reading, which would be administered in grades three through eight. These tests would guarantee, the president reasoned, that improvements occurred each year. That Bush would propose such a model was not surprising given that he had inherited and extended the same approach while governor of Texas. Opinions regarding annual testing varied in the nation's fifty states and in part depended on the partisan stripes of the particular state official. Even though state policymakers quietly fretted over Bush's new testing proposals, fearing they would drain state capacity and undermine their reform agendas that incorporated testing and standards in different ways, many muted their criticisms.

Top among state-level supporters were members of the Education Leaders Council (ELC), a group of reform-minded and typically Republican-leaning governors and state school chiefs that had formed in the mid-1990s. In a letter to Boehner shortly after his committee completed its work on the bill in May, the ELC expressed its support for NCLB and for Boehner, especially. The ELC noted how the chairman had stood up "to the inside-the-Beltway interest groups and their allies in Congress who are attempting to block some of the key provisions of the Bush plan." The letter concluded, "We are in your corner" (House Committee on Education and the Workforce 2001b). That support continued into the fall when the ELC's chief executive officer, Lisa Graham Keegan, joined forces with former Secretary of Education Bill Bennett, Chester Finn of the Fordham Foundation, and the Heritage Foundation's Krista Kafer in a memo to the House-Senate conference. They urged its members not to let obstructionist groups distract them from their task (Bennett et al. 2001).

Other state organizations, such as the Council of Chief State School Officers (CCSSO), which represents the leaders of state education departments across the political spectrum in nearly all fifty states, argued that annual testing was at best unnecessary and at worst counterproductive.[5] In early May, Gordon Ambach, executive director of the CCSSO, agreed that holding states accountable was a good idea. How to do that, however, was less clear. "The federal interest here is in accountability related to the use of federal funds," Ambach argued. "In our judgment, to meet the federal requirement . . . it is not essential to have six separate data points [meaning testing in grades three through eight] for reading and math for every year from virtually every schoolroom in the country" (Olson 2001). To bolster his case, Ambach noted that Texas was the only state with annual testing that scored in the top ten in math or reading on the 1996 and 1998 federal National Assessment of Educational Progress (NAEP) tests, which provided reliable cross-state comparisons. Referring to the grade three through eight requirement, he argued, "Where the state is testing at all grade levels now, that's fine. But where states like Maryland and Virginia and New York and Vermont have testing at most of those grade levels, but not all, we object to a requirement that they would have to test at those other grade levels" (Olson 2001).

As the House-Senate conference commenced in mid-July, many state leaders remained uneasy that Bush's testing proposal would undermine their agendas. For example, on July 17, the *New York Times* (Wilgoren 2001) reported that top education officials in all fifty states "said that the testing plan originally proposed by President Bush ignores the fact that virtually every state has developed comprehensive new standards and testing systems." The article also quoted Finn, who described the political challenges accompanying the testing requirement: "States have just gone through the agony of rejiggering their state testing programs, and are going to fight fiercely against rejiggering it yet again." Attempting to deflect this sort of criticism, Kress responded that the federal requirement would not usurp state power but actually buttress state efforts and ultimately raise achievement of low-income and other at-risk children. His logic argued that NCLB would build upon and expand state capacities rather than weaken them.

In some respects, both Kress and the critics were right. Nearly all states had made progress in developing standards and assessments during the 1990s. As of 2001, for example, forty-nine states had established content standards and were linking them to testing in key subjects. Some consequences attached to these test results included increasing state intervention in schools that were persistently failing to meet accountability targets (Fletcher 2001d). Those accomplishments notwithstanding, much work remained for the states to complete. Even though nearly all had established content standards and testing regimes, in most cases, each state's tests did not necessarily reflect the content present in its standards (Citizens' Commission on Civil Rights 2001). As education researchers and policymakers would say, tests and standards were frequently not aligned. Further, some state policy entrepreneurs found it politically difficult to preserve license to push their testing plans amidst growing local criticism. North Carolina, for example, had eliminated three of its standardized exams in response to parents, teachers, and legislators who argued schools were spending too much time—up to six weeks of the school year—on exam preparation and administration (Fletcher 2001a). In advancing their agendas, state policymakers were constantly taking stock of their own license and capacity to act. They feared that a highly prescriptive ESEA would complicate their efforts to convince state citizens and local school districts to continue supporting the standards and accountability movement.

Beyond the politics, even with strict accountability, testing, and consequences for failure, some states still struggled to demonstrate results. Reading and math achievement of their lowest performing students often improved slowly, if at all. And achievement gaps between advantaged and disadvantaged students continued to persist. Kathy Christie, an analyst at the Education Commission of the States, commented in late May that "Many of these components have been in place, and things have not exactly moved ahead like a fast train. . . . These are issues with which nearly every state has been struggling" (Fletcher 2001d).

While some people characterized NCLB's requirement for annual testing as a heavy-handed federal mandate, Bush continued to stress how states would possess flexibility to develop their own tests. That may have calmed some critics who feared a national exam, but it also created additional problems. If the flow of federal education dollars depended in part on state test results, how would the law recognize the inherent variation that potentially fifty different state testing systems would create? What "proficient" meant in one state would not necessarily be the same in another, as past evidence had shown.[6] In relying on state capacity to develop tests, which was really Bush's only practical option, given the unthinkable alternative of a national exam for all students (Jennings 1998), the authors of NCLB strained to overcome one of the most difficult roadblocks for expanding federal involvement in the nation's schools.

Beyond testing, federal officials also struggled to invent an approach to measure student achievement gains across these fifty different state testing systems. Devising this formula for AYP was a perpetual snag in the legislative process during 2001. The nub of the problem flowed from the noble concerns about educational equity that Bush and past presidents had used to justify the ESEA. Whatever formula emerged for measuring AYP, the law needed to require states to show that all student groups—disadvantaged, racial minorities, limited English proficient, and others—were making progress. That would avoid the potential for grand averages, which lumped all students together, to make state, district, and school results appear encouraging when, in reality, disadvantaged students continued to lag behind. To that end, members of Congress considered a formula that would define a school as needing improvement, or "failing," as some said, if it did not meet AYP targets for all student groups. The end goal was to have all students achieving at proficient levels after a specified number of years. In practice, crafting this plan further illustrated the capacity barriers federal officials face as they try to leverage state capacity to expand federal involvement in the nation's schools.

The trouble began in April, after work in the Senate revealed a stunning flaw in the AYP formula that the White House and legislators had worked out.[7] Mark Powden, staff director for Chairman Jeffords of the Senate Committee on Health, Education, Labor, and Pensions, applied the tentative formula retroactively to

Connecticut, North Carolina, and Texas. He chose those three states because nearly all observers agreed that they had made much progress in narrowing achievement gaps between student groups. The exercise revealed that the tentative AYP formula would label almost all schools in these states as failures. Education writer Thomas Toch (2001) quoted one staffer present at the meeting who said the results produced "stunned silence." Another Senate staffer I interviewed, who was deeply involved in the AYP discussions, told me, "It was the worst meeting ever. I left just wanting to cry." Even some of Bush's Republican allies, such as Scott Jenkins, Michigan Governor John Engler's education adviser, weighed in on this issue. Jenkins expressed concern that getting the AYP issue right was absolutely critical: "If you set this adequate yearly progress at a somewhat unrealistic standard, and then you're going to tie rewards and sanctions to that," he argued in mid-May, "you could potentially create some perverse incentives for both states and local school districts to try and game the system" (Olson and Robelen 2001). That could threaten the integrity of the standards movement and undermine the agendas that policy entrepreneurs in the states, including elected officials and business leaders, had worked to build during the 1990s.

The AYP problem delayed the Senate bill for weeks and eventually staffers and legislators produced a new formula. To some state groups, the revised approach appeared worse than the original plan. David Griffith, director of Governmental and Public Affairs at the National Association of State Boards of Education (NASBE), said this about the AYP fix in mid-May: "It's been explained to me, and I still don't understand the formula" (Gorman 2001d). Bush education adviser Kress later called the results of this recovery effort "Rube Goldbergesque" (Toch 2001).

Not only did the apparent AYP solution prove confusing, in what New York Yankee great Yogi Berra might have called "déjà vu all over again," it also failed to solve the original problem that Powden had discovered. Scholars affiliated with the National Bureau of Economic Research published a study about the AYP provision later that summer. That work found the revised formula would produce massive numbers of failing schools in some of the most celebrated reform states. Absent a consensus on how to best gauge school progress, the authors of the study argued, "It would be foolish to cut short the state experimentation and impose a single federal formula" (Kane and Staiger 2001).[8] Michael Cohen, who had penned the crucial NGA memo that helped set the agenda of the Charlottesville education summit and who by this time had served as an assistant secretary of education for Bill Clinton, concurred in early September when he stated, "The notion that the conference committee can be wise enough to write a single formula that will intelligently work in all states without strange, unintended consequences is fanciful" (Fletcher 2001c).

On testing, AYP, and other issues, representatives from the states continued to lobby the conference committee members as their work dragged into fall and early winter. Governors pressed for revisions to the AYP formula and urged congressional negotiators to include greater flexibility in the law. If the federal government was committed to annual testing, they reasoned, then the law should at least allow for a combination of state and local exams rather than state tests alone. In fact, some states already possessed such systems. That option would alleviate some of the capacity worries that state leaders anticipated. In part, concerns over cost drove these arguments as state budgets entered danger zones amidst the national economic slowdown in the fall of 2001 (Schemo 2001; Chaddock 2001; Associated Press 2001a).

In early October, the NGA sent a relatively lukewarm letter to the conference leaders—Boehner, Miller, Kennedy, and Senator Judd Gregg (R-NH)—pledging its commitment "to providing the best possible education for children" while implicitly noting the capacity limitations that federal policymakers faced.[9] The NGA reminded the conferees that they must consider the governors' views if they hoped to produce a workable ESEA reauthorization. In concluding, the letter offered this blunt reminder: "Without conference negotiations yielding results that are workable and effective for states, successful education reform is not achievable" (National Governors' Association 2001b).

In separate September and October letters addressed to NCLB conference members and to Senate and House appropriators working on the education budget for fiscal year 2002, the CCSSO (2001a, 2001b, 2001c) advocated for flexibility on AYP and any federal requirements regarding teacher qualifications. The CCSSO also wanted the conference to preserve the Harkin-Hagel amendment, which had passed on the Senate floor to address special education, specifically to require the federal government to fully fund its commitment to IDEA. Finally, the CCSSO pleaded for greater funding to support what appeared to be the inevitable requirement for annual testing, which NASBE projected could cost as much as $7 billion to implement (Associated Press 2001b).

While the governors and state chiefs did not pull their support for the bill and while the chiefs and governors on the ELC continued to endorse the original Bush proposals enthusiastically, by October, the NCSL became a vocal critic. In a letter, dated September 26, to conference committee leaders, the NCSL (2001a) criticized the developing conference report on nearly all levels, focusing in particular on the capacity demands of the proposed law. It called the annual testing requirement "an egregious example of a top-down, one-size-fits-all federal reform" and said neither the House nor Senate bill offered "an acceptable alternative threshold for AYP." Other contentious points included full funding for IDEA and the bill's data collection and reporting requirements. Stressing capacity issues, the NCSL said that the federal requirement "ignores the price of hardware, software and maintenance by again shifting the costs to the states." It quantified that claim by noting how "the majority of states (38) do not have a sophisticated statewide data system with the capacity to process and store this enormous amount of information." The NCSL concluded by emphasizing its key policymaking role in the nation's federal system before explaining its fears that NCLB would undermine state agendas. "Do we support flawed federal legislation because others have supported it? Or do we voice our honest opinion that this 'reform' stops us in our tracks and sends us off on a new and not necessarily successful course? We choose to do our duty by withholding our support for this legislation."

While the NCSL recognized its position was unpopular—"We're clearly out by ourselves on this now," said Shreve (Mollison 2001)—its criticisms, albeit coming relatively late in the legislative process, were not necessarily erroneous or without support.[10] In its own rebuke of the legislation, which appeared during the first week of November, the American Association of School Administrators (AASA) raised similar issues (Hunter 2001), as did the AASA's Bruce Hunter in an interview with me. The nation's governors, Republicans and Democrats alike, had related concerns about the bill's requirements, but the NGA remained on the fence and refused to endorse or oppose it even into the mid-fall.[11]

With staffers working essentially around the clock, the NCLB conference committee finally reported out a bill on December 11. Two days later, the full House passed it 381 to 41. On December 18, the Senate followed suit in an 87 to 10 vote. As adopted, NCLB contained nine titles and forty-five separate authorizations that extended from fiscal year 2002 to 2007. It was several hundred pages long and included major provisions regarding testing, AYP, teachers, and funding and flexibility that further deepened federal involvement in the nation's schools. In table 6.1 and the rest of this section, I draw on several sources to summarize some of NCLB's key elements (Center on Education Policy 2002; House Committee on Education and the Workforce 2001a; Riddle 2002a, 2002b).

NCLB's testing components mirrored the original proposal that was offered by Bush in January 2001. By the 2005–2006 school year, the law requires all states to develop and administer annual tests in math and reading in grades three through eight and at least once in grades ten through twelve. All states are also required to participate in the fourth and eighth grade NAEP tests in reading and math. Previously, state participation in NAEP had been optional. The law did not link direct consequences to NAEP scores, but all observers recognized that those results would offer an informal validity check on state tests. In other words, states reporting high levels of achievement on their own tests but performing woefully on the federal NAEP would certainly be challenged to explain the discrepancy (Riddle 2002b).

Student test results were directly connected to AYP. The long-range goal was that all students would be performing at state-defined proficient levels or better by the 2013–14 school year. Schools, school districts, and states would have to show that students across different groups—classified by race, gender, economic disadvantage, disability, and students learning English as a second language—were progressing toward that goal. Disaggregating scores aimed to highlight achievement gaps that remained between these students and their more advantaged (typically white and higher income) peers. The law also recognized that requiring annual positive movement in scores across all groups was essentially a statistical impossibility as some studies had shown during the legislative debate of 2001. Thus, the "Y" in AYP did not necessarily imply a yearly calculation of scores. States could show progress if rolling averages, calculated over two- to three-year periods, were steadily increasing. That was far from a perfect solution, however, as analyses by Kane and Staiger (2002) and others have shown.

TABLE 6.1
Major components of the No Child Left Behind Act of 2001

Testing and Student Achievement.

By 2005–6, states are required to administer annual statewide tests in reading and math for grades 3 to 8 and at least once in grades 10 to 12.

State test scores must be disaggregated at the school, school district, and state levels into a number of student categories: racial group, gender, economic disadvantage, disability, and for students learning English as a second language.

States must set annual targets for increasing achievement and closing gaps between groups so that by the 2013–14 school year, all students are proficient in math and reading.

States must participate in the grades 4 and 8 NAEP tests in reading and math.

Schools Needing Improvement. A school failing to meet state performance objectives for two consecutive years becomes a school in need of improvement.

Schools in the first year of needing improvement will receive technical assistance from the state, and students will be given the option of transferring to another public school.

Schools in need of improvement for a second consecutive year will continue to receive technical assistance; students can transfer to another public school; and parents will have the option to use a portion of the school's federal Title I money to pay for supplemental educational services from a state-approved provider.

Schools in need of improvement for a third consecutive year will, in addition to the measures noted above, be required to make major changes in the school's personnel and possibly its organization.

Schools in need of improvement for a fourth consecutive year must undergo a major organizational overhaul, which could include closing and re-opening it from scratch, converting it to a charter school, or turning over control of the school to a private management company or the state.

Teachers.

By 2005–6 states must have highly qualified teachers in all classes where core subjects are taught.

By 2002–3 all new teachers hired with federal Title I money must be highly qualified.

Funds are made available to school districts to recruit, retain, and train teachers and principals.

Funding and Flexibility.

Formula changes will direct additional federal Title I funds to the poorest school districts.

Districts may shift up to 50 percent of their funding for teaching improvement, innovation, technology, and safe and drug free schools among those programs or into their Title I programs.

Schools with 40 percent of their students in poverty may bundle their Title I money into schoolwide projects to improve education for all students at the school.

A number of demonstration projects are created to test the results from relaxing various federal requirements.

Even though members of Congress wrestled with the AYP formula for almost a year, the final result still remained technically complex (Riddle 2002b). That was partly because states had options for how to establish their baseline levels of achievement (from which they would be expected to improve) and because NCLB included safe harbor provisions that allowed schools to comply with AYP rules even if achievement for all pupil groups did not increase on schedule. These exceptions were potentially important because of the law's other provisions, outlined in the second part of table 6.1, that would affect schools in need of improvement.

Testing and AYP captured much of the spotlight during 2001. But equally important, and perhaps even more challenging to achieve, were requirements concerning teacher qualifications. Starting in fall 2002, the law required all new teachers hired with Title I money to be "highly qualified" (Stedman 2002). Among other things, that meant teacher aides needed to have completed at least two years of college. Within four years, the law required all Title I teachers, past and present, to be highly qualified. The law also stipulated that all regular classroom teachers in core subjects must meet a more rigorous standard of qualifications no later than the end of the 2005–2006 school year.[12] For new teachers, that meant having full state certification, which would disallow emergency or provisional waivers of certain requirements. Also, the law required new teachers to have at least a bachelor's degree and to prove their competence in the subject areas they taught, either by passing a test or having a college major in the relevant subjects. Veteran teachers also would have to demonstrate subject-matter competence based on standards the states would determine.

If the annual testing plan, AYP formula, and teacher provisions demanded much of state capacity, how was it that members of Congress and the Bush administration hailed NCLB's new flexibility? That claim grew primarily out of provisions allowing school districts to transfer up to 50 percent of their funds from four separate programs into Title I.[13] The Straight A's pilot program in NCLB provided additional flexibility for specific states and school districts. Under its provisions, called the State and Local Flexibility Demonstration Act, the federal government would select up to seven states to combine all of their state administration and state activity funds from eight separate programs. Participating states could use these program funds for any purpose and possess this authority for five years, provided they continued to meet the law's AYP requirements. This demonstration program also allowed a limited number of school districts in these seven states to combine funds from four specific programs and use them for any purpose.[14] Other funding provisions in NCLB included changes in Title I allocation formulas that better targeted funds to the neediest schools and districts, especially those in large cities.

Overall, NCLB attempted to borrow state capacity to deepen federal involvement in the nation's schools. The law also built on preexisting federal capacity that the IASA of 1994 had put in place. In an interview during late October 2001, Michael Cohen told me he was making "probably only slightly a partisan statement" in saying "80 percent of [Bush's] proposals were already law." In an op-ed published on the day Bush signed the bill, William Taylor and Dianne Piché (2002) of the Citizens' Commission on Civil Rights agreed. They noted how No Child Left Behind's "basic provisions are not novel" and they "build on Congress' last revision of the ESEA."

IMPLEMENTING NCLB

A complete analysis of NCLB's implementation would fill several volumes. Indeed, through Bush's first term and into his second, several authors began to examine the law's impact on students, schools and their teachers, school districts, and states (U.S. Department of Education 2004; Center on Education Policy 2003, 2004, 2005; National Conference of State Legislatures 2005; Fast and Erpenbach 2004; Erpenbach, Fast, and Potts 2003; Peterson and West 2003; Hess and Finn 2004; Meier and Wood 2004). I refer readers to those sources for some of the policy details so that I can remain focused here on the intersections between federalism and the education agendas of Washington and the American states. The evidence in this final section illustrates that the borrowing strength model explains much of the variation in NCLB's early implementation. The fourth, fifth, and sixth expectations from chapter 2 and table 5.1 are most relevant, so I organize the ensuing discussion around them.

The fourth expectation I derived from the borrowing strength model is that accurate assessments of state license and capacity will increase the likelihood that federal policy entrepreneurs will enjoy success when they borrow strength. Immediately after NCLB's passage, the evidence suggested that federal attention to state concerns in 2001 had helped get the law off to a reasonable start, even though future work to develop its crucial supporting regulations was still forthcoming.

Based on extensive interviews after NCLB became law, reporters at *Education Week* concluded most state officials generally supported NCLB and believed it "mirrors the push in many states for greater accountability and results in education" (Olson 2002b). State leaders also enjoyed the promises for new funding, especially to support reading in the early grades. In the language of the borrowing strength model, these reactions illustrate how federal actions can help state policy entrepreneurs bolster license and capacity to pursue their agendas at home. When federal policy appears consistent with state objectives, states can gain license to promote their own efforts. Still, these state officials expressed concerns regarding capacity. They doubted they could meet the requirements for hiring high-quality teachers and they worried "about how much they will have to change their testing and accountability systems, and whether the federal money set aside for that purpose will be enough" (Olson 2002b). That latter concern was important considering, at the beginning of 2002, only nine states had reading and math tests aligned with standards in grades three through eight as the law required (Olson 2002d).

Specific state organizations also weighed in as the law was getting off the ground. The NGA, which had withheld its overall judgment during the conference debate, announced its "appreciation" for the Congress and White House's efforts, and noted the new law "builds upon the work already done by governors" (National Governors' Association 2001a). The governors did, however, use this opportunity to press for full federal funding of special education, which the Harkin-Hagel amendment had guaranteed before the conference committee removed it from the bill. The NCSL did not relent in its opposition. Jane Krentz, a Democratic legislator from Minnesota and chair of the NCSL's Education, Labor, and Workforce Development Committee, said that both Democratic and Republican members of her group disliked the bill. "It's more an issue of states' responsibilities versus the feds, and us being really, really tired of unfunded mandates," she said (Robelen 2001).

Conversely, members of the nation's business community were enthusiastic. Recall that these policy entrepreneurs had been key players in the standards movement in the states. Many business leaders no doubt concurred with the comments of Edward B. Rust Jr., chairman of the BRT's Education Task Force and chairman and CEO of State Farm Insurance Companies, who concluded: "Passage of this legislation will show that, at long last, America has gotten serious about providing a quality education for all of its students" (The Business Roundtable 2001). On the day Bush signed the bill, Rust pledged that, "The BRT will continue to work with the states to ensure that these reforms yield real benefits for America's students" (The Business Roundtable 2002a). Similarly, Susan Traiman of the BRT also noted this point in my interview with her. Seeing opportunities to push their reform agendas in the states, in January 2002, the BRT quickly published an NCLB "tool kit" for business leaders. The kit included information and strategies that would, as the accompanying cover letter explained, "help business leaders seize specific opportunities to partner with educators and political leaders in the next year to implement reforms called for by the legislation" (The Business Roundtable 2002b).

Several of NCLB's key deadlines, such as those for implementing annual testing and guaranteeing that schools possess highly qualified classroom teachers, are only coming to pass as this book goes to press. Thus, it is difficult to state precisely whether federal efforts to borrow state capacity have produced policy successes as defined by the law. That said, one success that analysts have identified is that NCLB has helped to sharpen the nation's attention on achievement gaps between advantaged and disadvantaged students (Center on Education Policy 2005). Even as NCLB's critics, who I discuss next, have expressed increasing concerns about the law's demands, policy entrepreneurs in the advocacy communities and governments have enjoyed expanded license to keep the country focused on this goal of expecting and ensuring high achievement for all students.

During Bush's first term and into his second, state criticism of NCLB's provisions, but not its overall goals, became more sustained. That does not mean that all states have revolted against the law. Shortly after taking office, Bush's second education secretary, Margaret Spellings, noted that many of the criticisms about NCLB centered around technical issues, not fundamental principles, that over time could be managed and worked out. "We've rounded a corner," she said (Robelen and Olson 2005). Still, state officials have felt the law strain their capacities and they have worried that it may undermine some of their other promising initiatives or reform agendas (Sack 2005; National Governors' Association 2005).

In describing the brewing state criticism, one Washington lobbyist who represents state interests and has been critical of NCLB put it this way: with NCLB, Bush and his advisers essentially found themselves trying to manage a stove that contained fifty simmering pots. When we spoke in 2004, this lobbyist suggested that strong-arming from top administration officials and the shuttle diplomacy of staff at the U.S. Department of Education, who spent many hours on the road and on the phone trying to field complaints and allay state worries about NCLB, had managed to keep things reasonably under control. But amidst growing state concerns and approaching NCLB deadlines, that would not be a sustainable strategy in the long run. At some point, the lobbyist believed, out in state capitals, these pots would start to blow.

As of 2005, the simmering indeed became a boil in some places. That has undermined some of the political success that Bush anticipated NCLB's passage would produce (see expectation four from chapter 2 and table 5.1). Some of the critiques have been especially powerful because they have come from states that have otherwise been strong Bush supporters. Virginia is a notable example. In January 2004, the state's Republican-controlled House of Delegates passed a resolution challenging NCLB claiming the law was a "sweeping intrusion" that would overwhelm Virginia's finances and throw the state from progress it had already made on increasing student achievement. Republican James H. Dillard, House Education Committee chairman, said bluntly, "The damn law is ludicrous" (Becker and Helderman 2004). State elected leaders and education officials in other Republican strongholds, Utah and Texas, expressed similar disdain for the law in 2005 (Gest 2005b; Dillon 2005b; Davis 2005).

Wanting to break with the past history of poor ESEA enforcement, Bush and his top education officials promised that they would work with the states but also that they would expect all to comply with NCLB's provisions. The rhetoric of Secretary of Education Rod Paige; Undersecretary Eugene Hickok, who served in Bush's first term; Spellings; and other officials has suggested as much (Wilgoren 2001; Paige 2002; Schemo 2003; Becker and Helderman 2004; Dillon 2005a). But because NCLB relies so heavily on borrowed state capacity, federal officials have frequently altered course in response to state complaints.

As the borrowing strength model predicts, the feedback processes that have ensued during NCLB's initial years of implementation have altered the agendas of federal officials while simultaneously enabling states to continue to push their own priorities. The fifth expectation from chapter 2 and table 5.1 notes that states will be likely to seek concessions from the federal government if federal borrowing strains their own license or capacity. State advocacy can foster negative feedback, which in turn can attenuate the agenda ambitions of federal policy entrepreneurs. As the sixth expectation maintains, those feedbacks can lead federal officials to modify policies that depend on borrowed strength if they come to believe they have overestimated state license or capacity to act.

Despite the promises of tough enforcement, which Washington's fundamental capacity deficits in education make extremely difficult to keep, federal policymakers began conceding ground to the states almost immediately after NCLB became law. State leaders won a key victory in 2001 when they lobbied for regulations allowing them to use a mix of state, local, and even off-the-shelf (i.e., commercially produced) tests to meet NCLB's requirements for annual state examinations. Some legislators on Capitol Hill, most notably Representative George Miller, claimed this approach essentially eviscerated the law's core by making it impossible to compare student gains from year to year or across districts within a state. One aide to Miller derided the decision by saying, "Everything we did in the bill was centered around the assumption that you have a statewide testing system. If you have local assessments, you've lost that. To me, and I know to Congressman Miller, that contradicts the whole intent of the reform effort" (Olson 2002c). On the Senate side, six Democrats wrote to Secretary Paige to say they were greatly concerned that allowing a combination of state and local tests would make it "virtually impossible" to compare student achievement across a state (Olson 2002a).

In contrast to Miller's reaction, policymakers and lobbyists representing the states were overjoyed at the result. Carnie Hayes, director of federal-state relations for the CCSSO, described this flexibility on testing as "excellent, absolutely excellent," and said that the regulations "will go a long way to making this work with the different states" (Olson 2002c). State officials believed that concession would alleviate part of their capacity burden and simultaneously bolster their ability to push their own agendas with local districts. Attempting to counter claims that this flexibility would produce bad data or substantially weaken the law, undersecretaries of education Hickok and Susan Neuman assured legislators and others that states would still have to demonstrate how local or off-the-shelf tests were aligned with state standards. The law's accountability provisions, they believed, would remain potent (Olson 2002c). Still, the larger point was that in granting this concession at all, the states won a policy victory, which revealed some of the difficulties that federal policymakers experience when they craft agendas that rely heavily on the capacities of other governments.

A similar concession occurred when a key NCLB deadline arrived in June 2003. By that date, all states were to have completed work on several components of their accountability plans. States submitted reports on their progress to Paige, and, in June, he and the president held a press conference to describe how far the states had come. Bush's remarks were adulatory to say the least. Among other things, the president noted, "In the past five months we have approved the accountability plans of 33 states . . . And today we mark an historic milestone of accountability—this morning, Secretary Paige has approved the plans of 17 more states, bringing us to a total of 100 percent of the accountability plans in place"

(White House Office of the Press Secretary 2003). Actually, the data did not support such a sweeping claim because many issues remained for most states to address. Most of the states still had much work to complete. Only eighteen, in fact, had completed work on all elements of their accountability plans that the federal education department had required. More accurately, then, Paige's approvals were provisional and would become final only after states tended to their unfinished business (Erpenbach, Fast, and Potts 2003; Olson 2003).

How can one explain the willingness of Bush and Paige to praise the states despite the president's and secretary's promise to honor deadlines and vigorously enforce the law? The logic of the borrowing strength model suggests that these concessions are a predictable outcome in situations where federal officials attempt to maintain license and capacity to pursue their agendas. Arguably, tough enforcement where states had indeed made progress just eighteen months after NCLB became law might have undermined the Bush team's license to maintain federal involvement in education as it had envisioned. Because the president and other federal policy entrepreneurs have relied so heavily on state capacity for NCLB to succeed and because they have counted on borrowed state strengths to help them achieve valuable political and policy objectives, alienating states this early in the implementation game likely would have been unwise. Keeping states on board with the overall goals and trajectory of NCLB was their larger ambition. And praising them for effort, if not absolute success, would help state leaders themselves maintain license with their constituencies to move forward with NCLB's particular approach to standards-based reform. Recognizing the potential to undermine their larger cause, as expectation six from chapter 2 and table 5.1 predicts, federal policymakers backed down.

Federal concessions have also emerged when persistent states have questioned the logic of NCLB's accompanying regulations. Since Bush signed NCLB, the U.S. Department of Education has fielded dozens of waiver requests from states that have petitioned for additional flexibility under the law. These requests can be nuanced and complicated. The two most comprehensive studies of this issue reveal that the department has stood firm on several matters. For example, federal education officials have not allowed states to adjust the order for implementing choice and supplemental services options for students who attend schools in need of improvement (see table 6.1). But the department has also granted flexibility, even in some unexpected areas (Erpenbach, Fast, and Potts 2003; Fast and Erpenbach 2004). For example, the department has approved state proposals that allow more forgiving state calculations of school progress and AYP.

In addition to granting specific state-level waiver requests, Secretaries Paige and Spellings have also responded to state concerns by issuing blanket revisions or policy updates that amended NCLB's regulations (Robelen 2004a, 2004b; Hoff 2005; Davis and Hoff 2005; CNN 2005). During Paige's tenure, for example, the department adjusted rules that made it easier for states to incorporate severely disabled students and English-language learners into their assessment systems. Other changes gave leeway to rural teachers who teach several NCLB-defined core subject areas and may have had major challenges meeting the law's definition of "highly qualified." During her first six months on the job, Spellings promised greater flexibility as long as states demonstrated increasing student achievement. She also extended by six months the deadline by which veteran Title I teachers needed to become highly qualified.

These unfolding policy adjustments, and their relationship to federal and state education agendas, provide support for the fundamental logic of the borrowing strength model. Washington's inability to extend its education agenda without state capacity opens the door to a dynamic interplay between state and federal policy entrepreneurs as they jockey to push their favored ideas. By focusing on the license and capacity needs of these individuals, the model can account for how feedbacks enter the system and agendas develop. That improves upon perspectives that would characterize NCLB implementation as yet another example of American federalism's marble cake in action. There is cooperation and negotiation to be sure, but by focusing on license and capacity, the borrowing strength model can more precisely describe and explain the processes that are driving those federal-state relationships. Further, in recognizing the capacity deficits that plague federal policy entrepreneurs in education, the borrowing strength model provides a tonic to a more simplistic view that NCLB represents a substantial power grab by federal policy entrepreneurs. Yes, they have extended Washington's involvement in American schools. But as the feedback processes associated with NCLB have shown, in terms of capacity, federal officials are still fundamentally quite weak when it comes to leveraging changes in the nation's schools.

In closing this discussion of NCLB implementation, let me consider one final point about policy feedbacks. Much of this section has focused on negative feedbacks that occur when states attempt to extract concessions and federal policymakers curtail their agenda ambitions in response. It is worth considering this chapter's findings in light of the long-run dynamics that I explored in chapters 3, 4, and 5. Recall a key point from that analysis, which noted how a strategic maneuver by the governors at Charlottesville in 1989 helped to move the federal education agenda more consistently in line with the standards movement that the states were leading. The states effectively leveraged federal license to help them advance their own standards-based agendas at that time.

Consistent with my premise that American federalism is a dynamic system, by pushing the federal government to embrace reforms organized around standards, states helped to unleash forces that eventually enabled Washington to assume higher levels of interest and involvement in education. Put another way, the state strategy in 1989 represented a calculated gamble. Getting Washington onboard served state policy entrepreneurs who were building education agendas across the country. That was the potential reward of this bet. The risk was that as state and federal education agendas continued to develop through processes of positive feedback and as federal officials borrowed new state strengths in the 1990s and beyond, federal policy entrepreneurs might someday attempt to more aggressively take advantage of the standards movement for their own purposes. That created the possibility that Washington's leaders might overreach and attempt to move state agendas in new directions. Interestingly, managing the risks associated with the governors' gamble of 1989 has fallen to other state officials. As of 2005, none of the governors who attended the Charlottesville summit are still state chief executives. Wisconsin's Tommy Thompson was the last sitting governor to have attended the Charlottesville summit. His tenure ended in 2001 when he joined Bush's administration as secretary of Health and Human Services.

HAVING DEVELOPED THE BORROWING STRENGTH MODEL AND USED IT TO EX-plain developments in the American education agenda since the 1960s, in the final two chapters I consider some broader implications of my findings. A question that most careful policy analysts or academics often ask about a research study is, "So what?" There are many ways to answer that question for the broad topic and sweep of time that I have considered. In the next chapter, I focus specifically on political implications. There, I address the effects that America's changing K–12 education agenda has had on institutional politics in the states and in Washington. I also consider how these agenda dynamics have altered the interest group environment in those settings.

NOTES

1. Portions of this chapter and the next previously appeared elsewhere (Manna 2004). I would like to thank Teachers College Press for permission to publish a revised version of that work here.
2. Education was a major staple of Bush's campaign speeches; in fact, he frequently identified it as his number one priority. See, for example, chapter 4 of this book and Bruni (2000). The most frequently run advertisement in the 2000 election campaign was a Bush education ad (Campaign Media Analysis Group 2000).
3. Clay Johnson, a key Bush aide who spearheaded the transition effort, noted in panel remarks at the August–September 2002 Annual Meeting of the American Political Science Association that the transition's policy teams had little or no contact with agency personnel; only top advisers were deeply involved.
4. In my interview with Goldberg, he noted, "We said that we'd be looking at the proposals that were being debated and see if they were consistent with the principles that the BCEE had articulated." He also emphasized that the BCEE represented an unprecedented effort: "To my knowledge this is a first," he said. Never before had the business community mounted an organized, systematic Capitol Hill effort specifically designed to shape federal education legislation.
5. While the CCSSO and ELC are technically different groups, their memberships do overlap in some respects. Some state chiefs are members of both groups, while some are members of the ELC but have withdrawn from the CCSSO. The ELC membership also includes other state leaders, such as governors. Most simply, the CCSSO's membership is comprised of the top school officer in each state, while the ELC members

share a common vision of reform but are not necessarily from comparable offices across the states. Interviews with Carnie Hayes of the CCSSO and Billie Orr of the ELC helped to clarify these characteristics.

6. In 1998, for example, Fletcher (2001a) reported that 26 percent of fourth graders scored proficient or better on Tennessee's state reading test, while 89 percent of Texas's fourth graders did. However, when one compares Texas and Tennessee using results from the NAEP for that same year, roughly 26 percent of Tennessee's students did indeed score at a proficient level, but only 29 percent of Texas's students did.

7. At this stage in the legislative process, the AYP challenges resided mainly in the Senate. The House bill included a couple of different options for AYP, the details of which were to be worked out in the conference.

8. Because of the non-linear progress that even improving schools sometimes make, the authors of the report argued in an op-ed piece that "the steady progress at the state level masked an uneven, zigzag pattern of improvement at the typical school. Indeed, we estimate that more than 98 percent of the schools in North Carolina and Texas would have failed to live up to the proposed federal expectation in at least one year between 1994 and 1999. At the typical school, two steps forward were often followed by one step back" (Kane and Staiger 2001).

9. By this time, Jeffords had left the Republican Party to become an independent. That caused the Senate to shift to Democratic control, which made Kennedy the chairman of the Senate education committee and Gregg the ranking member.

10. Shreve also qualified that conclusion by saying, "But a lot of people told me they empathize, and they wish that they could have been so bold" (Mollison 2001).

11. Mollison (2001) also quoted NGA director of federal-state relations Frank Shafroth, who described the governors' positions in early October: "Governors aren't saying it's bad or it's good yet, [but] I don't see any way the governors will sign off on anything that's just dumped on them." A handful of my interview respondents with information on this issue also mentioned the frustration that the governors felt, even though governors tended to keep these opinions under wraps.

12. These core academic subjects are English, reading or language arts, mathematics, science, foreign languages, civics and government, economics, arts, history, and geography.

13. The four programs are (1) Teachers, (2) Technology, (3) Safe and Drug Free Schools, and (4) the Innovative Programs Block Grant.

14. These are the same four programs noted in the previous note.

PART III

IMPLICATIONS

7

Borrowing Strength and Education Politics

PREVIOUS CHAPTERS HAVE DESCRIBED HOW DYNAMIC INTERACTIONS BE-
tween the federal government and the states have expanded the nation's education
agenda since the first ESEA became law. These changes have also influenced
American politics. For several years after 1965, state and federal education politics
followed patterns dominated by legislative committees, agency bureaucrats, and
key interest groups—collectively, the famed iron triangles of political science
(Salisbury 1990; Baumgartner and Leech 1998). How times have changed. Certainly, the triangle's players remain important, especially in areas such as program
implementation. However, the expanding federal and state education agendas
have prompted more groups and high-profile leaders to attend to the nation's
schools.

The three sections in this chapter focus on the political changes that policy entrepreneurs have fostered as they pushed their education agendas. The first section
describes how, in maneuvering to advance their agendas, policy entrepreneurs in
Washington and state capitals have altered the relationships between key state institutions. The second section takes a parallel look at institutions but focuses on
how agenda dynamics have influenced political relationships between the president and Congress. The final section focuses on the burgeoning impact of interest
group influence in debates over education policy. There, I focus particular attention on changes in the American business community, given that the nation's captains of industry have become increasingly important policy entrepreneurs in
both federal and state venues where education agendas take shape.

EDUCATION AGENDAS AND INSTITUTIONAL POLITICS
IN THE STATES

Education agendas in Washington and the states continue to influence the relationships between governors, state legislators, state education agencies (SEAs),
and state boards of education. The vertical functional networks of state and federal education bureaucrats that had dominated education policy implementation

for several years after 1965 began to come under fire during the late 1970s and early 1980s. As chapter 5 argued, during those decades governors and other state leaders became more interested in the substance of K–12 education policy. Cracks in these networks emerged with the increasing agenda status of education and the political consequences associated with education policymaking.

Scholarly work across several policy areas has described how dissatisfaction with the red tape of federal grants has threatened bureaucratic control of these programs and increased the attractiveness of block grants (Baumgartner and Jones 1993, chapter 11; Conlan 1998, chapters 7, 8). The argument in this section is different, however, and focuses on how the changing agenda status of an issue, not just discontent with policy implementation, can produce political stresses that reshape state arenas of action. Specifically, as education has climbed the nation's agenda, it has changed previously dominant patterns of policy control and, in the process, produced a new education politics in the states. To assess those changes, one first needs to understand the policy environment in the states that federal-state interactions in education have traditionally fostered.

Dating to the first ESEA, federal money to support K–12 education has consistently flowed to the states via their SEAs. This pattern has persisted throughout the ESEA's life. One consequence has been that federal education officials interact with a limited range of state officials. As Gerald Tirozzi told me, "When I was assistant secretary [for elementary and secondary education] in the Clinton administration we worked almost exclusively with the state chiefs." Alex Medler, then the acting head of the federal education department's charter schools office, agreed. He noted to me that,

> Up here we lobby Congress all of the time; we've got fifty people who do that. But there's this view that we shouldn't lobby the states. . . . The view up here is that the Department of Education shouldn't be lobbying [state] legislatures directly on these kinds of things [charter school grants]. They want us to communicate to the state departments, and then they communicate to the legislatures, and then the laws can get changed.

The flow of federal aid to state departments and these lines of communication between federal and state education officials have fostered state bureaucratic structures paralleling federal priorities. By and large, state education departments have been organized, in the words of two of my interview respondents, to "mimic the federal structure" and produce "state clones of federal policy that [have] affected the way state programs were formulated."[1] Other individuals I interviewed, as well as some published authors (Robelen 2002), have used the term "silos" both to describe patterns of state education administration and to emphasize that federal money tends to flow toward separate program-oriented functions. Those relatively independent streams of money discourage state administrators from integrating the various activities they oversee.[2]

Remarkably, despite the important influences federal programs have had on the organization of state education bureaucracies, it was not until 1994 that a comprehensive study addressed this topic. Using data from fiscal year 1993, researchers at the GAO (1994) found that, on average, federal funding has important organizational and personnel impacts on state education departments. The GAO consistently noted, however, that much variation existed among the states. For example, across all states, roughly 41 percent of state education department operating funds derived from federal sources; but individual state-level totals ranged from 6 percent in Maine to 77 percent in Michigan. Similarly, in terms of personnel, the GAO reported that, on average, the salaries of 41 percent of employees in state departments came from federal dollars; but again, across the states the numbers ranged from 10 percent in Connecticut to 81 percent in Iowa. Figure 7.1 presents the data on all states by showing the extent to which SEAs rely on federal funds for their administrative budgets and their staffing.

The GAO identified two primary reasons for this state variation. First, not all state education departments operate the same mix of federal programs. This occurs because all states do not participate in the same federal education programs

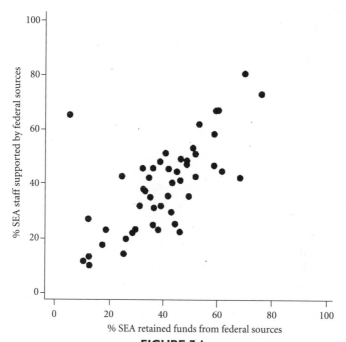

FIGURE 7.1
Federal financial support for SEA staff and administrative budgets, fiscal year 1993
Note: Each data point represents an individual state.
Source: Adapted from GAO (1994).

and because states sometimes have other administrative agencies, not their SEAs, that run these programs. Second, a single high-dollar program can skew overall spending and staffing patterns. Michigan provides a good example of both. As the GAO (1994, 8) authors explained, "Michigan's SEA operates three federal programs not common to most SEAs—Vocational Rehabilitation, Disability Determination Service, and Student Loans. . . . If these three federal programs are subtracted from the operating funding, the federal share of Michigan's SEA operating funding is reduced [from 77 percent] to about 33 percent."

Even with the careful caveats that pepper the GAO's analysis, it is clear that federal dollars can assert an important—in some cases hugely important—role on the policies and regulations that SEAs produce. And as my interviews made clear, the folk wisdom that SEAs are essentially creatures of the federal government animates the thinking of public officials and opinion leaders in the Washington education policy community. These patterns of state organization, and the federal dollars supporting them, have produced unintended political consequences that have become increasingly important as federal and state education agendas have expanded.

These political consequences become easy to see when one considers that, at the state level, four primary agents typically have some direct responsibility for developing a state's education agenda: state boards, SEAs, the state legislature, and the governor. The similarities across states typically end there, however. One of my veteran interview respondents made this point quite nicely when she noted, "One of the huge trends or controversies going back even before and back to the original ESEA was how to answer the question: 'Who is the state?' If you look at state constitutions and statutes you see lots of variation in how education is handled."

In some states, for example, the governor appoints members of the state board of education and even perhaps the state's chief school officer. In other states, the chief is an elected official who appears on the ballot alongside candidates for other statewide offices, such as governor and attorney general. Still other states involve a set of decision makers—the governor, state legislature, and state education chief, perhaps—to choose board members. Frequently, the terms of these appointed officials do not perfectly overlap the terms of governors and state legislators (NASBE Study Group on Education Governance 1996).[3]

By channeling federal dollars and most federal-to-state communication about policy through state education departments, federal education policy has essentially organized its efforts around one component of the states' governing apparatus. In an interview, David Shreve of the NCSL characterized the federal strategy to me this way: "By sending its money to the SEA, the federal government has picked a winner and a loser, and for good or ill, has altered the dynamic balance of the governance structure." He continued by describing to me a blind spot that the federal focus on state departments reveals. "The problem," he said, "is that when the feds see education they see a monolithic system and are oblivious to the great diversity in governance structures. That comes through in ESEA and IDEA. They see that system and they think that they need to give all of their money to the chiefs; they send it all to them."

Independently, the governors have expressed concerns that parallel Shreve's comments. In an NGA (2005) policy statement on education reform, for example, they note that K–12 education policy

> is broadly defined in state constitutions, specified in state statutes, and implemented by school districts. Current federal education programs bypass the authority of the state to determine education policy for these programs by sending the funds directly to state education agencies for local distribution, which often results in inconsistency and a loss in the states' ability to maximize leverage for important policy changes.

Certainly, one can craft a reasonable argument to justify the general federal strategy of engaging the states primarily through their education departments. The constitutional, statutory, and administrative divisions of labor within states and the policy and leadership functions that state departments are theoretically designed to handle often make them, at first glance at least, obvious recipients for federal funds and attention (Kaagan and Usdan 1993). For roughly a decade or so after the first ESEA became law, the relatively low profile that education had in state legislatures and governors' offices created incentives for federal policymakers to rely heavily on SEAs as conduits for federal efforts.

When governors and state legislators started to become more interested in education reform, they began to recognize the political challenges they faced in attempting to develop their own education agendas. Initially, at least, these state policy entrepreneurs found their agenda ambitions somewhat stifled by their very own SEAs, which possessed valuable data and much fiscal autonomy on account of their close ties to federal programs. This institutional mismatch, which federal funding streams and involvement in K–12 education have fostered, has created two enduring political consequences.

First, by channeling resources through state education departments, federal involvement has stoked political resentments and mistrust between state-level education leaders. In particular, the institutional independence federal resources facilitate in SEAs often frustrates governors and state legislators as these latter actors attempt to advance their agendas.

While Shreve agreed that the federal government sometimes has good rationales for channeling program dollars through SEAs, he emphasized the potential negative consequences for state-level education debates.[4] "I can tell you," he said, "that I've sat in hearings at the state level and heard testimony from education agency employees who respond to a [state] senator's question by saying 'I don't have to answer that because it's federal money you're talking about.' If there's one thing that a state legislator hates to hear it's something like that." These kinds of resentments have contributed to the problem of lagging capacity in state education departments that I discussed in chapter 5. As their education bureaucracies expanded, state politicians felt these organizations were largely beyond their direct control because, in several states, federal dollars supported most major activities that occurred inside the SEAs. That created disincentives for states to pass their own capacity-building measures, even as they pushed ahead with reforms in the legislative arena that demanded more from their bureaucracies.

Simultaneously, state school chiefs, who typically do not command the public profile and media spotlight of governors or state legislators, can harbor resentments of their own. They sometimes perceive governors' and legislators' self-promotion strategies as cheap political grabs designed to score points even while these same politicians pay little attention to the mundane, but critically important, details of program design and implementation that agencies struggle with every day (Kaagan and Usdan 1993). Tirozzi, who was a former head of the Connecticut state education department before joining the Clinton administration, told me that, often, and in his own specific case, governors and state school chiefs do get along well; but given the diversity in state education governance, this does not always happen. Some governors, he noted, "do one thing like pass a law for testing and they say that they're the education governor." David Griffith, director of Governmental and Public Affairs at NASBE, characterized a similar dynamic that sometimes plays out between governors and state boards. He explained, "There is always talk about abolishing state boards; governors use the rhetoric that they'll take over and the buck will stop here. But governors also like to have the boards as a punching bag. They can distance themselves from failure, but still take credit for success."

The second enduring political consequence of federal involvement is that it has created incentives for state leaders to borrow federal license as they advance their own agendas. That can help them to prevail in state-level political battles over the content of state education agendas. As a result, when these state actors position their organizations to claim credit for successes and deflect blame for failures, citizens and federal officials can find it difficult to hold states accountable for educational results. That difficulty has intensified since 1994 when federal involvement began to focus more on academic performance.

The defensive and sometimes buck-passing tendencies that governors, legislatures, SEAs, and, to some extent, state school boards develop manifest themselves in many ways. The results can reveal how state actors, in appealing to federal officials, can actually produce deeper federal interest and involvement in education. One example of this political maneuvering emerged during the early 1980s. Shortly after Secretary of Education Ted Bell's commission published *A Nation at Risk,* the governors were holding their annual meeting not far from where then Vice President George Bush was vacationing at his Maine home. Bush and Bell capitalized on the serendipity of those two events to host an informal meeting with the governors in Kennebunkport.

The governors used this meeting to air several complaints and to press for a national rating system of state education performance. In his memoirs, Bell (1988, 136) recalled the governors' frustration with SEAs that prompted this somewhat unusual request for greater federal oversight of state activities:

[The governors] said they had no information that told them where their states stood educationally in comparison to others. Lacking this, they were defenseless when their state superintendents and commissions of education insisted that students in *their* state were above the national average in academic achievement. If you believed these top-level state school officers, just about every state in the country was above the national average! Though many of the seriously concerned governors knew this was far from true, there was little they could do without data to support their efforts for change.

Bell responded and produced what became known as the "Wall Chart," a regular compilation of statistics in which the federal education department compared the educational performance of states on several indicators. After resisting this sort of state-by-state comparison for years, the CCSSO soon reversed course and "approved a plan to conduct regular comparisons of the educational performance of the states rather than permit the federal government to preempt interstate performance comparisons" (Jung and Kirst 1986, 97–98).

A second example centers on events from 1989 to 1994. Recall from chapter 5 that the governors were quite assertive and crafty during the buildup to the Charlottesville summit and in the implementation of its agreements. Part of the governors' political strategy was to mold the summit's agenda to fortify and extend their influence over education policymaking at the state and the federal levels. It is telling that the NEGP, the major institution to emerge from the summit's work, contained no members from state education departments or state legislatures. Only in 1994, when federal law codified the NEGP, did state legislators join its ranks. Even then, the governors outnumbered them by a two-to-one margin and still controlled the panel's chair.

Finally, examples of state posturing in federal debates were apparent in 2001 during the legislative process that produced NCLB. As part of its lobbying effort, the NCSL sent a letter to members of Congress that, among other things, raised concerns about education governance (National Conference of State Legislatures 2001a). In part, the letter argued,

ESEA remains the only major federal program in which a sub-state agency is specifically identified as the recipient of federal funds. Both pieces of legislation [House and Senate versions of the bill] directly endow state education agencies with unprecedented authority [that] . . . in both the short and long terms, impact overall state policy and state budgets. . . . Picking winners and losers in internal state affairs is not an appropriate role for the federal government.

One of my interview respondents and a friend of the state chiefs called the NCSL's use of "sub-state agency" a "gratuitous slap" against the CCSSO. In a related development, debates over NCLB's funding streams drew the CCSSO and the nation's governors into a battle over who should control federal dollars. An amendment to the Senate version of the bill, from George Voinovich (R-OH) and Evan Bayh (D-IN), proposed language that would have given governors more direct control over federal funds. The CCSSO and its allies pushed to keep the language more amenable to state departments. In the end, the Senate failed to adopt the amendment.

Mapping out the complicated political environment in which state actors operate provides some insight into the political strategies they sometimes adopt to develop and press their education agendas. With federal education agendas expanding, savvy state officials recognized new opportunities to borrow strength to expand their own agendas and win battles against other state actors. Beyond state capitals, the expanding federal education agenda has also produced important consequences for national politics inside the Washington Beltway. In the next section, I examine the connections between education's increasing agenda status and the political relationships between members of Congress and presidents.

EDUCATION AGENDAS AND INSTITUTIONAL POLITICS IN WASHINGTON

High school civics books typically portray the three branches of American government as separate institutions with divided powers. In contrast, political scientists have grown to appreciate the overlapping nature of the presidency, Congress, and the courts (Pickerill 2004; Coleman 1999). Jones (1994, 284) has described the American national government as a "separated system," and argues that grasping how it operates "logically requires attention to the institutional context within which any one part of the system does its work." Jones's formulation provides great insight for understanding the changing political battles between the White House and Congress over the federal education agenda.

For nearly twenty-five years after the first ESEA became law, members of Congress and their staffs tended to dominate federal education policy vis-à-vis the White House. In the separated system, presidents found themselves overmatched for two main reasons. The first reason is that members of the House and Senate, many of whom serve several terms, have faced greater incentives to maintain a complicated menu of federal education programs. Especially before the standards movement caught on, federal policy was primarily a complicated scheme involving complex formulas and many disconnected programs that allocated annual bundles of money to states and school districts. Many of those programs still remain, to be sure, but the onset of the standards movement has enabled federal policymakers to focus their efforts and attention. The peripheral and programmatic federal approach, which chapter 4 described, made it difficult for presidents to wrap their arms around the federal policy apparatus.

In contrast, members of Congress were and still are hugely attentive to the particular benefits that have flowed to their districts or states and they have worked doggedly to maintain the revenue streams that accompany federal programs. Thus, federal education policy has provided members with numerous opportunities to advertise successes with constituents and to build support in Washington by joining colleagues to defend mutually popular programs. Congressional scholars have noted generally how these two activities help members to achieve the twin goals of electoral success and influence on Capitol Hill (Mayhew 1974; Fenno 1978; Arnold 1990).

Not only do members hold regular hearings to study the details and track records of specific programs, many also develop strong loyalties to programs they helped to craft. Those preferences become drilled into their staffs, who keep a watchful eye over proposed changes that might harm a particular member's sacred cow. Long-time Washington education insider Chester "Checker" Finn described to me how these staffers, many fresh out of college, "are programmed by the people they work for to pay attention to those things—to defend the Checker Finn School Uniform Program. Or to make sure that others are there to support it; so when Checker Finn retires it becomes the Paul Manna School Uniform Program." Further, John Barth, a veteran of congressional and executive branch education politics, echoed these ideas. He told me that the funding formulas for federal education programs have been critically important because they "gave members of Congress something they could take home to their constituents. When I worked on the Hill, every time there was a proposal for a tweak in the funding formulas it'd lead to 435 CRS [Congressional Research Service] analyses about how it would affect each congressional district. That plays a formidable role in the political debate."

Given that presidents occupy the only at-large political office in the United States, they simply do not possess the incentives or the institutional resources to be this attentive to the cacophony of federal education programs that exist. Without an overall organizing frame for federal efforts, which would come later with standards, presidents remained at a disadvantage in their duels with members on Capitol Hill.

A second reason why congressional politicians tended to dominate education policymaking in the twenty-five years after the first ESEA has been due to institutional changes on Capitol Hill. During the early 1970s, congressional reforms allocated to members more staff resources and dispersed power among committee and subcommittee chairs, creating a newly empowered cadre of legislators (Smith and Deering 1990, 45–54). Those institutional changes emerged amidst the presidencies of Richard Nixon, Gerald Ford, and Jimmy Carter, three leaders who devoted relatively little developed attention to education, which Finn (1977) and the data in table 3.2 illustrate.

These presidents also faced major governing challenges. Nixon confronted the deepening quagmire in Vietnam and near-certain impeachment before resigning over the Watergate scandal. Ford faced one of the most difficult governing situations in the history of the United States after entering the White House even though he had not been popularly elected as a president or vice president. In his one term, Carter dealt with national economic stagnation, the Iranian hostage crisis, and a primary challenge from Senator Edward Kennedy in 1980. Thus, an increasingly capable and independent Congress combined with presidents who rarely focused on K–12 education enabled legislators to continue to dominate this policy area. Christopher Cross, former Republican staff director on the House education committee, described to me a conversation that captured quite succinctly the relative balance of power that existed across the 1970s. In an interview, Cross said, "I can recall Al Quie saying to me in about 1973 or 1974 that he felt no reason to support the White House [education] proposals just because he was the ranking [Republican] member [of the House education committee]."

If congressional dominance characterized education politics in the separated system through the 1970s and into the 1980s, by the 1990s things were certainly changing. By then, federal license to become more involved in the nation's schools had grown; presidents possessed a more visible and effective bully pulpit with the maturing Department of Education; and citizens started warming to an expanded federal role in the nation's schools. In addition, even amidst dozens of individual programs that continued to operate, federal interest and involvement in education became more coherently organized around supporting work on education standards and increasing student achievement.

Collectively, those changes helped presidents to improve their negotiating position on education relative to policymakers on Capitol Hill. Today, presidents do not single-handedly dominate national education politics. But with substantial media attention focused on the White House and more institutional resources at their disposal, presidents' powers of persuasion, arguably their most significant advantage in the nation's separated system (Neustadt 1980; Tulis 1987; Kernell 1993), have expanded. And as a result, they now enjoy greater opportunities to convince the public and other policymakers to see educational issues from their perspective. Not all presidents since 1989 have enjoyed great political success on education, though. Drawing on my personal interviews and the accounts in Jennings (1998), in the next several pages I contrast the experiences of George H.W. Bush, Bill Clinton, and George W. Bush to illustrate some of the reasons why presidential success on education has varied.

Across his four years in the White House, President George H. W. Bush missed several opportunities to advance his policy priorities (Campbell and Rockman 1991). The president enjoyed astronomically high approval ratings after the Persian Gulf War but nevertheless was not able to gain more control of the Washington policy agenda and secure reelection in 1992. In education policy, specifically, Bush presided over the successful Charlottesville education summit and had promised to be the "education president." Even so, he was unable to build on the momentum he appeared to possess in 1989. Four problems were most nettlesome for him.

Bush's first problem was that Lauro Cavazos, his education secretary, was a holdover from the Reagan administration. Cavazos served Bush until December 1990 and was generally an ineffectual member of Bush's cabinet (Douglas 1990; Mashek 1990; Jennings 1998), who never capitalized on the federal education department's bully pulpit as Ted Bell and William Bennett had done during the 1980s. Thus, after Charlottesville, during the very time Bush could have been building his own political capital and using it to advance his education agenda with Congress, he was without a persuasive spokesman. Bush's second education secretary, Lamar Alexander, was a strong replacement and took office in March 1991. That meant the post of education secretary remained vacant for almost three months, which also included much of the buildup to and execution of the Persian Gulf War. Perhaps Bush could have enjoyed more of a post-war bounce on education had he possessed an effective secretary to help leverage the president's high overall approval ratings during the war.

The second problem preventing Bush from gaining leverage with Congress was the political pinch on education that he failed to escape. Though he tried, Bush never warmed to the conservatism that Ronald Reagan and Reagan's most vociferous supporters espoused. That made many Republicans suspicious. They saw Bush's embrace of voluntary national standards as anathema to their commitment to reduce the federal role in education. On the other side of the aisle, congressional Democrats opposed Bush's support for expanded educational choice, which the president had advocated to placate conservatives. It was quite a tight spot and in part explains why Bush's primary education reform proposal, called America 2000, failed to take off. The plan originally tried to placate several interests by embracing standards and school choice. When the Democrats, who controlled Congress, eviscerated the bill's choice provisions, Bush and his team lost their interest in the effort, and it was defeated.

The partisan dynamics that emerged over America 2000, which Jennings (1998) documents in detail, suggest an interesting comparison to the events surrounding *A Nation at Risk*. Whereas the latter effectively borrowed strength from the states by employing the rationales that state policy entrepreneurs had been using in their advocacy, Bush's focus on choice prevented him from enjoying the same sort of boost. Recall from chapter 1 that in the late 1980s state movements supporting charter schools and vouchers were still in their infancy. Had Bush built America 2000 on the foundation of standards rather than choice, that would have enabled him to build on his own license coming out of the Charlottesville summit. He also would have been able to borrow strength from the governors who supported standards, which might have enabled him to weather the conservative criticisms that ultimately did-in America 2000. Absent more widespread support, the proposal died in a Senate filibuster led by the chamber's most conservative GOP members (Schwartz and Robinson 2000). Bush did help to push a standards-based agenda in other ways, but that occurred without the fanfare of a major legislative enactment (Jennings 1998, 32).

The related partisan dynamics that accompanied the burgeoning federal budget deficit compounded Bush's political problems. Congressional Democrats believed the government's budget woes should not undermine the federal commitment to education, while Republicans frequently branded Democratic proposals as too expensive. Those financial constraints frequently left Bush with few political options. His programmatic proposals were too small to satisfy Democrats but too large for members of his own party, many of whom still favored eliminating the Department of Education (Jennings 1998, 13–32).

A third problem confounding Bush was that, unlike every other president serving after 1965 (including Gerald Ford), Bush was the only chief executive never to have had the opportunity to work through an ESEA reauthorization. It is hard to overstate the importance of that fact of the nation's legislative calendar because the "secular time" during which presidents govern can powerfully constrain or enable their ambitions.[5] The ESEA reauthorization process provides a natural opportunity for policymakers to move federal agendas in new directions and claim credit for successes. Absent this opportunity, Bush assumed the more difficult task of building policy momentum on his own, something he and Alexander attempted to do, albeit unsuccessfully, with the president's America 2000 strategy.

A fourth and final problem lingered from the events surrounding the Charlottesville summit. Governors enjoyed the results of that meeting, which provided the president with a chance to borrow strength from their subsequent efforts. Inside the Washington Beltway, though, Bush provoked resentment from many members of Congress when he omitted them from the planning stages of Charlottesville and the development of national education goals that occurred afterward (Vinovskis 1999b). Even though the president chose this route for good reasons, which helped to preserve his institutional autonomy, in hindsight, it may have prevented him from building needed political bridges to Capitol Hill that could have paid long-run dividends. With conservatives opposing his agenda and Democrats controlling the House and Senate education committees, it is no wonder Bush failed to have much policy or political traction on education in Washington, even as the standards movement plowed ahead in the states.

Overall, despite greater license to act and a maturing bully pulpit on education, Bush's poor strategic choices along with the circumstances confronting his administration prevented the self-proclaimed education president from achieving his goals. This result occurred even though potential accomplishments appeared within reach after the Charlottesville summit. Had Bush more effectively borrowed license from the states to take advantage of the momentum after that historic meeting, perhaps he could have enjoyed more success.

Unlike Bush, President Bill Clinton used education to achieve several successes in his dealings with Congress. Clinton's efforts helped to establish more balance between the two branches in this policy area. Substantively, he was a formidable player in Washington's education policy debates during the 1990s. Recall that before becoming president, he was a leader at the Charlottesville summit where he helped the governors persuade Bush to support national education goals. One of the great ironies of Bush's presidency, in fact, is that he invited Clinton to attend his 1990 State of the Union speech, where, on account of Clinton's efforts at Charlottesville, the president openly praised the man who eventually would deny him a second term. Clinton was also intimately familiar with the trajectory of changes under way in state education policy. In the White House, he assembled an experienced education team. His only education secretary, former South Carolina governor Richard Riley, was known nationally and regionally (through the SREB) as an educational leader. Michael Cohen, who had been the NGA staffer who helped the governors develop their pre-summit strategy for 1989, was one of Riley's top advisers at the Department of Education before becoming an assistant secretary there.

One should remember that Clinton's major education policy achievements—Goals 2000 and the passage of IASA, which reoriented the ESEA toward an emphasis on standards—occurred in 1994 when Democrats still controlled the House and Senate. Some congressional Democrats chafed when Clinton defended the IASA's linkage to state academic and performance standards but compromised on what were called opportunity-to-learn standards. The governors opposed the latter because they likely would have placed large capacity burdens on states to provide additional resources to schools. Negative feedback from the governors moved Clinton to argue against opportunity-to-learn standards. Despite that bump, congressional Democrats voted for the reauthorization overwhelmingly in both houses. That support was critical, given that Republican support sank to the lowest level since the first ESEA of 1965 (Jennings 1998, 127). Vociferous GOP opposition flowed primarily from the linkage between education and related social issues such as school prayer, sex education, and home schooling, and the Republicans' continuing opposition to deepening federal involvement in America's schools.

It is unclear whether an ESEA linked to education standards and the Goals 2000 architecture to support it would have become law had Republicans controlled Congress in 1993 and 1994. However, if the GOP's performance on education after 1994 is any guide, there is little evidence to suggest they would have completely eviscerated Clinton's education agenda. As the 1990s unfolded, Republicans suffered from two major liabilities that allowed the president to curtail congressional dominance on education and to expand federal interest and involvement in the nation's schools.

The first liability was that Republicans espoused an education message that contradicted the preferences of most Americans. Many of my interview respondents across the political spectrum reflected on the disconnect between Republican positions in the 1990s and general public sentiment regarding education. Additionally, recall figure 1.1, which showed that by the early 1990s and for the rest of the decade public opinion began to mirror elite views about education's national importance. Public support emboldened Clinton, who relied heavily on direct appeals to Americans and data from public opinion polls, sometimes even "daily polling," according to a former Clinton education official I interviewed. With Americans generally behind him, the NEGP maturing, and his own political capital in education growing, Clinton possessed much license to extend the federal agenda.

The Republicans' public relations problem on education was severe. As one GOP congressional staffer told me, "The Republicans had said what they wanted to do on education, but they didn't explain it very well. People saw their positions and thought that the Republicans were calling for the elimination of public education or something like that." After Clinton secured a second term, moderate Republican House member Michael Castle of Delaware, himself a past governor, argued that, "Most of the [Republican] proposals [in 1995 and 1996] began with the words 'abolish,' 'eliminate,' or 'cut.' Thus, Americans were left with the impression that Republicans wanted to eliminate the federal role in education" (Jennings 1998, 175).

Those political missteps not only alienated potential GOP supporters but they also boomeranged to activate their opponents. As Gerald Sroufe of the American Educational Research Association told me, "Past arguments that the Republicans had made about eliminating the Department of Education forced the coalition favoring it and federal programs to come together." Sroufe said those groups "did telemarketing campaigns to raise awareness." Joel Packer, a veteran lobbyist with the National Education Association (NEA) agreed. In an interview, he told me, "In 1995 and after, when the Republicans took over control of Congress, fights over education increased the importance of the federal role in the public's mind." That built momentum for greater federal interest and involvement in education, the very outcomes Republicans opposed and Clinton favored.

A second major Republican liability was that after 1994, the education vision of GOP leaders on Capitol Hill conflicted with the preferences of two important state policy entrepreneurs: members of the business community and several key Republican governors. In 1995, when congressional Republicans proposed killing Goals 2000, Clinton and his team met with leaders of the BRT to help preserve the law. In a parallel development, at the NGA's annual meeting in the summer of 1995, Republican governors Tommy Thompson of Wisconsin and John Engler of Michigan and IBM's CEO Louis V. Gerstner Jr., the meeting's keynote speaker, opposed eliminating Goals 2000 and the NEGP as congressional Republicans had desired (Broder 1995; Jennings 1998, 158–60). Clinton's strategy of borrowing strength from the states by using Goals 2000 and the IASA to take advantage of their license and capacity helped him minimize potential state-level Republican opposition to his agenda. In the process, he gained added leverage in his dealings with Congress.

When Clinton clashed with Capitol Hill Republicans on education, the results nearly always broke in his favor—and sometimes with great political impact. An explicit example of this emerged during the federal budget debate in 1995. Clinton firmly resisted cuts that Republicans had proposed for education and other areas. Betting that the president would blink first, House and Senate Republican leaders refused to relent. The standoff persisted well into 1996 and ended up shutting down some nonessential but nevertheless popular federal functions. It became a political disaster for Republicans just as the gears of the 1996 election season began turning.

After Clinton's reelection in 1996, Republicans, especially those from politically moderate districts, began to realize how their education positions had disadvantaged them both nationally and in their battles against the White House. That recognition turned Clinton's second term into a bidding war over education. If one omits the GOP's successful challenge to a one-time $5 billion school construction proposal that Clinton included in his fiscal year 1998 budget, congressional Republicans actually appropriated more money for K–12 education than

Clinton requested in each year of his second term. This contrasted with his first term when, in three of four years (even when Democrats controlled Congress), appropriations were lower than the president's requests.[6]

In short, across his tenure, Clinton's education successes were essentially the product of his own political acumen and policy knowledge, the incompetence of his rivals, and the opportunities available in his times. He managed to engage with citizens' concerns about education and to mobilize the capabilities of the executive branch with a strong education secretary. By taking advantage of federal license to act in education, which Charlottesville and the NEGP had helped to build, and by using the IASA and Goals 2000 to borrow capacity from the states, by supporting standards-based reform, Clinton was consistently able to outmaneuver his congressional rivals.

As was addressed in chapter 6, President George W. Bush enjoyed much success launching his education agenda on Capitol Hill. Bush's opportunities to lead and his personal ability on education made him less like his father and more like Clinton. Unlike his father's administration, Bush entered office with an immediate opportunity to enjoy concrete policy success on education, given that the ESEA reauthorization was past due. As noted in chapter 6, Bush and his team devoted many hours to education during his presidential transition period so they could seize upon this moment.

Further, during 2001, even though Bush's education secretary, Rod Paige, was relatively ineffective in dealing with Congress and only a marginal player in the development of NCLB, the president himself was able to personally compensate for Paige's weaknesses or to rely on skilled aides, such as Sandy Kress, and key congressional lieutenants.[7] Until Bush's father appointed Alexander to serve in the nation's top education post, the elder Bush lacked a parallel brain trust when Cavazos proved lackluster.

Finally, also unlike his father, who alienated members of both parties with America 2000, Bush managed to form a strong coalition of Democrats and Republicans to support NCLB. Boehner was a rock-solid ally. According to my interview respondents, centrist Republicans, including Castle, who as a governor had been known as an education reformer, found themselves with added clout. On the other side of the aisle, Bush managed to earn the support of key liberals such as George Miller in the House and Kennedy in the Senate (Broder 2001a; Crowley 2001). Having Kress, a New Democrat, as his key White House adviser also enabled Bush to leverage support from Senator Lieberman and Senator Evan Bayh (D-IN). Their Three-R's proposal, which had been defeated in 2000, paralleled what Bush eventually proposed with NCLB (Gorman 2000; Rotherham 2001).

Bush's education challenges did differ from Clinton's, though, in an important way, as, perhaps, his toughest opposition on Capitol Hill came from within his own party. The president and Boehner faced immediate challenges from Republican conservatives who feared that NCLB would expand federal interest and involvement too deeply into the nation's schools. These members remained committed to promoting federal block grants and greater school choice options for parents. From the beginning of the 107th Congress, it was clear that conservative legislators would not accept the president's plan blindly, or with too much compromise. Representative Bob Schaffer (R-CO) provided a sampling of these views: "In my estimation, school choice is the only real salvation for America's schoolchildren. The heart of [Bush's] plan is a substantial step toward school choice. If the government needs more tests in order for America's schoolchildren to get school choice, then that's OK. [But without the choice provisions] then there's not much left to vote for" (Gorman 2001b, 552).

That sort of opposition created headaches for Bush because of his willingness to give on school vouchers and block grants in exchange for securing the testing and accountability provisions that he favored strongly. Bush addressed conservative concerns throughout the legislative process and expressed his views in the strongest terms to select House members, even Majority Whip Tom Delay (R-TX), who were uncomfortable with expanded federal involvement in education and the president's reluctance to fight aggressively for school choice (Clymer and Alvarez 2001).

Democrats had long considered vouchers a poison pill, which led Bush and his allies to offer other quasi-voucher approaches to fund tutoring in after-school programs at public, private, and nonprofit organizations (see table 6.1) rather than full-blown vouchers that House conservatives such as Schaffer, Peter Hoekstra (R-MI), and Jim DeMint (R-SC) favored. Conservatives became irate when the House education committee voted to remove vouchers from the developing bill. Schaffer argued that "Without the ability to exercise real accountability, real choice, this testing is nonsense" (Alvarez 2001b). In their four-page dissenting view, which was contained in the committee report that accompanied HR 1, the bill that was the working version of NCLB, Schaffer and Hoekstra joined Tom Tancredo (R-CO) to warn that "Republicans cannot afford to abandon their passion for children and free-market education so easily to the teacher unions and the education bureaucracy." Unfortunately for these men, voucher supporters fared no better on the floors of either chamber. On May 23, Majority Leader Dick Armey's (R-TX) amendment to provide private school choice for students who attend low-performing public schools failed 155 to 273. On June 12, Senator Judd Gregg offered an amendment to create a low-income school voucher demonstration program that also failed 41 to 58.

A similar trajectory of debate and eventual conservative compromise emerged regarding Republican proposals for block grants. Representative DeMint, who twice voted no on NCLB (once in the House education committee and once on the House floor) before finally voting for the conference report, personified this process. During 2001, DeMint was strongly committed to a GOP plan known as Straight A's. That proposal would have converted much federal education aid into block grants to the states. He pressed the issue in committee but lost the debate to moderates and Bush's Republican allies. When DeMint threatened to refight this battle on the House floor, Boehner and Bush both personally intervened to avert a political scuffle they feared would have rocked the bipartisan spirit that still prevailed as of late spring. Not wanting to cross his president, DeMint relented, and was satisfied with Bush's promise to fight for other issues, such as tuition tax credits. In the end, DeMint and his allies were pleased that the conference report did contain a version of Straight A's, albeit in a much more stripped-down form than they had proposed (Gorman 2001a).

Overall, the debates at the committee, floor, and conference levels illustrated the waning clout of congressional conservatives in the national debate over the federal education agenda. Their decline represented quite a shift from the 1980s and 1990s (Bell 1988; Jennings 1998). Even though some Republicans in Congress loathed a growing federal involvement in the nation's schools, these critics could not complain about the political results. In May 2001, for example, Senator Mitch McConnell (R-KY) reminded his fellow Republicans that Bush "has taken us [from] a 20-point deficit on education to a point in which we lead on education" (Alvarez 2001c).[8] In an interview the following month, Sally Lovejoy, who was Boehner's top staffer on the House education committee, concurred in a personal interview. She described to me the president's influence in light of the party's experiences during the 1990s: "Back in 1994, we [Republicans] came in and cut the crap out of education. We were against the existence of the Department of Education. Battles over education spending were part of the government shutdown. So those were the positions of the hard-core conservatives. We didn't dig ourselves out of that hole until Bush. He got the Republican Party out of this slump on education."

As Bush's time in office has unfolded, he has managed to prevent NCLB critics from reopening the legislation in advance of its next scheduled reauthorization. Although members of Congress have proposed several bills to change the law and despite growing concerns in the states from Democrats and Republicans alike about NCLB's capacity demands, Republican leaders in Congress have kept these proposals from moving forward (Manna, forthcoming.).

In his second term, state concerns over NCLB have sapped Bush's license to expand the law's reach. By early 2005, at least fifteen states had proposed legislation challenging NCLB (Gest 2005a). That has provided license for Bush's education opponents in Congress to put the brakes on his agenda. Additionally, the bipartisan spirit that persisted in 2001 had completely evaporated as Democrats argued that Bush reneged on the funding promises he made during NCLB's passage (Mikkelsen 2003; Stevenson 2004). In early 2005, Miller, who had been a key Democratic ally of Bush's in 2001, concluded that after NCLB's first year, Bush "walked away from those commitments to resources to the schools." In addition, just three years after NCLB became law, Miller said, "The tradition of bipartisanship agreement has been shredded" (Sandalow 2005).

Congressional opposition undermined the president's proposals to bring high schools more directly into the NCLB's framework. That plan, for Bush's second term, was met with lackluster enthusiasm and outright opposition from congressional Democrats and Republicans alike. As it did in 2001, much early opposition for this additional federal involvement came from the conservative wing of the

GOP. Representative Mike Pence (R-IN), leader of the conservative Republican Study Committee in the House, took a stab at Bush's agenda by saying the country needed to "reverse the expanding federal role in primary and secondary education, which conservatives believe is a state and local function" (Robelen 2005b). By May 2005, House Republican leaders said that they had no plans to take legislative action on the proposals before the end of the year. Castle, chair of the Education Reform Subcommittee, said, "Maybe next year, I don't know when, there's the possibility of legislation" (Robelen 2005a).

It is hard to say whether Bush's second-term difficulties with NCLB will have longer-term implications for the institutional relationship between future presidents and congresses. More generally, the evidence does show that the borrowing strength model is likely to remain a valuable tool for understanding how this relationship continues to unfold. Bill Clinton and George W. Bush were able to borrow license and capacity to expand the federal education agenda. Positive feedback helped them to advance their agendas and bolster the institutional position of the president on this issue. Bush's eventual difficulties have shown that members of Congress can also borrow strength in ways that can foster negative feedbacks and attenuate the agenda ambitions of their institutional rival down the street on Pennsylvania Avenue. State concerns over NCLB have provided license to Capitol Hill critics of the law who hope to advance their own views about the proper combination of federal interest and involvement in the nation's schools.

INTEREST GROUPS, IDEA MAKERS, AND EDUCATION POLITICS

One final issue to consider, which has and will continue to influence the institutional dynamics that the previous two sections described, is the growth of educational interest groups in the United States. Policy entrepreneurs who populate these groups can wield key influence and play "an important role in structuring the choices available to policymakers and the public's understanding of what is at stake in a public policy debate" (Baumgartner and Jones 1993, 190). As earlier chapters and the first two sections of this one have shown, some of these policy entrepreneurs attempt to maneuver within the halls of government. This final section notes how they can operate on the outside, as well.

For Clinton and George W. Bush, in particular, the "thickening" (Skowronek 1997, 31) of the interest group environment in Washington created opportunities as they attempted to expand the federal education agenda. Business groups, especially, have had major influence, so their evolving role, which has shifted dramatically since the 1960s, deserves special attention here. Before exploring the role of business and how it has changed, I begin this section by briefly summarizing the general transformation of educational interests that has occurred since the 1970s, the period when the iron triangles in education and other policy areas began to break down.

In general, scholars have documented the proliferation of organized interest groups in the American political system. Even though claims of an "interest-group explosion" are present in academic work for nearly every decade of the 1900s (Baumgartner and Leech 1998, 102), the number of organized interest groups and associations in several policy areas has increased in recent years. Education is no exception. For example, in 1980, the *Encyclopedia of Associations* listed 976 such educational groups. By 1990, that number had grown to 1,292. In 1995, it had stabilized somewhat at 1,312 (Baumgartner and Leech 1998, 103). Those numbers do not include many all-purpose groups and think tanks, which have expanded their own work on education during this time.

With the stakes in education rising as the federal government and the states have developed their education agendas, these groups have expanded the volume and range of voices that policymakers hear. In addition, new organizations with new ideas (or old ideas in new garb) have also sprung up. Some leaders at these new groups frequently disparage what they see as an old-guard educational establishment, known pejoratively as "The Blob." Many Blob members wear that label with a snicker and bit of pride, but their critics argue they put their own interests ahead of the nation's students.

Many groups with long histories, such as the NEA and the AFT, the CCSSO, and NASBE as well as several groups representing local interests, such as the AASA and the National School Boards Association, continue to remain active and influential in Washington's political circles and sometimes even national election campaigns. These groups no longer dominate the field, though, because new diverse organizations across the political spectrum have been able to find niches in the policy debate. One interview respondent described this shift to me by saying that Washington politicians now frequently "go out and get alternative groups and pull them in. They get a teacher who wrote them a letter complaining about the system. In general, they're running away from the establishment." Overall, education is like other policy areas now that the sometimes impenetrable iron triangles of the past have become more diffuse and fluid policy networks (Salisbury 1990; Baumgartner and Leech 1998; Milward and Provan 2000; O'Toole 2000b; O'Toole and Meier 2004).

Predictably, many newly influential groups in Washington have emerged as the projects of policy advocates or individuals with years of education policy experience in national or state politics. A partial list of these groups, which were founded or significantly expanded in the 1990s, includes one I mentioned in chapter 5, the ELC, and others, such as Achieve, the Center on Education Policy, the Thomas B. Fordham Foundation, the 21st Century Schools Project at the Progressive Policy Institute, the National Center on Education and the Economy, the Education Trust, and the Center for Education Reform. With education's importance rising on state and federal agendas, policy entrepreneurs at these groups have found no shortage of elected officials, government staffers, and reporters interested in their published work and events. In recent years, members of the nation's business community, who helped to found Achieve, have been perhaps as influential as all of these groups. Given the political implications of the business community's increasing role in helping to set state and federal education agendas, I now turn to describing how this particular group's position has evolved.

Despite a history of interest and involvement in state and local education issues from the beginning of the twentieth century through World War II, business leaders were first indifferent and then outright hostile to the increased federal presence in the nation's schools that was proposed in the 1960s. During the first ESEA debate in 1965, for example, Theron J. Rice, legislative action manager for the U.S. Chamber of Commerce, sent to all members of the House of Representatives a short letter and accompanying ten-page memo describing why members should oppose the bill. Rice argued that the ESEA would pose an "unprecedented threat of federal domination and standardization of elementary and secondary education" (Chamber of Commerce of the United States 1965). This hostility contrasts sharply with the enthusiastic support, described in chapter 6, that business leaders offered during debates in 2001 over NCLB.

Business opposition in 1965 and subsequent indifference to the mushrooming of federal education efforts through the 1970s were derived from three main sources according to Timpane and McNeil (1991, 1–3).[9] Financial self-interest was the first key source. Business leaders feared an expanded federal education agenda would produce higher taxes from federal, state, and local governments as policymakers responded to new mandates and initiatives. A second source was the growing number of stakeholders involved in educational decision making. Those additional players frustrated business leaders who did not possess the political or policy knowledge in education that would enable them to navigate such crowded waters. Business groups were typically risk averse in education policy and avoided entering highly charged political debates over educational issues involving race and desegregation. The third source was the nation's capable and plentiful domestic labor force and lack of significant international competition. American economic strength did not create any sense of urgency among the captains of U.S. industry; they saw no need to help improve the quality of schooling that the nation's young people received. Collectively, these three factors resulted in business leaders playing little or no role in debates over federal education policy for essentially a quarter century after the first ESEA became law.

Things were different at the state level, however. Starting in the late 1970s, as state leaders, especially governors, began to recognize education as a critical economic development issue, business leaders became engaged policy entrepreneurs who tried to influence state education agendas. Growing concerns prompted their reentry into education politics, first with state-level politicians through the 1980s and subsequently at the federal level in the 1990s, especially after 1994, as federal involvement expanded. Concerns over maintaining a well-trained workforce were paramount. This focus on economic competition, enhanced after *A Nation at Risk* appeared, was symbolized by increasing business requests that the federal government expand the available number of H1-B visas to enable firms to import more highly skilled workers from other nations (Goldberg and Traiman 2001).

Another concern building in the mid-1990s was what business leaders perceived as a painfully slow process of educational change occurring across the nation's fifty states. That observation proved especially frustrating because the path to improvement business leaders favored, holding students to higher standards, appeared so obvious to them by that time. These views emerged in sharp relief at the 1996 national education summit when several business executives stormed out of a meeting amidst what they believed was unnecessary political hair-splitting by the nation's governors. Reflecting on that event and debates over educational standards in 2001, Susan Traiman of the BRT explained to me, "The business community recognizes that based on our nation's politics and history education is a state and local function. But it is maddening to business leaders that all of the states have to figure this [standards] out on their own."

The business community's return to state education politics in the 1970s and 1980s and subsequent federal attempts in the 1990s to borrow strength from the states to expand federal involvement in education ushered in a new period of business interest in federal education policymaking. Unlike their involvement in the 1960s, though, which opposed the expanding federal role, business leaders have become enthusiastic supporters of Washington's burgeoning education agenda focusing on standards and accountability. The political leverage business leaders have provided to federal policy entrepreneurs from both major parties is hard to overstate. The previous section described how they were instrumental in helping President Clinton weather Republican attacks on his agenda in the 1990s. A decade later, business groups have remained steadfast supporters of NCLB, working to prevent the law's critics from undermining support for policies that promote high standards and educational accountability.

It is difficult to identify exactly when business groups began to reengage education policy on the national political stage. Without question, though, a crucial early event in this transformation occurred in June of 1989 when President Bush spoke to members of the BRT in Washington, DC. According to Traiman, "At that meeting [Bush] challenged the CEOs to get involved in education. The CEOs said 'yes,' but in saying that they didn't really know what 'yes' meant. So they spent a year thinking about it; thinking about how big companies—because that's what the BRT is made of—could have positive influence. They saw the place that they could get involved was in state policy, not federal. State policy was creating the infrastructure for reform." Most critically, that infrastructure contained emerging standards and testing systems.

In 1994 and subsequent years, when Clinton pressed for Goals 2000 and the IASA, he found a natural ally in the business community. Throughout the 1990s, Clinton and his advisers engaged in systematic efforts to warm business leaders to the idea that federal policy could properly borrow strength from the states to accelerate the standards movement. Part of this strategy involved reaching out to state and local business groups. From his position at the NAB, Milton Goldberg described to me how this frequently worked: "When Dick Riley was secretary [of education], his staff would often call over here. If Riley were going out to give a speech they'd call in advance and ask us who the business leaders [involved in education] were in the community, what they were working on, what their interests were. So when Riley would go out to a place like Indianapolis, for example, he could talk about these things in his speech."

Attempts by Riley and other Clinton advisers to embrace business created important political capital for the administration (a source of license) that proved especially valuable after Republican electoral successes in 1994. Business executives, who tended to ally with Republicans in state and federal politics, pushed state leaders to stay focused on standards-based reform and, in essence, attenuated some of the influence that national-level Republicans had over these state-level politicians. Business leaders helped keep the states moving ahead and provided a counterweight to groups on the political right that opposed standards-based reform. In an interview with me, John Barth, who worked with the NGA between stints with the NEGP, explained that some business leaders even "threatened to withhold campaign contributions [from state politicians] if states did not keep reforms on track." My interviews with Traiman and the Education Trust's Kati Haycock also explored examples of business influence on state-level politicians.

By 2001, acting through organizations such as the BRT, NAB, and BCEE, business leaders had become national players on education like never before. They remained committed to education standards; and because they saw how federal involvement could help state accountability systems to develop and mature, they supported federal policy that borrowed strength from the states. That support has been important for helping NCLB's advocates defend the law even as criticism has mounted (The Business Roundtable 2005). For example, as the law was entering its third year, president and CEO of the U.S. Chamber of Commerce, Tom Donahue (2004), said this about NCLB: "We strongly support the No Child Left Behind legislation because it works to create a K through 12 system that is more competitive with the educational systems of other industrialized nations and will lead to a better educated and more highly skilled American workforce in the future."

Comparing Donahue's remarks with Rice's advocacy in 1965 (which I quoted earlier) reveals in a nutshell how much business interests have changed. Leaders of the BRT, the U.S. Chamber of Commerce, and hybrid groups like Achieve, which is comprised of business representatives and state governors, have become key policy entrepreneurs wielding influence in federal and state education debates. Not only do these leaders stand firmly behind the expanded federal agenda in education that NCLB symbolizes, they also remain positioned to assert much influence in the future as federal and state agendas continue to develop.

IN ONE OF THE CLASSIC WORKS IN POLITICAL SCIENCE, E. E. SCHATTSCHNEIDER (1935) famously claimed that new policies create new politics. Even though he reached this conclusion after studying revisions to the United States tariff of 1929–30, Schattschneider also asked rhetorically, "Is this not true, in varying degrees, of nearly all other policies also?" (Schattschneider 1935, 288). For education policy, at least, based on the evidence in this chapter, it appears that Schattschneider's keen insights remain on target.

Since 1965, the developing education agenda in the United States and the dynamic relationships between policy entrepreneurs across the nation's federal system have created new education politics in Washington, DC, and the fifty states. In pushing their education agendas and borrowing strength to seize opportunities, policy entrepreneurs in the states, the federal government, and the American interest group community have engaged their adversaries in sometimes high-profile political battles. Those disputes have influenced policy to be sure. This chapter has shown that they have also helped to shape the fortunes of individual politicians and some of the long-run relationships between federal and state institutions that govern the nation's schools.

In the next chapter, I shift my attention from the political trenches to draw out some of the broader implications of the borrowing strength model of agenda setting. Up to this point in the book, I have tried to provide insights about how federalism influences agenda setting and about how education agendas have developed in the nation's capital and the states. I have argued that the borrowing strength model provides a compelling and concise way to understand these two topics. That said, no model is perfect. In developing any theory of complex social processes, one must simplify the world or explanations become intractable and conceptually imprecise. In offering some final thoughts on the borrowing strength model, the concluding chapter considers some of these simplifications and suggests how others might pick up where I have left off and subject my ideas to further tests. If, indeed, federalism is ever changing and requires frequent reinvestigation (Grodzins 1966), mine will hardly be the last word on the subject.

NOTES

1. These two quotes are from my interviews with two veterans of education debates in Washington, Jack Jennings and Kati Haycock, respectively.

2. See also Christopher Cross's comments, published as a discussant's response, in Hill (2000, 42).

3. NASBE publishes an annual chart that summarizes state education governance structures. It is available at http://www.nasbe.org/Educational_Issues/Governance/Governance_chart.pdf (accessed summer of 2005).

4. Jack Jennings and Chester Finn also raised this issue of interinstitutional trust in my interviews with them.

5. Skowronek (1997, 30) explains the relationship between secular time and presidential performance this way: "Presidential leadership in secular time will refer to the progressive development of the institutional resources and *governing responsibilities* of the executive office and thus to the repertoire of powers the presidents *of a particular period* have at their disposal to realize their preferences in action." (Emphasis mine.)

6. U.S. Department of Education (2002). Many thanks to my interview respondent, Donna Wong of the Congressional Budget Office, for helping me to interpret these numbers.

7. During the No Child Left Behind debate, Kress let slip to a reporter that Paige was "a little bit on the periphery" of the administration's discussions (Scheiber 2001). Interview respondents both on and off Capitol Hill commented on Paige's relative ineffectiveness in dealing with members of Congress.

8. Many of my Democratic interview respondents expressed dismay at this reversal. Jeff Mazur described to me the frustration that Democrats felt in mid-June: "Just this week there were poll results that said that Bush was low on everything except education. Democrats were mad as hell about that. 'How could we let that happen?' they said."

9. I also explored these reasons in interviews with Buzz Bartlett, Christopher Cross, Chester Finn, Janet Hansen, Susan Traiman, and Michael Usdan.

8

SETTING THE AGENDA IN THE
AMERICAN FEDERAL SYSTEM

The authors of the U.S. Constitution have received much deserved praise for designing a government grounded in realistic assumptions about human behavior. James Madison and the other founders reasoned that people tend to privilege their own interests and the interests of likeminded others. In addition to other mechanisms and institutions, the founders created the American federal system to strike a delicate balance between guaranteeing majority rule and protecting minority rights. Still, it was impossible to foresee how future generations of policy entrepreneurs would adapt to the constitution's constraints. Initially, the founders celebrated Madison's compound republic for its arresting tendencies. More than two centuries later, American federalism retains its ability to stifle change. However, as the policy entrepreneurs chronicled in this book would attest, the system has also proven capable of fostering sometimes even dramatic changes in government agendas. Positive and negative feedback are both possibilities, then, and how those processes play out depends on how these entrepreneurs maneuver to advance their priorities.

Beginning with the premise that American federalism is a dynamic and flexible system, I have argued that the compound republic provides actors in Washington, DC, and state capitals with opportunities to develop and push their agendas. When actors at one level of government expand their interest and involvement in a policy area, officials elsewhere do not necessarily suffer a corresponding loss of their own power or authority. Savvy and creative policy entrepreneurs have recognized that agenda expansions in one part of the federal system may actually provide them with opportunities to push their own favorite ideas in the arenas where they work. These opportunities are especially important when entrepreneurs lack license or capacity to act, but can leverage those assets from another level of government to ameliorate their own weaknesses.

Education policy has provided a useful case to test what I have called the borrowing strength model of agenda setting. I maintain that this model represents a strong conceptual improvement over other understandings of the American system embodied in general notions of cooperation or zero-sum perspectives of federalism that I reviewed in chapter 2. Still, as I suggested at the end of the previous chapter, mine will certainly not be the last word on federalism or agenda setting. With that recognition, the two sections in this final chapter are designed to provide launching pads for others who may wish to explore more deeply some of this book's fundamental claims. The first section suggests ways to extend the borrowing strength model. The second sums up the basic take-home points that I hope readers will continue to ponder as they set my book aside and move on to others.

EXTENDING THE BORROWING STRENGTH MODEL

The borrowing strength model of agenda setting provides a focused way to understand policy and political changes across time and governments. Because the model serves as a starting point for explaining the rich process of agenda setting in the American federal system, it is ripe for future extensions and applications. This section, which is organized around three specific questions, presents some of those opportunities.

A first question to ask about the model could be: When is borrowing strength likely to occur? In previous chapters, I argued that policy entrepreneurs will be more likely to borrow strength when they think it will help them achieve political gains and make good policy. That claim begins to suggest an answer to this first question, but it leaves much room for future work. An interesting extension would be to develop a more sophisticated microlevel behavioral model of borrowing strength. That would help to fill out the model by drawing on classic and more recent works that have studied policy decision making in other contexts (Simon 1947; Allison 1971; Jones 2001).

As a generic start, recall that, in chapter 2, I listed several things that might move a policy entrepreneur to borrow strength. Those factors included opportunities for electoral success, enhanced prestige with colleagues in or out of government, and the ability to make good policy. Those reasons may relate to other elite behaviors, too, such as selecting a particular campaign strategy, pushing for a certain committee seat in Congress, seeking a specific bureau assignment in an administrative agency or advocacy group, and deciding whether to run for higher office. It would be worth considering, then, whether the factors motivating policy entrepreneurs on these other choices are the same that motivate them to borrow strength to push their agendas.

One way to analyze the factors that move entrepreneurs to borrow strength would be to focus more intently on the entrepreneurs themselves—as others have done (Mintrom 2000)—to consider three separate issues: the extent to which entrepreneurs are risk seeking or risk averse in a particular policy area; the quality and amount of information entrepreneurs possess about the license and capacity of other governments; and the amount of borrowing strength needed to overcome what an entrepreneur perceives to be a government's license or capacity weakness. Relating these three factors could generate several hypotheses about the likelihood that an entrepreneur would attempt to borrow strength to make up for a license or capacity deficit. Consider two prototypical cases.

Case 1 is a risk-seeking entrepreneur who has good information about other governments' capabilities and only needs to borrow a bit to ameliorate the deficits she perceives. Borrowing strength would be a likely outcome for this entrepreneur. Case 2 is a risk-averse policy entrepreneur who lacks good information about the license and capacity of other governments and who believes he faces large license and capacity deficits. That entrepreneur would be less likely to borrow strength. These two cases are perhaps easy to consider because they represent end points on a continuum ranging from high to low probability of borrowing strength. Systematically analyzing these end points and others occupying intermediate locations along this continuum would be one way to better understand the forces that motivate entrepreneurs as they build their agendas.

A second question would be: Can the borrowing strength model incorporate local governments into its framework? I believe the short answer to this question is, "yes." In this book, my own substantive interests moved me to focus on federal-state relationships in education. The important developments in K–12 education policy that have shaped the American education agenda have emerged primarily from activities in state capitals and Washington, DC. It made much sense to focus my analytical lens on those two levels of government to describe these changes.

An additional reason for my focus is that, formally speaking, local governments are technically creatures of the states. In designing the U.S. Constitution, the nation's founders obsessed over the proper relationship between the national government and the states, but they opined no specific role for local governments in the system. That formal view of federalism and the importance of the federal-state interactions uncovered in previous chapters does not mean, however, that officials at those levels are the only ones who borrow strength. Local governments remain critically important players in the United States (Burns 1994; O'Toole 2000a). It was for that reason that I developed the borrowing strength model using a tight collection of general concepts and basic processes that in principle one could apply to governments at all levels. In fact, I believe that subsequent empirical studies that include local governments would actually support my basic claims. Let me illustrate what I mean by briefly returning to education policy and discussing one general and one specific example.

Reflecting on the explosion of state policy in the education reform decade of the 1980s, Elmore and Fuhrman (1990, 155) have addressed the claim that state efforts during this time would mean "traditions of local control of education would finally die." That prediction was incorrect, Elmore and Fuhrman argued, because "evidence on the implementation of the reforms suggests that local policymakers were just as active as state policymakers in generating initiatives. Far from a zero-sum game, state and local relations in education resemble a basketball game where everyone on the starting team, as well as on the bench, scores in double figures." The overall environment, which Elmore and Fuhrman characterized as "governance busyness," produced more, not less, local activity and potential power for local governments. Reflecting on the same period, Odden and Marsh (1990, 177) agreed by noting that the local response to state reform "was characterized more by 'strategic interaction' with state reform direction, both in responding to and affecting the content of state policy locally." Those patterns persisted into the 1990s (Mintrom and Vergari 1997, 152). Some have argued that with the coming of NCLB, local school boards, for example, have seen their actual power whither and their futures become uncertain (Howell 2005). A key factor determining those futures will be how school board members, superintendents, and other local policy entrepreneurs maneuver in this environment. Events from Philadelphia, in fact, illustrate how federal education law can provide these policy entrepreneurs with opportunities to borrow strength to advance their own agendas.

As noted in chapter 6, NCLB requires local school districts to hire only highly qualified teachers in core subjects. But other than a federal requirement that teachers possess a college degree and content-area preparation, state certification guidelines and teacher assessments essentially define what "highly qualified" means. Some local districts attempting to eliminate teacher shortages have used NCLB's teacher requirements to push state governments to revisit their licensure laws. In Philadelphia, schools chief Paul Vallas and others successfully argued that the Pennsylvania Board of Education should consider as "highly qualified" teachers who have college degrees in their subjects but are involved in alternative certification programs. Vallas claimed that the federal act gave him leverage to argue for changing state laws to include alternative programs. With those adjustments, he would be able to draw teachers from programs such as Teach for America, as he did when he was superintendent of the Chicago Public Schools (Mezzacappa 2002).

Vallas's advocacy illustrates how local school district leaders are sometimes quite creative and savvy in defending their priorities. Here, a local leader used a federal mandate about teacher quality to gain leverage in state-level debates over teacher licensure. Clearly, by imposing its mandate, federal leaders asserted their power. However, Pennsylvania retained primary control of the licensure process and exercised that power in a way that actually helped Philadelphia leaders to advance their own agendas. These interactions reveal borrowing strength in ways that link local, state, and federal officials. Thus, describing state-local relationships in zero-sum terms would likely mischaracterize the political and policy dynamics at work, just as zero-sum portrayals of state-federal relations often miss the mark.[1]

A third question one might ask to extend the borrowing strength model would be: Does the model generalize to other policy areas? In their important study of agenda setting, Baumgartner and Jones (1993, 47) summarize the potential pitfalls of works examining single policy areas. They note how even "The best longitudinal studies [of the public agenda] have usually been limited to only a single issue. . . . No matter how well done or how theoretically informed many of these studies may be, their applicability to other areas or to other issues is easily questioned." Whether insights from my own analysis can inform research and practice in other policy areas is, thus, a relevant question.

There are several reasons why I believe this book can provide general insights for scholars and policymakers alike. Conceptually, I have stated my central claims in general terms. The processes at the core of the work—advocacy of policy entrepreneurs, positive and negative feedback, and borrowing strength—build on research that scholars of political development, agenda setting, and federalism have already considered in other policy contexts. To that extent, even though this book focuses on changes in the American education agenda, its conclusions travel beyond that domain. Consider these examples.

One application would be to use the borrowing strength model to explore changes in social welfare policy. Both welfare and education are domestic policy areas, which would likely facilitate fruitful comparisons between them. But compared to education, because federal and state governments share much more of the budgetary and programmatic responsibilities in welfare—Medicaid is a big ticket item for both levels of government, for example (Holahan, Weil, and Wiener 2003), the model would be forced to perform in a much different context. As a general strategy for extending the model, seeking policy areas with different configurations of federal and state funding would help identify other areas to explore.

A second application would be to consider policies such as environmental protection or workplace safety. Federal and state governments play roles in both areas, obviously, but these areas tend to involve different tools of government. Unlike education and welfare, governments tend to rely less on grants and more on social and economic regulation to achieve their environmental and workplace safety objectives (Salamon 2002). It would be interesting to examine how the borrowing strength model performs in policy areas dominated by tools of government other than grants, and in areas that combine a relatively balanced mix of several different tools.

Scholars and analysts of social welfare, environmental policy, and workplace safety may quibble with some of the conjectures I have presented here. My point is not to tell researchers in these fields that their theoretical or empirical approaches need major overhauls. Rather, my goal is to invite these experts to consider the borrowing strength model as a way to understand how federalism and agenda setting interact to produce policy and political results in several different fields. Examining my claims in more areas will help to sharpen the model and test its versatility. It will also help knowledge—rather than more metaphors of federalism or stand-alone case studies of agenda setting—to accumulate because the borrowing strength model is organized around a generic set of basic concepts. That result would avoid some of the less useful tendencies in previous work that other scholars of federalism (Anton 1989) and agenda setting (Baumgartner and Jones 1993) have identified.

FUNDAMENTAL CLAIMS ABOUT AGENDA SETTING IN A
FEDERAL SYSTEM

This book began with two questions. If states and localities are the primary care-takers of K–12 education, how have federal policymakers so expanded their reach into the country's schools since 1965, the year the first ESEA became law? And, more generally, how does the American federal system create opportunities for policymakers across the country to advance their agendas even in areas where they may struggle to wield influence?

It was puzzling over the first question that moved me to consider the second. Like many people who had analyzed federal education policy (Sundquist 1968; Thomas 1975; Finn 1977; Kaestle and Smith 1982; Thomas 1983; Graham 1984; Brademas 1987), I began by assuming that machinations inside the Washington Beltway would provide answers about how the nation's education agenda had changed since 1965. Federalism and state policy entered the analysis only after prodding from other researchers, doing additional reading, and, most important, talking with people who have worked to craft government education agendas through the years.

Energized by the analytical possibilities federalism seemed to offer, I returned to the library to see how scholars of agenda setting had described federalism's in-fluence on policy and political agendas in the United States. The silence was deaf-ening. While scholars sometimes recognized federalism's importance, they typically either ignored it (Riker 1993; Light 1999); acknowledged it but suggested it was a highly complex topic that future scholars should examine (Kingdon 1995); or explored it but organized their arguments around zero-sum character-izations of the American compound republic (Baumgartner and Jones 1993) that federalism scholars had criticized but, unfortunately, had not tackled with sharp theorizing. With this as the state of the art, the overall theoretical and empirical challenges of my research project became clear: to integrate in general terms what scholars knew about federalism and agenda setting and then to use those insights to explain dynamics in the American education agenda. My efforts have produced several major claims about federalism and agenda setting in the United States. I conclude with the following main ideas.

The United States is a compound republic. This is perhaps too obvious to state, but it bears repeating because the claim is so fundamental to any understanding of how the country's government works. The American political system is composed of much more than national institutions and the groups and voters that pressure them. Leaders in Washington, DC, can wield great power, but they remain funda-mentally weak in several policy areas. Thus, one should not neglect the important ways that state governments and federalism can influence policy and political agendas. The states' emergence as increasingly professional and capable actors is perhaps the most frequently overlooked fact of American political development in the last fifty years.

Recognizing more explicitly the interconnectedness of federal and state policymakers is useful because it will help scholars remember that American federalism is a dynamic system. It will also help them produce more complete models of policymaking, agenda setting, and the development of the American state. Policymakers themselves will be able to improve their efforts by regularly reminding themselves that their work is intimately connected to the efforts and agendas emanating from elsewhere. To conclude glibly that "those folks in Washington are just out of touch" or that "the states are laggards" may make policymakers feel good as they vent frustrations with one another. But those views are simplistic and ignore the diverse sets of pressures that exist and shape agendas across the compound republic. Policymakers can complain, for sure, but they should not lose sight of that larger reality.

Agendas take shape when policy entrepreneurs mobilize license and capacity to promote government interest and involvement in a policy area. This sentence summarizes the basic model of agenda setting that has organized this book. Agendas are not self-generating. Governments become interested and involved in certain areas because policy entrepreneurs agitate for their interests and sometimes succeed. Those entrepreneurs can anticipate more success promoting an agenda if they possess license to justify a government's interest and involvement and if they can mobilize government capacities to take concrete action.

For scholars of agenda setting, these claims should not be controversial because they build upon conceptualizations other researchers have considered. Policymakers, as well, likely recognize the need to muster claims and capabilities if they hope to promote agendas in favored areas. Even though the model I outline in chapter 2 is relatively straightforward, it represents an important advance because it provides a way to capture federalism's flexibility and link agenda setting processes across levels of government. The next claim illustrates how.

Policy entrepreneurs can build their agendas by borrowing strength from other levels of government to ameliorate their license or capacity deficits. The allocation of labor in the American compound republic and formal divisions between governments create constraints that can limit policy entrepreneurs as they try to promote their agendas. In short, federalism can be a source of negative feedback that stifles agenda development. However, the system's structure can also promote positive feedback processes that expand agendas. Borrowing strength is the mechanism that entrepreneurs at one level of government can use to leverage arguments and capabilities from another. American federalism is important, then, and not simply because it allows entrepreneurs to shop for new venues if they experience defeat, as previous scholarly treatments of agenda setting have shown. Instead, these entrepreneurs can continue building agendas in their present location if they successfully borrow license or capacity from somewhere else. Overall, the concept of borrowing strength is theoretically appealing because it identifies a clear but generic mechanism to explain how feedback processes can play out and influence agendas across levels of government. Thus, there is no need to construct new metaphors or build separate models for federal, state, and local arenas. Many behaviors across these levels are consistent with the single model I have proposed.

The generality of the borrowing strength model of agenda setting can also provide insights for policymakers. The model helps to reveal possible strategies they can use to circumvent obstacles as they promote their ideas. Borrowing strength also encourages them to think more comprehensively about their location in the American federal system and to appreciate the strategies and tactics other policy entrepreneurs employ to promote or attenuate agenda development. Finally, because public officials commonly have careers at different levels of government and in nongovernmental organizations, a generic model of agenda setting provides a powerful analytical device these individuals can use as they develop their own strategies and tactics to defend their favored ideas.

Federal and state officials face great challenges and potential risks when they attempt to borrow strength from one another. Even though borrowing strength offers a way for policy entrepreneurs to build agendas, seeking leverage from another level of government is neither easy nor without potential costs. Theoretically, this means there likely exist systematic reasons why borrowing strength would be more likely to occur in some instances and policy areas than others. As I noted in the previous section, that would be one area for future researchers to consider more deeply.

The challenges associated with borrowing strength should remind federal policymakers that capable leadership and intrusive bumbling are essentially two sides of the same coin. Borrowing strength that properly leverages arguments or capabilities emanating from the states can create synergies that generate major successes. At the same time, though, attempting to borrow state strengths that seem apparent but actually do not exist can produce costly losses. A general rule of thumb this book implies would be for federal officials to borrow strength only when they can accurately assesses and ably leverage state license and capacity. If these conditions hold, federal officials should enjoy political and policy success. However, attempting to borrow strength that does not exist or borrowing ineffectively by identifying an inappropriate leverage point can create political and policy disasters for federal officials. In the process they may hamstring or derail promising state initiatives. Collectively, evaluating state license and capacity, identifying key points of influence, and then borrowing effectively are all easier said than done. Federal policy entrepreneurs need to proceed with caution.

State-level policy entrepreneurs face their own challenges and risks associated with borrowing strength. Leveraging federal license and capacity to propel state agendas forward can facilitate greater federal involvement in their affairs than state officials may desire. Federal officials may misinterpret or overinterpret advances from state policymakers and push subsequent federal agendas that move states in directions that governors, state legislators, career officials, and those outside of government neither anticipated nor desired. As many state entrepreneurs recognize, federal and state agendas do not always move together in harmony. State officials must remember that borrowing strength may help them promote their agendas, but in the end it can sometimes create more problems than the effort is worth.

The American compound republic is not a zero-sum system. Developments in American federalism and changes in policy agendas have produced more than simply new arrangements of public authority in the United States. Apparent oscillations between the aggrandizement of power in Washington, DC, during the New Deal or the decentralization of authority to states with devolution during the 1990s make it tempting to study federalism's progressive march from one era to the next. That focus can be useful because identifying central tendencies associated with particular periods is a valuable pursuit. However, seeing gains at one level of government as necessarily corresponding to losses at another is too narrow a view of American federalism. In the short run, agenda changes may increase powers for some governments and decrease them for others, but over time creative policy entrepreneurs across the system can leverage these changes to promote their own priorities. The result can be new powers and expanded agendas across levels of government instead of zero-sum trade-offs between them. Generations of scholars have sometimes explicitly recognized that American federalism is not always a zero-sum system (Grodzins 1966; Beer 1978; Elazar 1984). But until now, nobody has offered a theory that captures the system's zero-sum and non–zero-sum features, even though some have urged others to try (Zimmerman 1992, 2001).

Probing how American federalism can encourage negotiation and power expansions across levels of government rather than focusing on models designed to highlight trade-offs within the system provides opportunities for future scholars, given that more and more policy areas have intergovernmental dimensions. Additionally, state policymakers should not feel helpless when confronting federal laws that seem overbearing; and federal officials should spend more time pondering why states sometimes do not follow federal mandates as expected. Laws and regulations, be they federal or state, are rarely the last word on a matter. They frequently open rather than close discussion about what items should be on a government's agenda and about what are the most appropriate ways to achieve desirable social outcomes.

As federal-state cooperation has emerged in education and other areas, state officials have not meekly followed assertive leaders in Washington who offer incentives that encourage states to cooperate. Policy entrepreneurs in the states have shaped cooperative arrangements to conform to their own agenda preferences, even as policy entrepreneurs in Washington have seen their own agendas expand in new ways. Sometimes, growing federal agendas and the institutions they produce can stifle state ambitions. But as the evidence in this book shows, at other times, states have used an assertive federal government to push their own agendas and prerogatives.

OVERALL, BY BRINGING TOGETHER SCHOLARSHIP ON FEDERALISM AND agenda setting, this book provides a theoretically driven argument to explain how American federalism can foster and hinder agenda change. Across the analysis, I have tried to address two broad groups in particular: scholars of federalism and agenda setting and people interested in American education policy. These groups are important because, collectively, they have attempted to answer two of the most challenging questions that democracies such as the United States regularly confront: How should political communities decide which issues deserve the most attention and public resources? And, how can a society provide its children with opportunities to receive an outstanding education? I can think of few questions that deserve greater attention than these. With any luck, this book has provided insights about both.

NOTE

1. It is also worth mentioning that Vallas has used NCLB to advance his priorities in local debates with Philadelphia's teacher union (Manna 2006). Recall that NCLB's overall objective is to increase math and reading achievement and to reduce achievement gaps between disadvantaged and more advantaged students. That focus has put pressure on union leaders who have tried to resist moves that would undermine seniority as a key factor determining teacher assignments. Superintendents like Vallas and Boston's Thomas Payzant (Manna 2006) have used concerns about achievement gaps to argue that district leaders need more flexibility to assign their best teachers to schools that need them most.

Appendix

In this appendix, I describe in detail my primary data sources. I invite interested readers to contact me with additional questions about the data or my analysis.

INTERVIEWS

The sixty elite interviews I completed for this book involved members of the education policy community in Washington, DC. Except for a couple of phone interviews, I conducted all interviews in person. The interviews themselves occurred between April 2001 and May 2002 with some brief follow-up conversations and e-mail exchanges with a handful of respondents between 2003 and 2005. Table A.1 identifies my respondents and their affiliations at the time of my initial interview with each one.

Because I was interested in changes in the American education agenda across time and in recent years, I attempted to identify respondents who had a long-term view and who were more knowledgeable about the details of contemporary events; some respondents provided both perspectives. Overall, as categorized in tables A.2, A.3, and A.4, the respondents brought a range of policy expertise and knowledge to the interviews. Collectively, the people I interviewed spoke from a variety of professional and political points of view. Fifteen of my respondents had worked on education policy issues for less than five years, but twenty-one had worked with such issues for longer than two decades. I also achieved a partisan balance by interviewing a relatively equal number of respondents who had experience working for Republicans or for Democrats in addition to a large number of respondents whose work was not affiliated with a partisan group. Several, as table A.3 shows, worked in multiple positions, both inside government—at the federal, state, and sometimes local levels—and outside.

After beginning with a handful of key contacts, I built my list of respondents using a snowball technique. Typically, my last question in each interview was, "Are there other people you would suggest I contact about my research?" As my year of interviews progressed, many names my respondents offered were people that I had already inter-

TABLE A.I
Interview respondents

Respondent	Position at Time of Interview
Gordon Ambach	Executive Director (Retired), CCSSO
John Barth	Acting Executive Director, NEGP
Buzz Bartlett	President and Chief Executive Officer, Council for Basic Education
Lisa Bos	Education Reform Project Director, Republican Study Committee, U.S. House
Michael Cohen	Senior Fellow, Aspen Institute
Christopher Cross	Immediate Past President and Chief Executive Officer, Council for Basic Education
Charles Edwards	Senior Editor, *Title I Monitor* and *Title I Handbook*
Amanda Farris	Professional Staff Member, Committee on Health, Education, Labor, and Pensions (Republican staff), U.S. Senate
Elizabeth Fay	Legislative Assistant, Sen. Evan Bayh (D-IN)
Chester Finn	President, Thomas B. Fordham Foundation
Milton Goldberg	Executive Vice President, NAB
Siobhan Gorman	Reporter, *National Journal*
Mark Graul	Chief of Staff, Rep. Mark Green (R-WI)
Dana Gray	Legislative Assistant, Rep. Lynn Rivers (D-MI)
David Griffith	Director of Governmental and Public Affairs, NASBE
Kara Haas	Legislative Assistant, Rep. Michael Castle (R-DE)
Samuel Halperin	Founder and Senior Fellow, American Youth Policy Forum
Janet Hansen	Vice President and Director of Education Studies, Committee for Economic Development
Kati Haycock	Director, The Education Trust
Carnie Hayes	Director of Federal-State Relations, CCSSO
Bruce Hunter	Associate Executive Director for Public Policy, AASA
Nathalia Jaramillo	Consultant, Council of the Great City Schools
John "Jack" Jennings	Founder and Director, Center on Education Policy
Craig Jerald	Senior Policy Analyst, The Education Trust
Krista Kafer	Senior Policy Analyst, Heritage Foundation
Michael Kennedy	Legislative Assistant, Rep. Thomas Petri (R-WI)
Victor Klatt	Vice President, Van Scoyoc Associates
Erika Lestelle	Legislative Assistant, Rep. Bob Schaffer (R-CO)
Dane Linn	Director of the Education Policy Studies Division, Center for Best Practices, NGA
Sally Lovejoy	Director of Education and Human Resources Policy, Committee on Education and the Workforce (Republican staff), U.S. House

TABLE A.I (*continued*)

Respondent	Position at Time of Interview
Jay Mathews	Staff Writer, *Washington Post*
Jeff Mazur	Legislative Assistant, Rep. Ron Kind (D-WI)
Denzel McGuire	Professional Staff Member, Committee on Health, Education, Labor, and Pensions (Republican staff), U.S. Senate
Alex Medler	Acting Director, Public Charter Schools Program, U.S. Department of Education
Alex Nock	Legislative Associate, Committee on Education and the Workforce (Democratic staff), U.S. House
Billie Jo Orr	President, ELC
Joel Packer	Lobbyist, NEA
Shawn Pfaff	Graduate Student, La Follette School of Public Affairs, University of Wisconsin
Jacqueline Raphael	Research Associate, Education Policy Center, Urban Institute
Diane Stark Rentner	Associate Director, Center on Education Policy
Michael Resnick	Associate Executive Director, National School Boards Association
Andrew Rotherham	Director, 21st Century Schools Project, Progressive Policy Institute
Jorge Ruiz-de-Velasco	Research Associate, Education Policy Center, Urban Institute
Cheryl Sattler	Editor, *Title I Monitor* and *Title I Handbook*
David Shreve	Program and Committee Director for Education, Labor, and Job Training, NCSL
Mike Sommers	Legislative Director, Rep. John Boehner (R-OH)
Gerald Sroufe	Director of Government Relations, American Educational Research Association
Michele Stockwell	Legislative Assistant, Sen. Joseph Lieberman (D-CT)
Kathleen Strottman	Legislative Assistant, Sen. Mary Landrieu (D-LA)
Gerald Tirozzi	Executive Director, National Association of Secondary School Principals
Thomas Toch	Writer in Residence, National Center on Education and the Economy
Susan Traiman	Director, Education Initiative, BRT
Michael Usdan	Senior Fellow, Institute for Educational Leadership
Dustin Valerius	Education Policy Analyst, ELC
Courtney Weise	Legislative Director, Rep. Jim DeMint (R-SC)
Arthur Wise	President, National Council for Accreditation of Teacher Education
Donna Wong	Budget Analyst, Congressional Budget Office

Note: Three additional respondents wished to remain anonymous. All legislative assistants had education policy as one of their responsibilities.

TABLE A.2
Position of interview respondents at time of interview

Position	N	%
Federal government		
Executive branch	1	1.7
Congressional staff	20	33.3
Other	1	1.7
Extragovernmental representing		
State groups	7	11.7
Local government groups	4	6.7
Business	3	5.0
Research and think tanks	16	26.7
Other	3	5.0
Media	4	6.7
Other	1	1.7
Total number of respondents	(60)	

viewed, which reassured me that I had identified several of the key people who were knowledgeable about my subject.

The interviews ranged in length, but most lasted approximately forty minutes. I also asked each respondent if I could identify him or her by name in the work. All respondents were given the opportunity to talk off the record at any time. I took handwritten notes and, immediately after the interview when possible, typed them up to reconstruct a transcript of the discussion.

Substantively, the interviews could best be described as loosely open-ended. Each began with me providing a brief overview of the research project. I then guided the discussion through a series of general topics, which I organized around the following five questions: (1) Why do you think K–12 education has become such an important issue for policymakers and elected officials in Washington? (2) How have policymakers in Washington attempted to gain influence in education, given that they provide such a small proportion of the money for it? (3) How would you describe the relationship between the federal government and the states on education policy? (4) What do you think about developments on education in the Republican Party? What about those that arose, in particular, during the 2000 election cycle? What about the Democratic Party? (5) Where do you think federal education policy is headed?

While these substantive questions provided an initial roadmap for entering the interviews, I asked several different follow-up questions to pursue interesting lines of discussion and to tap each respondents' particular expertise. For example, my discussions with representatives of the business community focused on the development of business interests in education and the efforts of business leaders in states and Wash-

TABLE A.3
Work experience of interview respondents

A. Years working in education	N	%
Less than 5	15	25.0
5 to 10	10	16.7
11 to 20	5	8.3
21 to 30	10	16.7
More than 30	11	18.3
Not ascertained	9	15.0
B. Previous positions in education	**N**	**%**
Federal government		
Executive branch	14	23.3
Congressional staff	12	20.0
State government	9	15.0
Local government	3	5.0
Extragovernmental organization	18	30.0
Educator (K–12 or higher education)	19	31.7
No previous position in education	13	21.7
Total number of respondents	(60)	

Note: The percentages in part B do not add to 100 because respondents could be coded into multiple categories if they held multiple prior positions in education.

ington, DC. Many of my meetings with current congressional staffers centered on the politics and policy issues of the moment. And sometimes I addressed several specific issues with people who were directly involved in particular events or chains of events that interested me, such as the development of *A Nation at Risk* or the Charlottesville summit and its aftermath.

CODING RULES FOR EDUCATION CONTENT

I worked with several different data sets to capture the education content of presidential speeches, congressional hearings, public laws, party platforms, and political advertisements in presidential elections. To allow for substantive comparisons across these data sets and to facilitate consistency in the coding, I applied the same coding rules to all data sets whenever possible. Given the nature of these data sources, which I describe

TABLE A.4
Partisan affiliations of interview respondents

A. In position at time of interview	N	%	
Works for Republican	11	18.3	
Works for Democrat	8	13.3	
Work is not affiliated with a party	41	68.3	
B. In previous positions in education	N	%	
Worked for Republican	8	13.3	
Worked for Democrat	11	18.3	
Worked for Republicans and Democrats	2	3.3	
Work was not affiliated with a party	16	26.7	
Not ascertained	10	16.7	
No previous position in education	13	21.7	
Total number of respondents		(60)	

in more detail momentarily, I applied the coding rules to different units of analysis across each data set.

I settled upon a final set of variables and coding rules after several trial runs using draft coding schemes and consulting with other researchers who had experience developing and using content coding rules. The final list of variables is as follows: *(1) emphasis:* the extent to which the item (i.e., a sentence in a presidential speech or party platform, a congressional hearing, or a political advertisement) referred to education; *(2) level:* the level of education (i.e., pre-kindergarten up through higher education) identified in the item; *(3) agent:* the entity identified in the item, if any, that was involved in the development, production, or execution of education policy; *(4) tone:* if identified, whether the agent was described in a positive, negative, or neutral way; and *(5) policy area:* the specific education policy area, if any, that the item addressed.

To test the reliability of the rules that accompanied each variable, I had a second person code a random sample (10 percent) of cases from my presidential speeches data set. I trained this coder, a graduate student in political science, on how to apply the coding rules. On independent passes with this sample of cases, the coder and I agreed 89 percent of the time on the emphasis variable; 89 percent on level; 76 percent on agent; 84 percent on tone; and 70 percent on policy area. After ensuing discussions of the items, the levels of agreement generally increased. The wider discrepancy on the policy area variable reflects, in part, the large number of possible content codes for that variable (see table 3.3, for example) and the fact that this second coder was not an education policy expert. Given these limitations, I felt that the level of agreement was strong, especially on the emphasis and level variables, which I relied on most heavily in previous chapters.

PRESIDENTIAL SPEECHES

The major presidential speeches I analyzed came from various editions of the *Public Papers of the Presidents* from 1961 to 2000. State of the Union messages and inaugural addresses comprised the vast majority of the speeches I considered. In a few instances, however, I coded other speeches that emulated these addresses—for example, Lyndon Johnson's "Address Before a Joint Session of Congress on November 27, 1963," which he delivered as he took office after John Kennedy's assassination (paralleling an inaugural address), and George H. W. Bush's "Address before a Joint Session of Congress on February 9, 1989" (paralleling a State of the Union address). I chose not to code Richard Nixon's 1973 State of the Union message due to its unusual format (rather than delivering the State of the Union as a single speech, in 1973 Nixon transmitted it to Congress in a series of six lengthy written messages, a format that rendered the item not comparable to the others in this series). I also double-counted two years, 1969 and 1977, because speeches by presidents of different political parties overlapped in purpose during these years: in 1969, exiting president Lyndon Johnson presented a State of the Union speech while incoming president Richard Nixon delivered an inaugural; the same scenario occurred in 1977 with Gerald Ford and Jimmy Carter. Separating out Republicans from Democrats within a single year, and thus double-counting, was needed to complete the regression analyses presented in table 5.2.

Substantively, I read all speeches for education content and singled out sentences that addressed education in some way. Thus, the individual sentence served as the unit of analysis. I then coded each sentence using the variables described in the previous section: emphasis, level, agent, tone, and policy area.

CONGRESSIONAL HEARINGS AND PUBLIC LAWS

Data on congressional hearings and public laws came from the Policy Agendas Project at the University of Washington's Center for American Politics and Public Policy. These data were originally collected by Frank R. Baumgartner and Bryan D. Jones with the support of National Science Foundation grant number SBR-9320922. Neither the National Science Foundation nor the original collectors of the data bear any responsibility for the analysis included in this book. I owe special thanks to Bryan Jones and his team of assistants who have always gone the extra mile to answer questions I encountered as I used these data. Full documentation on the original data sets is available from the website of the Policy Agendas Project. It may also be found in Baumgartner and Jones (1993) and Baumgartner and Jones (2002b).

Each observation in the congressional hearings data set, which contains more than 74,000 cases, is a single hearing. Each observation in the public laws data set, which contains approximately 17,000 cases, is a specific public law. From these comprehensive collections of hearings and public laws, I developed a search algorithm to capture a pool of possible cases for my analysis. My search strategy paralleled approaches other authors have employed to analyze data from the Policy Agendas Project (Baumgartner and Jones 2002b). I would be glad to share the details of this algorithm with interested readers; they are also described in the appendix of my Ph.D. dissertation (Manna 2003).

I applied my education content coding scheme for the emphasis and level variables to these hearings and public laws. I chose not to try to code my other variables to avoid generating codes that would contain significant measurement error. To accurately code for my other variables would have required me to read in great detail the actual hearings transcripts and public laws. The sheer number of cases involved made that approach intractable.

To ensure accurate coding of the emphasis and level variables, I made extensive use of the congressional hearings abstracts available in Lexis-Nexis, the descriptions of public laws that appear in each year of *CQ Almanac*, and the topic descriptions from the original Policy Agendas Project data sets. In particular, the hearings abstracts were quite good and contained content descriptors, short summaries of testimony, and witness affiliations, all of which helped me to apply my education content codes. Unfortunately, even with the abstracts in hand and after experimenting with some coding probes, I concluded that I did not have enough information to apply the education codes for variables other than emphasis and level.

Finally, let me offer two additional clarifications. As of this writing, the public laws time series of the Policy Agendas Project ended at the year 1998. To obtain data on 1999 and 2000, I used the public laws search engine of the Thomas website, http://thomas.loc.gov/, and identified all public laws passed in those two years. Scanning the summaries of each law, I was able to identify relevant laws that enabled me to extend the time series in figures 3.2 and 4.2 up through 2000. Also, to avoid biasing upward the counts of hearings and public laws, I omitted hearings and public laws that dealt exclusively with the operations of the Washington, DC, Public School System (subtopic code 2014 in the Policy Agendas Project documentation). That was appropriate because these hearings parallel the actions of a local school board and typically have little to do with whether education is rising or falling on the national political and policy agendas.

PRESIDENTIAL CAMPAIGN ADVERTISEMENTS

The data to produce figure 3.3 are from John Geer's coding of advertisements from the Julian P. Kanter Political Commercial Archive at the University of Oklahoma. I am grateful to Geer, who has made these data available and has answered my questions about them. Full documentation for the original data is available in Geer (1998a). Geer bears no responsibility for the interpretations or use of the data that appear in this book.

Each observation in the Geer data set is a single advertisement produced for a general election campaign. I used Geer's comprehensive list of content codes to identify a subset of these advertisements for analysis. Then I applied my own coding rules using only my level variable to analyze the ads. Lacking the actual advertisements, I was not confident I could accurately apply my coding rules for the other variables.

I decided to omit two of Geer's content categories that, at first glance, looked like possible candidates for my analysis: code 374, "cares about programs for kids/school lunch program," and code 319, "supports research." I omitted those categories after consulting with Geer, who indicated that category 374 coded generally for children's programs, not exclusively school lunches. Similarly, category 319 may have included research regarding K–12 education, research at colleges and universities, and other sorts of research issues not connected to education. Omitting these categories seemed prudent because they were not as clearly and exclusively about education as the others. I would be glad to provide interested readers the complete list of categories I used to identify the collection of advertisements I coded. That list is also available in Manna (2003).

The data to produce analyses of advertisements in the 2000 presidential election (the results appear in table 3.1) come from the Wisconsin Advertising Project (WiscAds) at the University of Wisconsin Department of Political Science. The project is supported by grants from the Pew Charitable Trusts under the direction of Kenneth Goldstein. Neither Pew nor the original collectors of the data bear any responsibility for the analysis included in this book. For additional information on the original database, readers should consult the WiscAds website located at http://www.polisci.wisc.edu/tvadvertising/Index.htm.

In 2000, the WiscAds team analyzed political campaign advertisements run on broadcast and cable television stations in the top seventy-five media markets in the United States. The advertisements came to the team in the form of storyboards and accompanying frequency data that were furnished by the Campaign Media Analysis Group, which uses an advanced satellite technology, originally designed by the United States Navy to track Soviet submarines, to capture advertisements from the airwaves and generate the storyboards. Each storyboard contains snapshots, at four-second intervals, of the visual images in the ad as well as a complete transcript of the spoken words in the entire ad. The frequency data capture the number of times each individual advertisement, as represented in a single storyboard, is aired.

Consulting with WiscAds researchers, I obtained all storyboards from 2000 that represented individual advertisements run by either the Bush or Gore campaigns or the Republican National Committee or Democratic National Committee on the candidates' behalf. Using the advertisement as the unit of analysis, I applied my education content coding rules for the variables previously mentioned: emphasis, level, agent, tone, and policy area. Additionally, I used the WiscAds frequency data to calculate the number of times each advertisement hit the airwaves during the campaign.

MOST IMPORTANT PROBLEM SERIES

Data to produce the 1960 to 2000 series describing education as one of the most important problems facing the nation (figure 1.1) came from election-year surveys of public opinion conducted by the National Election Studies at the University of Michigan. These data are based on work supported by the National Science Foundation under grant numbers SBR-9707741, SBR-9317631, SES-9209410, SES-9009379, SES-8808361, SES-8341310, SES-8207580, and SOC77-08885. Any opinions, findings, and conclusions or recommendations expressed in this book are my own and do not necessarily reflect those of the National Science Foundation or the National Election Studies. For interested researchers, I would be happy to provide the recode commands I used to prepare these data for analysis. Finally, I should note that the wording of the most important problem questions varies slightly across some of the surveys I examined. Interested readers can contact me or consult the National Election Studies codebooks, available at http://www.umich.edu/~nes/, for details on these minor differences.

References

Abramson, Paul R., John H. Aldrich, and David W. Rohde. 2002. *Change and continuity in the 2000 elections.* Washington, DC: CQ Press.

Agranoff, Robert, and Michael McGuire. 2001. American federalism and the search for models of management. *Public Administration Review* 61 (6):671–81.

Aldrich, John H., John L. Sullivan, and Eugene Borgida. 1993. Foreign affairs and issue voting: Do presidential candidates "waltz before a blind audience"? In *Controversies in voting behavior,* eds. R. G. Niemi and H. F. Weisberg. Washington, DC: CQ Press.

Allison, Graham T. 1971. *Essence of decision: Explaining the Cuban missile crisis.* New York: HarperCollins.

Alvarez, Lizette. 2001a. Bush's education plan taps an unlikely source, Lieberman. *New York Times,* January 23.

———. 2001b. House Democrats block voucher provision. *New York Times,* May 3.

———. 2001c. Senate takes on Bush's education bill as some conservatives grumble. *New York Times,* May 2.

American Federation of Teachers. 2001. Making standards matter: A fifty-state report on efforts to implement a standards-based system. Washington, DC: American Federation of Teachers.

Anton, Thomas J. 1989. *American federalism and public policy: How the system works.* New York: Random House.

Arnold, R. Douglas. 1990. *The logic of congressional action.* New Haven, CT: Yale University Press.

Associated Press. 2001a. Report: States cutting education. *CNN.com,* November 19. http://www.cnn.com (accessed November 21, 2001).

———. 2001b. Testing could cost states as much as $7 billion. *USA Today,* May 10. http://www.USAToday.com (accessed May 18, 2001).

Bacharach, Samuel B., ed. 1990. *Education reform: Making sense of it all.* Needham Heights, MA: Allyn and Bacon.

Bachrach, Peter, and Morton Baratz. 1962. The two faces of power. *American Political Science Review* 56 (4):947–52.

Baumgartner, Frank R., and Bryan D. Jones. 1993. *Agendas and instability in American politics.* Chicago: University of Chicago Press.

———. 2002a. Positive and negative feedback in politics. In *Policy dynamics,* eds. F. R. Baumgartner and B. D. Jones. Chicago: University of Chicago Press.

————, eds. 2002b. *Policy dynamics.* Chicago: University of Chicago Press.

Baumgartner, Frank R., and Beth L. Leech. 1998. *Basic interests: The importance of groups in politics and in political science.* Princeton, NJ: Princeton University Press.

Beamer, Glenn. 1999. *Creative politics: Taxes and public goods in a federal system.* Ann Arbor, MI: University of Michigan Press.

Becker, Jo, and Rosalind S. Helderman. 2004. VA seeks to leave Bush law behind. *Washington Post,* January 24.

Beer, Samuel H. 1978. Federalism, nationalism, and democracy in America. *American Political Science Review* 72 (1):9–21.

Bell, Derrick, ed. 1980. *Shades of brown: New perspectives on school desegregation.* New York: Teachers College Press.

Bell, Terrell H. 1988. *The thirteenth man: A Reagan cabinet memoir.* New York: The Free Press.

Bennett, William J., Lisa Graham Keegan, Chester E. Finn Jr., and Krista Kafer. 2001. Memo to House and Senate ESEA conferees and congressional leaders re: Recommendations for improving ESEA legislation. October 3.

Berke, Joel S., and Michael W. Kirst. 1972. Intergovernmental relations: Conclusions and recommendations. In *Federal aid to education: Who benefits? Who governs?,* eds. J. S. Berke and M. W. Kirst. Lexington, MA: Lexington Books.

Berkman, Michael B. 1993. *The state roots of national politics: Congress and the tax agenda, 1978–1986.* Pittsburgh: University of Pittsburgh Press.

Birkland, Thomas A. 1997. *After disaster: Agenda setting, public policy, and focusing events.* Washington, DC: Georgetown University Press.

Blum, Justin. 2001. Bush touts education plan at DC school. *Washington Post,* January 25. http://www.washingtonpost.com (accessed February 15, 2001).

Borman, Geoffrey D., Samuel C. Stringfield, and Robert E. Slavin, eds. 2001. *Title I: Compensatory education at the crossroads.* Mahwah, NJ: Lawrence Erlbaum.

Bowling, Cynthia J., and Deil S. Wright. 1998. Change and continuity in state administration: Administrative leadership across four decades. *Public Administration Review* 58 (5):429–44.

Boyd, William Lowe. 1990. How to reform schools without half trying: Secrets of the Reagan administration. In *Education reform: Making sense of it all,* ed. S. B. Bacharach. Needham Heights, MA: Allyn and Bacon.

Brademas, John. 1987. *The politics of education.* Norman, OK: University of Oklahoma Press.

Broder, David S. 1995. Just plain dumb. *Washington Post,* August 2.

————. 2001a. Long road to reform. *Washington Post,* December 17.

————. 2001b. Salvaging real education reform. *Washington Post,* July 15.

Bruni, Frank. 2000. The 2000 campaign: The Texas governor; after convention, Bush chides Gore for divisive tone. *New York Times,* August 19.

Budge, Ian, and Richard I. Hofferbert. 1990. Mandates and policy outputs: U.S. Party platforms and federal expenditures. *American Political Science Review* 84:111–32.

Burns, Nancy. 1994. *The formation of American local governments: Private values in public institutions.* New York: Oxford University Press.

Bush, George W. 2001. No child left behind. Washington, DC: The White House.

Campaign Media Analysis Group. 2000. 2000 presidential election. *The CMAG Eye,* November/December, 36.

Campbell, Angus, Philip E. Converse, Warren E. Miller, and Donald E. Stokes. 1960. *The American voter.* New York: John Wiley and Sons.

Campbell, Colin, S. J., and Bert A. Rockman, eds. 1991. *The Bush presidency: First appraisals.* Chatham, NJ: Chatham House Publishers.

Carter, Jimmy. 1982. *Keeping faith: Memoirs of a president.* New York: Bantam Books.

Center for Education Reform. 2005. All about charter schools. January 25. http://www.edreform.com/index.cfm?fuseAction=document&documentID=1964 (accessed June 6, 2005).

Center on Education Policy. 2002. A new federal role in education. Washington, DC: Center on Education Policy.

———. 2003. From the capital to the classroom: State and federal efforts to implement the No Child Left Behind Act. Washington, DC: Center on Education Policy.

———. 2004. From the capital to the classroom: Year 2 of the No Child Left Behind Act. Washington, DC: Center on Education Policy.

———. 2005. From the capital to the classroom: Year 3 of the No Child Left Behind Act. Washington, DC: Center on Education Policy.

Chaddock, Gail Russell. 2001. Education law biggest in 35 years. *Christian Science Monitor,* December 18. http://www.csmonitor.com/2001/1218/p1s2-usgn.html (accessed January 23, 2002).

Chamber of Commerce of the United States. 1965. Letter to members of the House of Representatives on federal aid to elementary and secondary education legislation. March 17.

Chubb, John E. 1985a. Excessive regulation: The case of federal aid to education. *Political Science Quarterly* 100 (2):287–311.

———. 1985b. The political economy of federalism. *American Political Science Review* 79 (4):994–1015.

Cibulka, James G. 2001. The changing role of interest groups in education: Nationalization and the new politics of education productivity. *Educational Policy* 15 (1):12–40.

Citizens' Commission on Civil Rights. 2001. Closing the deal: A preliminary report on state compliance with final assessment and accountability requirements under the Improving America's Schools Act of 1994. Washington, DC: Citizens' Commission on Civil Rights.

Clark, David L., and Mary Anne Amiot. 1981. The impact of the Reagan administration on federal education policy. *Phi Delta Kappan,* December, 258–62.

Clymer, Adam, and Lizette Alvarez. 2001. Congress reaches compromise on education bill. *New York Times,* December 12. http://www.nytimes.com (accessed December 12, 2001).

CNN. 2005. Deadline extended for teacher aides. *CNN.com,* June 16. http://www.cnn.com (accessed June 17, 2005).

Cobb, Roger W., and Charles D. Elder. 1983. *Participation in American politics: The dynamics of agenda-building.* Baltimore: Johns Hopkins University Press.

Cohen, Michael. 1987. State boards in an era of reform. *Phi Delta Kappan,* September, 60–64.

———. 2002. Unruly crew: Lessons from the Clinton administration's attempts to cajole the states into complying with federal mandates for standards-based reform. *Education Next,* Fall, 43–47.

Coleman, John J. 1999. Unified government, divided government, and party responsiveness. *American Political Science Review* 93 (4):821–35.

Congressional Quarterly. 1966. *CQ almanac 1965.* Washington, DC: CQ Press.

———. 2000. *CQ almanac 1999.* Washington, DC: CQ Press.

Conlan, Timothy. 1998. *From new federalism to devolution: Twenty-five years of intergovernmental reform.* Washington, DC: Brookings Institution.

Council of Chief State School Officers. 2001a. Letter to House-Senate conferees on the No Child Left Behind Act. September 26.

———. 2001b. Letter to members of the House Labor, Health and Human Services, and Education Appropriations Subcommittee. September 26.

———. 2001c. Letter to senators regarding the FY 2002 ESEA labor, health and human services, and education appropriations bill. October 29.

Cross, Christopher T. 2004. *Political education: National policy comes of age.* New York: Teachers College Press.

Crowley, Michael. 2001. Teddy bear. *The New Republic,* August 2. http://www.thenewrepublic.com (accessed August 9, 2001).

Dahl, Robert A. 1956. *A preface to democratic theory.* Chicago: University of Chicago Press.

———. 1961. *Who governs? Democracy and power in an American city.* New Haven, CT: Yale University Press.

Davis, Michelle R. 2005. Utah is unlikely fly in Bush's school ointment. *Education Week,* February 9.

Davis, Michelle R., and David J. Hoff. 2005. Questions linger over NCLB policy shifts. *Education Week,* April 20.

Derthick, Martha. 1987. American federalism: Madison's middle ground in the 1980s. *Public Administration Review* 57 (1):66–74.

———. 2001. *Keeping the compound republic: Essays on American federalism.* Washington, DC: Brookings Institution.

Dillon, Sam. 2005a. "Soccer mom" education chief plays hardball. *New York Times,* April 28. http://www.nytimes.com (accessed April 28, 2005).

———. 2005b. Utah vote rejects part of education law. *New York Times,* April 20. http://www.nytimes.com (accessed April 25, 2005).

Donahue, John D. 1997. *Disunited states: What's at stake as Washington fades and the states take the lead.* New York: Basic Books.

Donohue, Tom. 2004. Opening address to the center for corporate citizenship education partnership conference. *U.S. Chamber of Commerce,* May 20. http://www.uschamber.com (accessed July 9, 2005).

Douglas, Carlyle C. 1990. A learning experience in education policy. *New York Times,* December 16.

Dow, Peter. 1991. *Schoolhouse politics: Lessons from the Sputnik era.* Cambridge, MA: Harvard University Press.

Downs, Anthony. 1972. Up and down with ecology—the "issue attention cycle." *The Public Interest* (no. 28):38–50.

Doyle, Dennis P., and Terry W. Hartle. 1985. *Excellence in education: The states take charge.* Washington, DC: American Enterprise Institute.

Educational Testing Service Policy Information Center. 1990. The education reform decade. Princeton, NJ: Educational Testing Service.

Elazar, Daniel J. 1984. *American federalism: A view from the states (3rd edition).* New York: Harper and Row.

———. 1991. Cooperative federalism. In *Competition among states and local governments: Efficiency and equity in American federalism,* eds. D. A. Kenyon and J. Kincaid. Washington, DC: Urban Institute.

Ellis, Joseph J. 2000. *Founding brothers: The revolutionary generation.* New York: Random House.

Elmore, Richard F., and Susan H. Fuhrman. 1990. The national interest and the federal role in education. *Publius* 20 (2):149–62.

Elmore, Richard F., and Milbrey W. McLaughlin. 1982. Strategic choice in federal education policy: The compliance-assistance trade-off. In *Policy making in education: Eighty-first yearbook of the national society for the study of education,* eds. A. Lieberman and M. W. McLaughlin. Chicago: University of Chicago Press.

Elmore, Richard F., and Milbrey Wallin McLaughlin. 1983. The federal role in education: Learning from experience. *Education and Urban Society* 15 (3):309–30.

Erpenbach, William J., Ellen Forte Fast, and Abigail Potts. 2003. Statewide accountability under NCLB. Washington, DC: Council of Chief State School Officers.

Evans, William N., Shelia E. Murray, and Robert M. Schwab. 1997. Schoolhouses, courthouses, and statehouses after Serrano. *Journal of Policy Analysis and Management* 16 (1):10–31.

Farkas, George, and L. Shane Hall. 2000. Can Title I attain its goal? In *Brookings papers on education policy,* ed. D. Ravitch. Washington, DC: Brookings Institution.

Fast, Ellen Forte, and William J. Erpenbach. 2004. Revisiting statewide educational accountability under NCLB. Washington, DC: Council of Chief State School Officers.

Federal News Service. 2001. Excerpt from Bush statement announcing start of his education initiative. *New York Times,* January 24.

Fellman, David, ed. 1976. *The Supreme Court and education (3rd ed.).* New York: Columbia University Press.

Fenno, Richard F., Jr. 1978. *Home style: House members in their districts.* Boston: Little, Brown and Company.

Fesler, James W., and Donald F. Kettl. 1996. *The politics of the administrative process (2nd ed.).* Chatham, NJ: Chatham House.

Finn, Chester E., Jr. 1977. *Education and the presidency.* Lexington, MA: Lexington Books.

Finn, Chester E., Jr., Andrew J. Rotherham, and Charles R. Hokanson Jr., eds. 2001. *Rethinking special education for a new century.* Washington, DC: Thomas B. Fordham Foundation and the Progressive Policy Institute.

Fiorina, Morris. 1981. *Retrospective voting in American national elections.* New Haven: Yale University Press.

Firestone, William A. 1990. Continuity and incrementalism after all: State responses to the excellence movement. In *The educational reform movement of the 1980s,* ed. J. Murphy. Berkeley, CA: McCutchan Publishing.

Fletcher, Michael A. 2001a. As stakes rise, school groups put exams to the test. *Washington Post,* July 9.

———. 2001b. Conferees agree on education package. *Washington Post,* December 12.

———. 2001c. Congress still divided on education reform. *Washington Post,* September 9.

———. 2001d. School accountability remains tough task. *Washington Post,* May 29.

Fuhrman, Susan H. 1987. Education policy: A new context for governance. *Publius* 17 (3):131–43.

———. 1994. Clinton's education policy and intergovernmental relations in the 1990s. *Publius* 24 (3):83–97.

Geer, John G. 1998a. Campaigns, party competition, and political advertising. In *Politicians and party politics,* ed. J. G. Geer. Baltimore: Johns Hopkins University Press.

190 References

ed. 1998b. *Politicians and party politics.* Baltimore: Johns Hopkins University Press.

General Accounting Office. 1994. Education finance: Extent of federal funding in state education agencies (GAO/HEHS-95-3). Washington, DC: Government Printing Office.

Gest, Justin. 2005a. No child growth proposals may stall: Some governors don't favor high school version. *Houston Chronicle,* March 1. http://www.chron.com (accessed March 3, 2005).

———. 2005b. Texas fined for no child defiance. *Houston Chronicle,* April 25. http://www.chron.com (accessed April 25, 2005).

Goertz, Margaret E. 1996. State education policy in the 1990s. In *The state of the states (3rd ed.),* ed. C. E. Van Horn. Washington, DC: CQ Press.

———. 2001. The federal role in an era of standards-based reform. In *The future of the federal role in elementary and secondary education,* ed. Center on Education Policy. Washington, DC: Center on Education Policy.

Goldberg, Milton, and Susan L. Traiman. 2001. Why business backs education standards. In *Brookings papers on education policy,* ed. D. Ravitch. Washington, DC: Brookings.

Goldstein, Amy, and Michael A. Fletcher. 2001. Bush's voucher plan liable to test hill accord. *Washington Post,* January 24.

Goldstein, Kenneth, and Travis N. Ridout. 2004. Measuring the effects of televised political advertising in the United States. *Annual Reviews of Political Science* 7:205–26.

Goodnough, Abby. 2001. State asks court to overturn school financing ruling. *New York Times,* October 26. http://www.nytimes.com (accessed October 26, 2001).

Gorman, Siobhan. 2000. A Bush-Lieberman education ticket? *National Journal,* September 9, 2809.

———. 2001a. Behind bipartisanship. *National Journal,* July 14, 2228–33.

———. 2001b. Bush's big test. *National Journal,* February 24, 549–53.

———. 2001c. The making of a Bush loyalist. *National Journal,* April 28, 1246–48.

———. 2001d. When the fine print changes. *National Journal,* May 12, 1418.

Gormley, William T. 2001. An evolutionary approach to federalism in the U.S. Paper presented at Annual Meeting of the American Political Science Association, August 31, at San Francisco, CA.

Graham, Hugh Davis. 1984. *The uncertain triumph: Federal education policy in the Kennedy and Johnson years.* Chapel Hill, NC: University of North Carolina Press.

Gray, Virginia. 1973. Innovation in the states: A diffusion study. *American Political Science Review* 67 (4):1174–85.

Gray, Virginia, and David Lowery. 2000. The institutionalization of state communities of organized interests. Paper presented at Annual Meeting of the Midwest Political Science Association, April 27–30, at Chicago, IL.

Grodzins, Morton. 1966. *The American system: A new view of government in the United States.* Chicago: Rand McNally and Company.

Guthrie, James W. 1983. The future of federal education policy. *Teachers College Record* 84 (3):672–89.

Halperin, Samuel. 1975. *Essays on federal education policy.* Washington, DC: Institute for Educational Leadership, The George Washington University.

Hartle, Terry W., and Richard P. Holland. 1983. The changing context of federal education aid. *Education and Urban Society* 15 (4):408–31.

Hedge, David M. 1998. *Governance and the changing American states.* Boulder, CO: Westview Press.

Hedge, David M., and Michael J. Scicchitano. 1994. Regulating in space and time: The case of regulatory federalism. *Journal of Politics* 56 (1):134–53.

Hedge, David M., Michael J. Scicchitano, and Patricia Metz. 1991. The principal-agent model and regulatory federalism. *Western Political Quarterly* 44 (4):1055–80.

Hehir, Thomas, and Sue Gamm. 1999. Special education: From legalism to collaboration. In *Law and school reform,* ed. J. P. Heubert. New Haven, CT: Yale University Press.

Hehir, Thomas, and Thomas Latus. 1992. *Special education at the century's end: Evolution of theory and practice since 1970.* Cambridge, MA: Harvard Educational Review.

Herring, Pendleton. 1965. *The politics of democracy: American parties in action (New ed.).* New York: W.W. Norton.

Hess, Frederick M., and Chester E. Finn Jr., eds. 2004. *Leaving no child behind: Options for kids in failing schools.* New York: Palgrave Macmillan.

Hill, Jeffrey S., and Carol S. Weissert. 1995. Implementation and the irony of delegation: The politics of low-level radioactive waste disposal. *Journal of Politics* 57 (2):344–69.

Hill, Paul T. 2000. The federal role in education. In *Brookings papers on education policy,* ed. D. Ravitch. Washington, DC: Brookings Institution.

Hirschman, Albert O. 1970. *Exit, voice, and loyalty: Responses to decline in firms, organizations, and states.* Cambridge, MA: Harvard University Press.

Hoff, David J. 2005. States to get new options on NCLB law. *Education Week,* April 13.

Holahan, John, Alan Weil, and Joshua M. Wiener, eds. 2003. *Federalism and health policy.* Washington, DC: Urban Institute.

House Committee on Education and the Workforce. 2001a. House-Senate panel approves H.R. 1 education reform bill. News release, December 11.

———. 2001b. State education reform leaders urge passage of H.R. 1 education bill. News release, May 16.

Howell, William G., ed. 2005. *Besieged: School boards and the future of education politics.* Washington, DC: Brookings Institution.

Hunter, Bruce. 2001. Letter to representative John Boehner (R-OH) on the ESEA conference. November 8.

Iyengar, Shanto, and Adam F. Simon. 2000. New perspectives and evidence on political communication and campaign effects. *Annual Reviews of Psychology* 51:149–69.

Jennings, John F. 1987. The Sputnik of the eighties. *Phi Delta Kappan,* October, 104–9.

———. 1988. Working in mysterious ways: The federal government and education. *Phi Delta Kappan,* September, 62–65.

———. 1998. *Why national standards and tests? Politics and the quest for better schools.* Thousand Oaks, CA: Sage.

———. 2001. Title I: Its legislative history and its promise. In *Title I: Compensatory education at the crossroads,* eds. G. D. Borman, S. C. Stringfield, and R. E. Slavin. Mahwah, NJ: Lawrence Erlbaum Associates.

———, ed. 1995. *National issues in education: Elementary and Secondary Education Act.* Bloomington, IN, and Washington, DC: Phi Delta Kappa and the Institute for Educational Leadership.

Jones, Bryan D. 2001. *Politics and the architecture of choice: Bounded rationality and governance.* Chicago: University of Chicago Press.

Jones, Charles O. 1994. *The presidency in a separated system.* Washington, DC: Brookings Institution.

Jones-Correa, Michael. 2000–01. The origins and diffusion of racial restrictive covenants. *Political Science Quarterly* 115 (4):541–68.

Jung, Richard, and Michael Kirst. 1986. Beyond mutual adaptation, into the bully pulpit: Recent research on the federal role in education. *Educational Administration Quarterly* 22 (3):80–109.

Kaagan, Steve, and Michael D. Usdan. 1993. Leadership capacity for state reform: The mismatch between rhetoric and reality. *Education Week*, May 5.

Kaestle, Carl F. 2001. Federal aid to education since World War II: Purposes and politics. In *The future of the federal role in elementary and secondary education*, ed. Center on Education Policy. Washington, DC: Center on Education Policy.

Kaestle, Carl F., and Marshall S. Smith. 1982. The federal role in elementary and secondary education, 1940–1980. *Harvard Educational Review* 52 (Special Issue):384–412.

Kafer, Krista. 2001. A small but costly step toward reform: The conference education bill. *Heritage Foundation Web Memo*, December 13. http://www.heritage.org (accessed June 13, 2001).

Kane, Thomas J., and Douglas O. Staiger. 2001. Rigid rules will damage school. *New York Times*, August 13. http://www.nytimes.com (accessed August 13, 2001).

———. 2002. Volatility in school test scores: Implications for test-based accountability systems. In *Brookings papers on education policy*, ed. D. Ravitch. Washington, DC: Brookings Institution.

Kernell, Samuel. 1993. *Going public: New strategies of presidential leadership*. Washington, DC: CQ Press.

Kettl, Donald F. 1997. The global revolution in public management: Driving themes, missing links. *Journal of Policy Analysis and Management* 16 (3):446–62.

King, Gary. 1998. *Unifying political methodology: The likelihood theory of statistical inference*. Ann Arbor, MI: University of Michigan Press.

Kingdon, John W. 1995. *Agendas, alternatives, and public policies (2nd ed.)*. New York: HarperCollins.

Kirst, Michael W. 1984. The changing balance in state and local power to control education. *Phi Delta Kappan*, November, 189–91.

———. 1995. Who's in charge? Federal, state, and local control. In *Learning from the past: What history teaches us about school reform*, eds. D. Ravitch and M. A. Vinovskis. Baltimore: Johns Hopkins University Press.

Krosnick, Jon. 1990. Government policy and citizen passion: A study of issue publics in contemporary America. *Political Behavior* 12 (1):59–92.

Krutz, Glen S. 2002. Omnibus legislation: An institutional reaction to the rise of new issues. In *Policy dynamics*, eds. F. R. Baumgartner and B. D. Jones. Chicago: University of Chicago Press.

Light, Paul C. 1997. *The tides of reform: Making government work, 1945–1995*. New Haven, CT: Yale University Press.

———. 1999. *The president's agenda: Domestic policy choice from Kennedy to Clinton (3rd ed.)*. Baltimore: Johns Hopkins University Press.

Long, J. Scott. 1997. *Regression models for categorical and limited dependent variables*. Thousand Oaks, CA: SAGE Publications.

Lowi, Theodore J. 1967. The public philosophy: Interest-group liberalism. *American Political Science Review* 61 (1):5–24.

———. 1994. Foreword: Political history and political science. In *The dynamics of American politics*, eds. L. C. Dodd and C. Jillson. Boulder, CO: Westview Press.

Maisel, L. Sandy. 1987. *Parties and elections in America: The electoral process*. New York: Random House.

———, ed. 1994. *The parties respond: Changes in American parties and campaigns.* Boulder, CO: Westview Press.

Majone, Giandomenico. 1989. *Evidence, argument, and persuasion in the policy process.* New Haven, CT: Yale University Press.

Manna, Paul. 2003. Federalism, agenda setting, and the development of federal education policy, 1965–2001. Ph.D. diss., Department of Political Science, University of Wisconsin-Madison.

———. 2004. Leaving no child behind. In *Political education: National policy comes of age,* ed. C. T. Cross. New York: Teachers College Press.

———. 2006. Teachers unions and No Child Left Behind. In *Collective bargaining in education: Negotiating change in today's schools,* eds. J. Hannaway and A.J. Rotherham. Cambridge, MA: Harvard Education Press.

———. Forthcoming. Control, persuasion, and educational accountability: Implementing the No Child Left Behind Act. *Educational Policy.*

Manno, Bruno V. 1995. Reinventing education in the image of the great society. In *National issues in education: Elementary and Secondary Education Act,* ed. J. F. Jennings. Bloomington, IN, and Washington, DC: Phi Delta Kappa International and the Institute for Educational Leadership.

Martin, Janet M. 1994. *Lessons from the hill: The legislative journey of an education program.* New York: St. Martin's Press.

Mashek, John W. 1990. Cavazos quits post. *Boston Globe,* December 13.

Mayhew, David R. 1974. *Congress: The electoral connection.* New Haven, CT: Yale University Press.

McLaughlin, Margaret J., and Martyn Rouse, eds. 2000. *Special education and school reform in the United States and Great Britain.* New York: Routledge.

Meier, Deborah, and George Wood, eds. 2004. *Many children left behind: How the No Child Left Behind Act is damaging our children and our schools.* Boston: Beacon Press.

Mezzacappa, Dale. 2002. Pennsylvania moves to raise teacher standard. *Philadelphia Inquirer,* November 15.

Mikkelsen, Randall. 2003. Bush, Kennedy part ways over school bill. *Washington Post,* January 8. http://www.washingtonpost.com (accessed January 8, 2003).

Miller, Warren E., and J. Merrill Shanks. 1996. *The new American voter.* Cambridge, MA: Harvard University Press.

Milward, H. Brinton, and Keith G. Provan. 2000. How networks are governed. In *Governance and performance: New perspectives,* eds. C. J. Heinrich and L. E. Lynn Jr. Washington, DC: Georgetown University Press.

Minorini, Paul A., and Stephen D. Sugarman. 1999. School finance litigation in the name of educational equity: Its evolution, impact and future. In *Equity and adequacy in education finance,* eds. H. F. Ladd, R. Chalk, and J. S. Hansen. Washington, DC: National Academy Press.

Mintrom, Michael. 2000. *Policy entrepreneurs and school choice.* Washington, DC: Georgetown University Press.

Mintrom, Michael, and Sandra Vergari. 1997. Education reform and accountability issues in an intergovernmental context. *Publius* 27 (2):143–66.

———. 1998. Policy networks and innovation diffusion: The case of state education reforms. *Journal of Politics* 60 (1):126–48.

Mollison, Andrew. 2001. State legislators now oppose Bush's education plan. *Cox Newspapers,* October 1. http://www.coxnews.com (accessed October 9, 2001).

Moore, John L., Jon P. Preimesberger, and David R. Tarr, eds. 2001. *Congressional quarterly's guide to U.S. Elections (4th ed.), volume 1.* Washington, DC: CQ Press.

Morehouse, Sarah M., and Malcolm E. Jewell. 2004. States as laboratories: A reprise. *Annual Reviews of Political Science* 7:177–203.

Murphy, Jerome T. 1982. Progress and problems: The paradox of state reform. In *Policy making in education: Eighty-first yearbook of the National Society for the Study of Education, part 1,* eds. A. Lieberman and M. W. McLaughlin. Chicago: University of Chicago Press.

Murphy, Joseph, ed. 1990. *The educational reform movement of the 1980s: Perspectives and cases.* Berkeley, CA: McCutchan Publishing.

NASBE Study Group on Education Governance. 1996. A motion to reconsider: Education governance at a crossroads. Alexandria, VA: National Association of State Boards of Education.

Nathan, Richard P. 1990. Federalism—the great "composition." In *The new American political system (2nd version),* ed. A. King. Washington, DC: American Enterprise Institute.

National Center for Education Statistics. 2004. *Digest of education statistics, 2003.* Washington, DC: Government Printing Office.

National Commission on Excellence in Education. 1983. A nation at risk: The imperative for educational reform. http://www.ed.gov/pubs/NatAtRisk/risk.html (accessed Spring and Summer 2002).

National Conference of State Legislatures. 2001a. Letter to congressional conferees regarding the re-authorization of the Elementary and Secondary Education Act. September 26.

———. 2001b. State fiscal outlook for FY2002: November update. December 3. http://www.ncsl.org/programs/fiscal/sfo2002.htm (accessed January 9, 2002).

———. 2005. Task force on No Child Left Behind final report. Denver, CO, and Washington, DC: National Conference of State Legislatures.

National Governors' Association. 2001a. Governors welcome education reform efforts, hopeful that Congress restores full funding for special education next year. News release, December 18.

———. 2001b. Letter to Chairman Boehner, Representative Miller, Chairman Kennedy, and Senator Gregg on the ESEA reauthorization, October 5.

———. 2005. Policy position: ECW-2. Education reform policy. http://www.nga.org (accessed July 5, 2005).

Nelson, Barbara J. 1984. *Making an issue of child abuse: Political agenda setting for social problems.* Chicago: University of Chicago Press.

Neustadt, Richard E. 1980. *Presidential power: The politics of leadership from FDR to Carter.* New York: John Wiley and Sons.

Nicholson-Crotty, Sean. 2004. Goal conflict and fund diversion in federal grants to the states. *American Journal of Political Science* 48 (1):110–22.

Nie, Norman H., Sidney Verba, and John R. Petrocik. 1976. *The changing American voter.* Cambridge, MA: Harvard University Press.

Odden, Allan, and David Marsh. 1990. Local response to the 1980s state education reforms: New patterns of local and state interaction. In *The educational reform movement of the 1980s,* ed. J. Murphy. Berkeley, CA: McCutchan Publishing.

Oleszek, Walter J. 1996. *Congressional procedures and the policy process (4th ed.).* Washington, DC: CQ Press.

Olson, Lynn. 2001. Bush test plan fuels debate over uniformity. *Education Week,* May 9.

———. 2002a. Negotiators retain heart of Ed. Dept. proposals. *Education Week,* March 27.

———. 2002b. States gear up for new federal law. *Education Week,* January 16.

———. 2002c. Testing rules would grant states leeway. *Education Week,* March 6.

———. 2002d. Testing systems in most states not ESEA-ready. *Education Week,* January 9.

———. 2003. "Approved" is relative term for Ed. Dept. *Education Week,* August 6.

Olson, Lynn, and Erik W. Robelen. 2001. Defining "failure" critical to Bush testing plan. *Education Week,* May 16.

Olson, Mancur. 1965. *The logic of collective action: Public goods and the theory of groups.* Cambridge, MA: Harvard University Press.

Oppel, Richard A., and Diana Jean Schemo. 2000. Bush is warned vouchers might hurt school plans. *New York Times,* December 22.

Orfield, Gary. 1978. *Must we bus? Segregated schools and national policy.* Washington, DC: Brookings Institution.

———. 1999. Conservative activists and the rush toward resegregation. In *Law and school reform,* ed. J. P. Heubert. New Haven, CT: Yale University Press.

Orren, Karen, and Stephen Skowronek. 1994. Beyond the iconography of order: Notes for a "new institutionalism." In *The dynamics of American politics,* eds. L. C. Dodd and C. Jillson. Boulder, CO: Westview Press.

Osborne, David, and Ted Gaebler. 1992. *Reinventing government.* Reading, MA: Addison-Wesley.

O'Toole, Laurence J., Jr., ed. 2000a. *American intergovernmental relations: Foundations, perspectives, and issues (3rd ed.).* Washington, DC: CQ Press.

O'Toole, Laurence J., Jr. 2000b. Different public managements? Implications of structural context in hierarchies and networks. In *Advancing public management: New developments in theory, methods, and practice,* eds. J. L. Brudney, L. J. O'Toole Jr., and H. G. Rainey. Washington, DC: Georgetown University Press.

O'Toole, Laurence J., Jr., and Kenneth J. Meier. 2004. Desperately seeking Selznick: Cooptation and the dark side of public management in networks. *Public Administration Review* 64 (6):681–93.

Paige, Roderick. 2002. Remarks to meeting of chief state school officers. *U.S. Department of Education,* January 9. http://www.ed.gov/news/speeches/2002/01/20020109.html (accessed January 14, 2004).

Passow, A. Harry. 1990. How it happened, wave by wave. In *Education reform: Making sense of it all,* ed. S. B. Bacharach. Needham Heights, MA: Allyn and Bacon.

Payzant, Thomas W., and Jessica Levin. 1995. Improving America's schools for children in greatest need. In *National issues in education: Elementary and Secondary Education Act,* ed. J. F. Jennings. Bloomington, IN, and Washington, DC: Phi Delta Kappa International and the Institute for Educational Leadership.

Peterson, Paul E. 1995. *The price of federalism.* Washington, DC: Brookings Institution.

Peterson, Paul E., and Bryan C. Hassel, eds. 1998. *Learning from school choice.* Washington, DC: Brookings Institution.

Peterson, Paul E., Barry G. Rabe, and Kenneth K. Wong. 1986. *When federalism works.* Washington, DC: Brookings Institution.

Peterson, Paul E., and Martin R. West, eds. 2003. *No child left behind? The politics and practice of school accountability.* Washington, DC: Brookings Institution.

Petrocik, John R. 1996. Issue ownership in presidential elections, with a 1980 case study. *Journal of Politics* 40 (3):825–50.

Pew Research Center for the People and the Press. 2005. Bush approval rating lower than for other two-termers; public's agenda differs from president's. Washington, DC: Pew Research Center for the People and the Press.

Pickerill, J. Mitchell. 2004. *Constitutional deliberation in Congress: The impact of judicial review in a separated system.* Durham, NC: Duke University Press.

Pierson, Paul. 1994. *Dismantling the welfare state? Reagan, Thatcher, and the politics of retrenchment.* New York: Cambridge University Press.

———. 2000a. Increasing returns, path dependence, and the study of politics. *American Political Science Review* 94 (2):251–67.

———. 2000b. Not just what, but *when:* Timing and sequence in political processes. *Studies in American Political Development* 14 (1):72–92.

Pipho, Chris. 1978. Minimum competency testing in 1978: A look at state standards. *Phi Delta Kappan,* May, 585–88.

Plank, David N., and Rick Ginsberg. 1990. Catch the wave: Reform commissions and school reform. In *The educational reform movement of the 1980s,* ed. J. Murphy. Berkeley, CA: McCutchan Publishing.

Polsby, Nelson W. 1984. *Political innovation in America: The politics of policy initiation.* New Haven, CT: Yale University Press.

Posner, Paul L. 1998. *The politics of unfunded mandates: Whither federalism?* Washington, DC: Georgetown University Press.

Radin, Beryl A., and Willis D. Hawley. 1988. *The politics of federal reorganization: Creating the U.S. Department of Education.* New York: Pergamon Press.

Raphael, Jacqueline, and Shannon McKay. 2001. Analysis of the flexibility partnership demonstration program state reports. Washington, DC: Urban Institute.

Ravitch, Diane. 1995. *National standards in American education: A citizen's guide.* Washington, DC: Brookings Institution.

———. 2001. The history lesson in Bush's school plan. *New York Times,* January 27.

Riddle, Wayne. 2002a. Education for the disadvantaged: ESEA Title I reauthorization issues. Washington, DC: Congressional Research Service.

———. 2002b. K–12 education: Highlights of the No Child Left Behind Act of 2001 (P.L. 107-110). Washington, DC: Congressional Research Service.

Riker, William H. 1986. *The art of political manipulation.* New Haven, CT: Yale University Press.

———, ed. 1993. *Agenda formation.* Ann Arbor, MI: University of Michigan Press.

Robelen, Erik. 2004a. Federal rules for teachers are relaxed. *Education Week,* March 19.

———. 2004b. States given more leeway on test rule. *Education Week,* April 7.

Robelen, Erik, and Lynn Olson. 2005. Spellings to listen, but not retreat, on NCLB. *Education Week,* February 9.

Robelen, Erik W. 2001. Congress set to pass sweeping education bill. *Education Week,* December 12. http://www.edweek.com (accessed December 18, 2001).

———. 2002. ESEA to boost federal role in education. *Education Week,* January 9.

———. 2005a. Bush high school plan not quite ready to graduate. *Education Week,* May 18.

———. 2005b. Bush's high school agenda faces obstacles. *Education Week,* February 9.

Rossiter, Clinton, ed. 1961. *The federalist papers.* New York: New American Library.

Rotherham, Andrew. 2001. The new 3 R's of education. *Blueprint Magazine,* February 7. http://www.ndol.org/ndol_ka.cfm?kaid=132 (accessed October 8, 2001).

Rudalevige, Andrew. 2003. No child left behind: Forging a congressional compromise. In *No child left behind? The politics and practice of school accountability,* eds. P. E. Peterson and M. R. West. Washington, DC: Brookings Institution.

Sack, Joetta L. 2005. State agencies juggle NCLB work, staffing woes. *Education Week,* May 11.

Salamon, Lester M., ed. 2002. *The tools of government.* New York: Oxford University Press.

Salisbury, Robert H. 1990. The paradox of interest groups in Washington—more groups, less clout. In *The new American political system,* ed. A. King. Washington, DC: American Enterprise Institute.

Salzer, James. 2001. Barnes cuts Bush's grade over vouchers. *Atlanta Journal and Constitution,* January 27.

Sandalow, Marc. 2005. Second chance for Bush to unite divided U.S. *San Francisco Chronicle,* January 19.

Schattschneider, E. E. 1935. *Politics, pressures and the tariff.* New York: Prentice-Hall.

———. 1960. *The semisovereign people: A realist's view of democracy in America.* New York: Holt, Rinehart, and Winston.

Scheiber, Noam. 2001. Rod Paige learns the hard way. *The New Republic,* June 21. http://www.tnr.com (accessed July 24, 2001).

Schemo, Diana Jean. 2001. Congress may ease plans for school accountability. *New York Times,* August 10. http://www.nytimes.com (accessed August 10, 2001).

———. 2003. Critics say money for schools falls short of promises. *New York Times,* February 5.

Schiller, Wendy J. 1995. Senators as political entrepreneurs: Using bill sponsorship to shape legislative agendas. *American Journal of Political Science* 39 (1):186–203.

Schneider, Mark, Paul Teske, and Michael Mintrom. 1995. *Public entrepreneurs: Agents for change in American government.* Princeton, NJ: Princeton University Press.

Schwartz, Robert B., and Marian A. Robinson. 2000. Goals 2000 and the standards movement. In *Brookings papers on education policy,* ed. D. Ravitch. Washington, DC: Brookings Institution.

Sheingate, Adam D. 2003. Political entrepreneurship, institutional change, and American political development. *Studies in American Political Development* 17 (2):185–203.

Simon, Herbert A. 1947. *Administrative behavior.* New York: Macmillan.

Skocpol, Theda. 1994. The origins of social policy in the United States: A polity-centered analysis. In *The dynamics of American politics,* eds. L. C. Dodd and C. Jillson. Boulder, CO: Westview Press.

Skowronek, Stephen. 1997. *The politics presidents make: Leadership from John Adams to Bill Clinton.* Cambridge, MA: Harvard University Press.

Smith, James A. 1991. *The idea brokers: Think tanks and the rise of the new policy elite.* New York: The Free Press.

Smith, Marshall S., Jessica Levin, and Joanne E. Cianci. 1997. Beyond a legislative agenda: Education policy approaches of the Clinton administration. *Educational Policy* 11 (2):209–26.

Smith, Marshall S., Brett W. Scoll, and Valena White Plisko. 1995. The Improving America's Schools Act: A new partnership. In *National issues in education: Elementary and Secondary Education Act,* ed. J. F. Jennings. Bloomington, IN, and Washington, DC: Phi Delta Kappa International and the Institute for Educational Leadership.

Smith, Steven S., and Christopher J. Deering. 1990. *Committees in Congress (2nd ed.).* Washington, DC: CQ Press.

Stedman, James B. 2002. K–12 teacher quality: Issues and legislative action. Washington, DC: Congressional Research Service.

Stephens, David. 1983–1984. President Carter, the Congress, and NEA: Creating the Department of Education. *Political Science Quarterly* 98 (4):641–63.

Stevenson, Richard W. 2004. Renewing his focus on schools, Bush proposes spending increase. *New York Times,* January 9. http://www.nytimes.com (accessed January 12, 2004).

Stone, Deborah A. 1989. Causal stories and the formation of policy agendas. *Political Science Quarterly* 104 (2):281–300.

———. 1997. *Policy paradox: The art of political decision making (2nd ed.).* New York: W.W. Norton.

Struggling toward opportunity: 40 years since Little Rock. 1997. *PS: Political Science and Politics* 30 (3):443–73.

Sundquist, James L. 1968. *Politics and policy in the Eisenhower, Kennedy, and Johnson years.* Washington, DC: Brookings Institution.

Taylor, William L., and Dianne M. Piché. 2002. Will new school law really help? *USA Today,* January 8.

The Business Roundtable. 2001. The Business Roundtable calls conference report a vital step forward for American education. News release, December 11.

———. 2002a. The Business Roundtable commits to help states, districts make new education reforms work. News release, January 8.

———. 2002b. Using the No Child Left Behind Act to improve schools in your state. Washington, DC: The Business Roundtable.

———. 2005. No Child Left Behind receives high marks at Business Roundtable forum. News release, February 9.

Thelen, Kathleen. 2002. How institutions evolve: Insights from comparative-historical analysis. In *Comparative historical analysis in the social sciences,* eds. J. Mahoney and D. Rueschemeyer. New York: Cambridge University Press.

Thomas, Norman C. 1975. *Education in national politics.* New York: David McKay Company.

———. 1983. The development of federal activism in education. *Education and Urban Society* 15 (3):271–90.

Tiebout, Charles M. 1956. A pure theory of local expenditures. *Journal of Political Economy* 64 (5):416–24.

Timpane, P. Michael, and Laurie Miller McNeill. 1991. *Business impact on education and child development reform.* New York and Washington, DC: Committee for Economic Development.

Toch, Thomas. 1991. *In the name of excellence: The struggle to reform the nation's schools, why it's failing, and what should be done.* New York: Oxford University Press.

———. 2001. Bush's big test. *Washington Monthly,* November. http://www.washingtonmonthly.com (accessed November 4, 2001).

Tulis, Jeffrey K. 1987. *The rhetorical presidency.* Princeton, NJ: Princeton University Press.

U.S. Department of Education. 2002. Budget history tables. Washington, DC: U.S. Department of Education.

———. 2004. The secretary's third annual report on teacher quality. Washington, DC. U.S. Department of Education Office of Postsecondary Education.

Van Horn, Carl E. 1996. The quiet revolution. In *The state of the states (3rd ed.),* ed. C. E. Van Horn. Washington, DC: CQ Press.

Vinovskis, Maris A. 1999a. Activities of the National Education Goals Panel, 1990–1992: Unpublished manuscript prepared for the National Education Goals Panel.

———. 1999b. Development of the six national education goals and creation of the panel to oversee them. Unpublished manuscript prepared for the National Education Goals Panel.

———. 1999c. The road to Charlottesville: The 1989 education summit. Washington, DC: National Education Goals Panel.

Volden, Craig, Jeff Cummins, and Nathan D. Woods. 2000. The political economy of education spending in American federalism. Paper presented at Annual Meeting of the Midwest Political Science Association, April 27–30, at Chicago, IL.

Walker, David B. 1995. *The rebirth of federalism: Slouching toward Washington.* Chatham, NJ: Chatham House Publishers.

Walker, Jack L. 1969. The diffusion of innovations among the American states. *American Political Science Review* 63 (3):880–99.

———. 1977. Setting the agenda in the U.S. Senate: A theory of problem selection. *British Journal of Political Science* 7 (4):423–45.

Warren, Donald. 1990. Passage of rites: On the history of educational reform in the United States. In *The educational reform movement of the 1980s,* ed. J. Murphy. Berkeley, CA: McCutchan Publishing.

Washington Post and ABC News. 2002. Post-ABC poll. *Washington Post,* September 28. http://www.washingtonpost.com/wp-srv/politics/polls/vault/stories/data092702.htm (accessed September 29, 2002).

Wawro, Gregory J. 2000. *Legislative entrepreneurship in the U.S. House of Representatives.* Ann Arbor, MI: University of Michigan Press.

Wear, Ben. 2003. Bush's impact aid plan has familiar ring. *Education Week,* February 26.

Weisberg, Herbert F., and Clyde Wilcox, eds. 2004. *Models of voting in presidential elections: The 2000 U.S. election.* Stanford, CA: Stanford University Press.

Weiss, Janet A. 1998. Policy theories of school choice. *Social Science Quarterly* 79 (3):523–32.

Weissert, Carol S., ed. 2000. *Learning from leaders: Welfare reform politics and policy in five Midwestern states.* Albany, NY: Rockefeller Institute Press.

White House Office of the Press Secretary. 2002. President signs landmark education bill. News release, January 8.

———. 2003. President highlights progress in education reform. News release, June 10.

Wilgoren, Jodi. 2001. Education plan comes under fire by state officials. *New York Times,* July 17. http://www.nytimes.com (accessed July 24, 2001).

Wilkerson, J. Harvie, III. 1979. *From Brown to Bakke. The Supreme Court and school integration: 1954–1978.* New York: Oxford University Press.

Wirt, Frederick M., and Michael W. Kirst. 1997. *The political dynamics of American education.* Berkeley, CA: McCutchan Publishing Corporation.

Wolbrecht, Christina. 2000. *The politics of women's rights: Parties, positions, and change.* Princeton, NJ: Princeton University Press.

Wood, B. Dan. 1991. Federalism and policy responsiveness: The clean air case. *Journal of Politics* 53 (3):851–59.

———. 1992. Modeling federal implementation as a system: The clean air case. *American Journal of Political Science* 36 (1):40–67.

Zimmerman, Joseph F. 1992. *Contemporary American federalism: The growth of national power.* New York: Praeger.

———. 2001. National-state relations: Cooperative federalism in the twentieth century. *Publius* 31 (2):15–30.

INDEX

Note: Page numbers followed by an *n* plus a number refer to notes. Page numbers followed by *f* refer to figures, and by *t,* tables.

North Carolina, 125, 137n8; and testing, 123
Northwest Ordinance of 1787, 17n4

Odden, Allan, 168
Ohio, 13
Oklahoma, 116n6
Oklahoma City bombing, 30
Oleszek, Walter, 48
Omnibus Budget Reconciliation Act of 1981, 72
open-enrollment policies, 107
Orr, Billie Jo, 103, 137n5

Packer, Joel, 154
Paige, Rod, 119, 132–34, 155, 164n7
party platforms, 60–66; Democrats and education, 62t–63t; Republicans and education, 64t–65t, 67n6
Paul Manna School Uniform Program, 149
Payzant, Thomas, 75, 174n1
Pence, Mike, 158
Pennsylvania, 168
Peterson, Paul, 43n3
Philadelphia: and NCLB, 168, 174n1
Piché, Dianne, 130
Pledge of Allegiance, 52
Policy Agendas Project, 181
policy entrepreneurs, 8, 14–16, 19, 28–29, 66, 171; and borrowing strength, 5, 33–40, 37f, 43, 114; expectations about, 39–40, 86–87, 92, 104, 166–67, 171; and interest groups, 158–59; and license, 29–31, 90; and softening up, 15, 33–35
policy venues, 27
Polsby, Nelson, 30
Posner, Paul, 29
Powden, Mark, 124–25
presidential campaigns: advertisements in, 51–53, 54t, 136n2, 182–83; and education, 51–53, 54t
presidential speeches, 67n4, 181; and education, 53–60, 56t–57t, 58t–59t, 92–95, 93t

presidents, 149; and bully pulpits for education, 78, 150; interest of, in education, 50–60, 92–95, 100
President's Reorganization Project (Carter), 78
property taxes: and school funding, 11
Public Law 89-10 (ESEA). See Elementary and Secondary Education Act (ESEA)
public laws: statements of purpose of, 72, 83
Public Papers of the Presidents, 181

Quie, Albert, 84n12, 150

Rabe, Barry G., 43n3
Raphael, Jacqueline, 116n10
Reagan, Ronald, 52, 60, 67n4, 79, 104–5, 151; and desire to abolish the Department of Education, 78, 80; and education, 69, 99–100; speeches of, 55, 57
redistributive policies, 30–31, 38, 43n3
Republicans, 66, 120, 153–58; and Department of Education, 151; party platform of, 64t–65t, 67n6
Republican Study Committee in the House, 158
Resnick, Michael, 100
Results in Education (NGA report), 102
Rice, Theron J., 160, 162
Riker, William, 20, 26, 43–44n4
Riley, Richard, 28, 75, 117, 152–53, 161–62
Robb, Charles, 97
Romer, Roy, 103
Rust, Edward B., Jr., 131

Salamon, Lester, 44n11
San Antonio School District v. Rodriguez (1973), 11
Schaffer, Bob, 156
Schattschneider, E. E., 39, 162–63
school boards (local), 168
school breakfast and lunch program, 49, 61, 71